Hiking

North

Carolina's

National

Forests

JOHNNY MOLLOY

Hiking North Carolina's National Forests

50 Can't-Miss Trail Adventures

in the Pisgah, Nantahala,

Uwharrie, and Croatan

National Forests

THE UNIVERSITY OF
NORTH CAROLINA PRESS
CHAPEL HILL

A *Southern Gateways Guide*
© 2014 Johnny Molloy
All rights reserved
Set in Caecilia and Gotham
Manufactured in the United States of America

The paper in this book meets the guidelines for permanence and durability of the Committee on Production Guidelines for Book Longevity of the Council on Library Resources.

The University of North Carolina Press has been a member of the Green Press Initiative since 2003.

Unless otherwise noted, all photos are by the author.

Library of Congress Cataloging-in-Publication Data
Molloy, Johnny, 1961–
    Hiking North Carolina's national forests : 50 can't-miss trail adventures in the Pisgah, Nantahala, Uwharrie, and Croatan national forests / by Johnny Molloy.
        pages cm. — (A Southern gateways guide)
    Includes index.
    ISBN 978-1-4696-1166-2 (cloth : alk. paper)
    ISBN 978-1-4696-1167-9 (pbk. : alk. paper)
    1. Hiking—North Carolina—Guidebooks.
    2. Forest reserves—North Carolina—Guidebooks.
    3. North Carolina—Guidebooks.
I. Title.
GV199.42.N662G745 2014
917.56—dc23   2013020447
Southern Gateways Guide™ is a registered trademark of the University of North Carolina Press.

cloth 18 17 16 15 14 5 4 3 2 1
paper 18 17 16 15 14 5 4 3 2 1

 This book is for all the trail builders and the hikers who trek through North Carolina's national forests, and John Bland.

Hike Summary Chart

Hike	Distance (miles)	Time (hours)	Difficulty
Pisgah National Forest			
1 Highlands of Roan	4.8	3.0	Moderate
2 Roan Gardens and High Bluff	0.5, 2.0	1.5	Easy
3 Hunt Fish Falls	6.0	4.0	Moderate
4 Little Lost Cliffs Loop	4.2	2.5	Moderate
5 Falls of Harper Creek Loop	9.4	6.0	Moderate to difficult
6 Tablerock Loop	3.6	2.5	Moderate
7 Tower of Babel at Linville Gorge	6.2	5.0	Difficult
8 Shelton Laurel Backcountry Loop	10.2	7.0	Difficult
9 Lovers Leap Loop	3.9	3.0	Moderate
10 Max Patch	2.7	1.5	Easy to moderate
11 Black Mountain Crest	7.6	5.0	Difficult
12 Douglas Falls	6.6	4.0	Moderate to difficult
13 South Mills River Loop	7.6	4.5	Moderate
14 Pink Beds Loop	5.3	3.0	Easy to moderate
15 Shining Rock Wilderness Loop	8.3	6.5	Difficult
16 Shining Rock High Country Hike	8.8	5.0	Moderate to difficult
17 Sam Knob Loop	3.9	2.5	Moderate
18 Middle Prong Wilderness Loop	8.1	6.0	Difficult
19 Falls of Graveyard Fields	3.2	2.0	Easy to moderate
20 Looking Glass Rock	5.6	4.0	Moderate to difficult
21 John Rock	5.4	3.5	Moderate
Nantahala National Forest			
22 Lower Falls Loop	6.4	4.0	Moderate
23 The Hangover	6.2	4.0	Moderate
24 Joyce Kilmer Memorial Forest	2.0	1.5	Easy
25 Falls of Snowbird Creek	10.6	6.5	Difficult
26 Wesser Bald Tower	2.2	1.5	Easy
27 Fires Creek Rim Loop	5.8	4.5	Difficult
28 Siler Bald	3.6	2.5	Moderate
29 Jackrabbit Mountain Loop	2.8	1.5	Easy

Highlights

Open balds, multiple panoramas

Catawba rhododendron gardens, high country forest, views

Three notable waterfalls, huge swimming hole

Huge waterfalls with mountain views, cliffs with high country vistas

Two amazing waterfalls, swimming

Panoramas from Little Tablerock and Tablerock

Gorge vistas and wilderness

Waterfall, Baxter Cliff, views, good backpacking circuit

Views of French Broad River Valley from Lovers Leap and other outcrops

360° mountain views, blackberries in season

Highest ridge in North Carolina, superlative vistas, rare spruce-fir ecosystem

Two dissimilar yet superlative waterfalls, solitude

Spring wildflowers, mountain streams, trout fishing, backpacking opportunities

High-altitude wetland, laurel and rhododendron blooms

Shining Rock Wilderness, cascades, views from Shining Rock and other outcrops

Continual mountain panoramas, high-elevation flora

Miles of mountain views, highland knob, high country stream

Designated wilderness, spruce-fir, trout fishing, swimming

High-elevation falls, views from meadows, highland stream

Grand views from notable granite dome

Sweeping vistas from granite face

Mountain lake, wilderness, Lower Falls, swimming, fishing

Joyce Kilmer-Slickrock Wilderness, views

Old-growth forest, huge trees

Three waterfalls, each different in size, shape, and flow; remote setting

360° panoramas from viewing tower

Solitude, views, northern hardwood forest

Nearly 360° views, restored bald

Mountain and lake views, adjacent recreation opportunities

Hike Summary Chart (cont.)

Hike	Distance (miles)	Time (hours)	Difficulty
Nantahala National Forest (cont.)			
30 Park Creek Loop	8.8	5.5	Difficult
31 Standing Indian	5.0	3.0	Moderate
32 Southern Nantahala Wilderness Hike	8.8	5.5	Difficult
33 Jones Knob via the Bartram Trail	5.4	3.5	Moderate
34 Cliffside Lake Double Loop	0.8, 1.9	2.0	Easy
35 Glen Falls	1.8	2.0	Moderate
36 Whiteside Mountain	2.0	2.0	Moderate
37 Chattooga Wild and Scenic River Hike	5.4	3.0	Moderate
38 Panthertown Backcountry Loop	7.4	4.0	Moderate to difficult
39 Schoolhouse Falls Loop at Panthertown	4.9	3.0	Moderate
40 Whitewater Falls	0.6	1.0	Easy
Uwharrie National Forest			
41 Birkhead Wilderness Hike	6.9	4.0	Moderate to difficult
42 Vistas of Badin Lake	5.1	3.0	Moderate
43 Uwharrie Trail	19.8	12.5	Difficult
44 Upper Dutchmans Loop	9.4	5.5	Difficult
45 Lower Dutchmans Loop	11.6	6.5	Difficult
46 Densons Creek Loop	2.1	1.5	Easy to moderate
Croatan National Forest			
47 Cedar Point Tideland Trail	1.4	1.5	Easy
48 Neusiok Trail: Oyster Point to Blackjack Shelter	4.8	2.5	Moderate
49 Boardwalks of the Neusiok Trail	7.0	4.0	Moderate
50 Neusiok Trail Beach and Bluff Hike	7.6	4.5	Moderate

Highlights

Nantahala River, wildflowers, backcountry

Great views from atop Standing Indian, Southern Nantahala Wilderness

Big Laurel Falls, Southern Nantahala Wilderness

Stellar views, solitude, Bartram Trail

Quiet mountain lake, views

Mountain vista, four waterfall views

Multiple views from open cliffs

Deep wooded gorge, swimming, fishing

Multiple views, multiple waterfalls

Three waterfalls, views from open mountainside

Two views of gigantic falls

Bluff views, wildflowers in season, wilderness

Lake views, fishing opportunities

Backpacking, wildflowers, winter views from multiple hilltops

Wildflowers, streams, big woods aura

Good backpacking loop, creekside hiking, wildflowers

Bluff views, wildflowers in season

Coastal estuary and forest

Tidal environment and swamp-bordered pinelands

Wetland boardwalks, pine flatwoods, trail shelter

Tidal river views, beach hiking, trail shelter

Contents

Uwharrie National Forest Hikes

Croatan National Forest Hikes

Acknowledgments

Thanks for the University of North Carolina Press, especially Mark Simpson-Vos. Thanks to all the people who have hiked with me in North Carolina's national forests through the decades, including Pam Morgan, John Cox, Bryan Delay, Kevin Thomas, Tom Lauria, John Harv Sampley, John Bland, and a whole lot more hikers unnamed.

Preface

What an honor to be asked by the University of North Carolina Press to write a hiking guide to North Carolina's national forests! And what a joy it has been to actually hike the hikes, then share them with you. I hope this guide leads you to as many enjoyable adventures as I have had in the Tar Heel State's four national forests—the Pisgah, the Nantahala, the Uwharrie, and the Croatan. I have been hiking the trails of these public lands for over three decades, seeing much beauty contained within. Immediately coming to mind are certain scenes—the tidal flats of Mill Creek nestled between wooded hills, where fiddler crabs scurry from my foot falls, or gazing out from the sandy beaches along the Neuse River. I recall walking through the magnificent shortleaf pine stands dividing noisy brooks and seeing the first wildflowers of a Piedmont spring. In the mountains I can see the crashing waterfalls and stone slabs that border them; I can feel chill air while gazing on a host of ridges splashed in autumnal paint. I can see grassy balds opening to a darkening summer sky. I recall a menagerie of superlative scenery that can be found along the hiking trails of these North Carolina national forests.

And what a task it was to capture the best scenes along the best hikes that together paint a mosaic of ecosystems within forest lands stretching literally from the mountains to the sea. I took the duty very seriously, drawing upon my years of experience within North Carolina's national forests as well as knowledge gleaned while authoring more than 50 outdoor guides throughout the United States, including a tent camping guide to North Carolina. I wanted to get it right. To this end I have included the hikes that must be done to paint an accurate picture of what North Carolina's national forests have to offer. I hope you will find that the hikes contained herein are truly *the* can't-miss hikes of North Carolina's national forests.

Throughout the process I kept looking for the best of the best and found some new sights that please this grizzled veteran—panoramas of the Pee Dee River basin from Dark Mountain, the massive swimming holes of Gragg Prong, and fascinating pitcher plants on the Neusiok Trail. After completing the task of writing this book, I came away with an even more profound respect for the wild lands of North Carolina's national forests. I hope you will, too. Happy hiking!

Map Legend

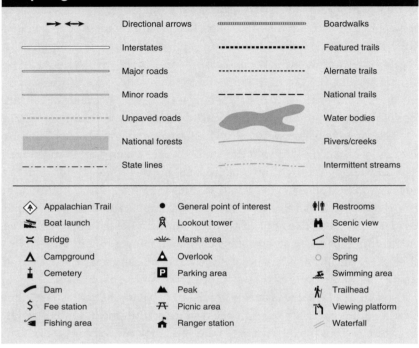

Directional arrows		Boardwalks
Interstates		Featured trails
Major roads		Alernate trails
Minor roads		National trails
Unpaved roads		Water bodies
National forests		Rivers/creeks
State lines		Intermittent streams

Appalachian Trail · General point of interest · Restrooms
Boat launch · Lookout tower · Scenic view
Bridge · Marsh area · Shelter
Campground · Overlook · Spring
Cemetery · Parking area · Swimming area
Dam · Peak · Trailhead
Fee station · Picnic area · Viewing platform
Fishing area · Ranger station · Waterfall

Hiking North Carolina's National Forests

Introduction

The national forests of North Carolina reflect the wealth of nature within the Tar Heel State. The Pisgah, Nantahala, Uwharrie, and Croatan represent each of the major physical provinces of North Carolina—the mountains, the piedmont, and the coast and coastal plain. Elevations of the national forests range from sea level along the White Oak River to 6,682 feet atop Mount Mitchell—the highest point in the East. The lands are laced with more than 1,700 miles of trails, including several national scenic paths, such as the famed Appalachian Trail. These trails travel through nearly a dozen designated wildernesses, three wild and scenic rivers, and other special places.

The very first tract of national forest in the eastern United States was purchased in North Carolina, in 1912, shortly after the passage of the Weeks Act. This federal law established the creation of national forests east of the Mississippi River. This first-ever public national forest parcel in the East was located near the town of Marion and is part of the Pisgah National Forest. Over time, more lands were purchased, mostly cutover lands from timber companies, but also old-growth forests in healthy shape. Today, the four national forests of the Tar Heel State contain 1.2 million acres, which translates to 4 percent of the state's acreage.

For North Carolinians from the city and the country, these forests are an increasingly important natural getaway. And well it should be. Hikers can trek trails, as can mountain bikers, equestrians, and four-wheelers. Auto tourists can ply remote roads and scenic byways. Campers can spend the night at a multitude of campgrounds scattered throughout the national forests. Boaters can tackle whitewater streams as well as more serene rivers and lakes. Anglers can vie for fish on the hundreds of miles of cold- and warm-water fisheries. Birders can explore high and low for their favorite species. It is truly a recreation haven for all.

However, recreation is just one component of North Carolina's national forests. They also contain an important reservoir of the nation's timber. Wooded watersheds protect drinking water supplies and reduce flooding. Furthermore, national forests safeguard rare plants and animals and create swaths of land that act as an umbrella for entire ecosystems.

Fact is, North Carolina's national forests are not managed as state or national parks. National forests are multifaceted, and user recreation is not the sole priority in their management, unlike state and national parks, which emphasize recreation and preservation generally, with cleared, easy-to-follow trails. National forests are managed using the multiple-use concept. As officially stated by the national forest website, the concept "advocates a conservation ethic in promoting the health, productivity, diversity, and beauty of forests and associated lands." This means managing for recreation, but also timber production, plant and animal species management, and soil and water management, with no single use emphasized to the detriment of others.

Thus, in national forests, you may find varied trails and trail conditions, from clearly marked and groomed interpretive nature trails like Cedar Point Tideland Trail or well-maintained paths like the Uwharrie Trail, to primitive, poorly marked, and seldom-hiked wilderness trails like the Old Butt Knob Trail in Shining Rock Wilderness.

Readers will find this book most helpful because not only do I construct a mosaic of wide-ranging hikes that reflect the biodiversity of nature and the multiplicity of hiking experiences in North Carolina's national forests, but I also vary the trail descriptions to fit the particular hike. For example, on an easy-to-follow hike I may emphasize historical or natural information that adds layers of understanding to the walk. In contrast, a difficult-to-follow hike through the remote wilderness on a faint path may be heavy on the nut and bolts of the hike, clearly indicating how to make your way through the untamed segments of North Carolina's national forests, rather than emphasizing interpretive information.

Generally speaking, national forest trails are more primitive than state or national park paths. This guide is written with that in mind, to get you to the trailhead, on the path, soaking in the surroundings, and back to the trailhead in one piece. In fact, the hiking trails of North Carolina's national forests *are* wild treasures that can intimidate the most seasoned hiker.

Nevertheless, what we see today in North Carolina's national forests was not always this way. Once these national forests were established, there was much work to do in replanting trees and cutting fire roads and trails. At first the work was slow. Ironically it was the Great Depression that sped the evolution of the forest. Many young men, unable to find a job, joined the Civilian Conservation Corps, which established work camps throughout North Carolina. For nearly ten years they made a mark on the forest. To this day, you can see their handiwork at places like Wayah Bald Tower.

Cutover forests began to recover. Through wildlife management programs, native species began to thrive. White-tailed deer lingered on the edge of clearings; black bear furtively fed on fall's mast. Lesser species came back, too. Pinelands and pocosins were reestablished. Today, a vast array of flora and fauna—from salamanders to falcons, from Venus flytrap plants to northern flying squirrels—call the Pisgah, Nantahala, Uwharrie, and Croatan home.

And now people, as recreationalists, can explore these Carolina wonderlands once again to fish for secretive brook trout, to listen to the wind whistle through highland spruce-fir woods, to smell the tangy salt air from underneath live oaks, and to see the changing of the seasons from pine-clad hills. And to best enjoy the Pisgah, Nantahala, Uwharrie, or Croatan, you must take to your feet. The rewards increase with every footfall along mountaintop meadows, into valleys of rhododendron where waterfalls roar among misted trees, in blooming laurel thickets, or along blackwater coastal streams.

Over the past century North Carolina's national forests have undergone many changes, but through it all, these public lands have shone. There is much to see and little time to see it all in our digital, hurried era. Yet, a respite into the back of beyond will revitalize both mind and spirit. To smell the autumn leaves on a crisp afternoon, to climb to a lookout, or to contemplate how pioneers lived at an old homesite will put our lives into perspective.

This book will help you make every moment and every step count, whether you are leading the family on a brief day hike or undertaking a challenging backpack into the remote reach of the forests. With your precious time and the knowledge imparted to you, your outdoor experience can be realized to its fullest.

Often, forest sightseers randomly pick a hike not knowing where it will lead. Or they follow the crowds wherever they go. Many times, I've been stopped with the question, "What's down this trail?" Choosing a hike at random in the vastness of North Carolina's national forests may result in a rigorous affair with only wasted time to show for your efforts.

This book presents fifty hikes from which to choose. Included are classics such as Shining Rock and Linville Gorge. However, many hikes are off the beaten path, offering more solitude on journeys to lesser-known yet equally scenic sights such as Douglas Falls and Rattlesnake

Landing. You have the opportunity to get back to nature on your own terms.

Two types of day hikes are offered: there-and-back and loop hikes. There-and-back hikes lead to a particular rewarding destination and return via the same trail. The return trip allows you to see everything from the opposite vantage point. You may notice different trailside features the second go-round, and returning at a different time of day may give the same path a surprisingly different character.

To some, returning on the same trail just isn't as enjoyable. With 1,700 miles of North Carolina national forest trails awaiting them, some hikers just can't stand the thought of covering the same ground twice. The loop hikes avoid this. Day hiking is the most popular way to hike in the national forests, but this guide offers hikes that can be backpacked, for those who want to see the cycle of the mountains go from day to night and back to day again. Backpackers must follow forest regulations and practice "Leave No Trace" wilderness use etiquette.

To enter the vast lands of the national forest, to enjoy the woods, and to have wilderness experience can unleash your mind and body. Here you can relax, find peace and quiet. Here you can grasp beauty and splendor: a white quartz outcrop with a window to the valley below, a deer disappearing into a laurel thicket, or shorebirds flying in formation. In these untamed lands you can let your thoughts roam free in eye-pleasing settings, without being hemmed in by our fast-paced existence. The national forests of North Carolina—the Pisgah, Nantahala, Uwharrie, and Croatan—are some of North Carolina's most precious natural resources. Get out and enjoy them.

How to Use This Guide

Each hike has its own unique description. A one-paragraph hike summary is located at the beginning of each hike. It gives an overview of what the hike is like—the terrain and what you might see along the way. Along with the hike summary is an information box that allows the hiker quick access to pertinent information: hike distance, time, difficulty, highlights, cautions, fees/permits, best seasons, other trail users, trail contacts, and GPS coordinates. Below is an example of a summary and box included with a hike:

---

14 • PINK BEDS LOOP

Hike Summary: On this hike, you can walk a historic section of Pisgah National Forest near what is known as the Cradle of Forestry. Travel a perched valley, walking along a ridge-rimmed wetland with rich plant life. Head down the upper South Fork Mills River Valley. The return trip takes you through thickets of mountain laurel and rhododendron, the Pink Beds, while crossing streams. Finally, explore numerous meadows where you might see wildlife on your return trip. Elevation changes along the hike are less than 200 feet, nearly unheard of in these highlands.

Distance: 5.3-mile loop

Hiking time: 2.5–3.5 hours

Difficulty: Easy to moderate

Highlights: High-altitude wetland, laurel and rhododendron blooms

Cautions: Wet trail from beaver dams

Fees/Permits: No fees or permits required

Best seasons: March through November; summer for programs
    at nearby Forest Discovery Center, fall for driest trail

Other trail users: Mountain bikers on second half of loop

Trail contacts: Pisgah Ranger District, 1001 Pisgah Highway,
    Pisgah Forest, NC 28768, (828) 877-3265, www.fs.usda.gov/nfsnc

Finding the trailhead: From the intersection of NC 280 and US 276 in Brevard,
    take US 276 north for 11.3 miles to the Pink Beds Picnic Area, on your right,
    .2 mile beyond the right turn to the Forest Discovery Center.

GPS trailhead coordinates: N35° 21.212′, W82° 46.728′

FROM THE INFORMATION BOX we learn the details of each hike. This hike is 5.3 miles long and forms a loop. **Hiking time** is the average time it will take to cover the route. Hiking time factors in total distance, elevation gain, and trail conditions. Factor in your own fitness level to the given hiking time. **Difficulty** gives you an idea of how challenging the hike will be: easy, moderate, or difficult. This rating is subjective, but I factored in the same elements for determining hiking time—distance, elevation gain, and trail conditions. A long-distance walk with considerable elevation change on a remote wilderness trail deserves "difficult," whereas a level walk on a graveled nature trail gets an "easy" rating. **Highlights** describes the can't-miss part of the trek. **Cautions** reviews any potential hiking hazards, so you can be aware on the front end. Obviously, this doesn't cover every potential pitfall of a given hike, but it does keep you apprised of any hike-specific hazards with which to contend, such as a wet trail from beaver dams on this example. **Fees/ Permits** lets you know ahead of time if there is a charge to park or enter a particular place, or whether a permit is required to hike or camp. **Best seasons** lets you know the time of year when this hike is most rewarding. **Other trail users** informs you as to whether the path is hiker-only or if you will be sharing it with mountain bikers or equestrians. **Trail contacts** details ways to reach the particular national forest ranger district of the given hike, including mailing address, phone number, and website. **Finding the trailhead** gives specific directions from a commonly known location to the hike's starting point. The **GPS trailhead coordinates** enable you to use your navigational aid to find the trailhead as well.

The hike description also includes a narrative of the hike. A detailed account describes trail junctions, stream crossings, and trailside features, along with their distance from the trailhead. This helps you keep apprised of your whereabouts and ensures that you don't miss those features noted. A summary of trail mileages is given at the narrative's end, so you can quickly scan the distance to major trail intersections or highlights. All of the above information should help you make the most of these can't-miss hikes in North Carolina's national forests. Now get out there and hit the trail!

Pisgah National Forest Hikes

Pisgah National Forest Hike Locator Guide

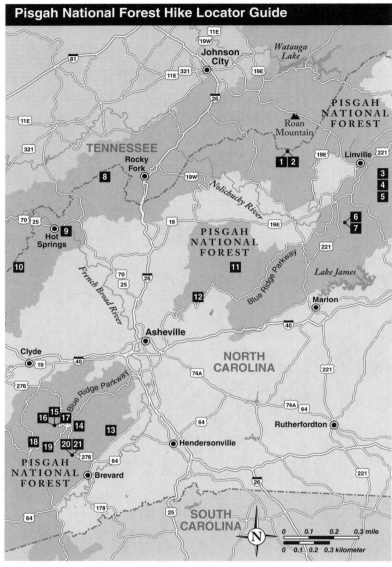

1. Highlands of Roan
2. Roan Gardens and High Bluff
3. Hunt Fish Falls
4. Little Lost Cliffs Loop
5. Falls of Harper Creek Loop
6. Tablerock Loop
7. Tower of Babel at Linville Gorge
8. Shelton Laurel Backcountry Loop
9. Lovers Leap Loop
10. Max Patch
11. Black Mountain Crest
12. Douglas Falls
13. South Mills River Loop
14. Pink Beds Loop
15. Shining Rock Wilderness Loop
16. Shining Rock High Country Hike
17. Sam Knob Loop
18. Middle Prong Wilderness Loop
19. Falls of Graveyard Fields
20. Looking Glass Rock
21. John Rock

1 • HIGHLANDS OF ROAN

Hike Summary: This spectacular hike travels over open meadows and rare spruce-fir forests to a rocky vista above 6,000 feet. You will leave Carvers Gap at the North Carolina–Tennessee state line and head northbound over two grassy balds. Rock outcrops provide more panoramas. Finally, the hike diverges from the Appalachian Trail (AT), and you follow a spur up to the top of Grassy Ridge, filled with more views. Reach a plaque memorializing a man who loved the highlands of Roan as much as you will after completing this trek.

This ridgeline dividing North Carolina and Tennessee is one of the most spectacular stretches of the entire Southern Appalachian Mountains. If the day is clear—and it is often not—then you will be rewarded with multiple 360° panoramas while hiking over a medley of landscapes, including dense spruce-fir forests, open grassy meadows, rock outcrops, brush thickets, gardens of rhododendron, and sometimes all of the above at once.

Also be apprised that this is one of the busier stretches of the AT, but deservedly so. If you're looking for solitude, visit during off times, such as weekdays or during the colder time of year. Leave Carvers Gap and pick up the AT, northbound, by walking through a wooden fence. Begin hiking a gravel track that generally works its way up the west slope of Round Bald. At .2 mile, the trail enters a dusky copse of red spruce and Fraser fir. Evergreen needles cover the coppery forest floor, also sprinkled with mossy rocks. Switchback uphill, emerging onto a grassy slope dotted with small islands of tightly tangled rhododendron and groves of spruce. Views open of Carvers Gap and Roan Mountain to your west. Top out on Round Bald at .6 mile, after a 250-foot climb. Panoramas open in all directions, with Carter County, Tennessee, to the north and Mitchell County, North Carolina, to the south. The views are limited only by the clarity of the sky. Often, fog or clouds roll over the ridgeline, obscuring the view, only to open again. The path descends to Engine Gap at 1.1 miles. Climb amid rock, stunted haw and beech trees, alder, and blueberry bushes. Open onto a prominent rock outcrop at 1.3 miles. Hikers are drawn to boulders that make for excellent seats in this amphitheater of the wild. A stellar vista opens into the Volunteer State. Just ahead you reach the official high point of Jane Bald, not nearly as grassy as Round Bald. Speaking of that, these balds are being kept from growing over by multiple means, including mowing, hand clipping, and even grazing goats!

Drop off Jane Bald, then climb to another striking view at 1.7 miles. Here, you can gaze back at the meadows through which you passed. Roan Mountain looms dark and imposing in the backdrop. Continuing on, stunted mountain ash trees rise above grasses. Carolina juncos flit among the wind-pruned vegetation. Your eyes fight between watching the rocky path at your feet and the changing panoramas in the distance.

At 1.8 miles, the AT splits near an outcrop. There has been a sign here in the past and may be one in the future. Here, the white-blazed AT leaves left and downhill, whereas the trail to Grassy Ridge heads right. Continuing northbound on the AT is a fine option. You will pass over plenty more clearings as well as wooded areas between here and US 19E, the end of that AT segment. However, this hike is aiming for Grassy Ridge and takes the lesser-used right fork. Ascend southeasterly, still straddling the Tennessee–North Carolina line. The path is rutted in places while making its way through low brush, wind-sculpted trees, and tightly grown thickets of rhododendron. Keep climbing, breaking the 6,000-foot barrier.

At 2.1 miles, open onto the grassy part of Grassy Ridge, pocked with

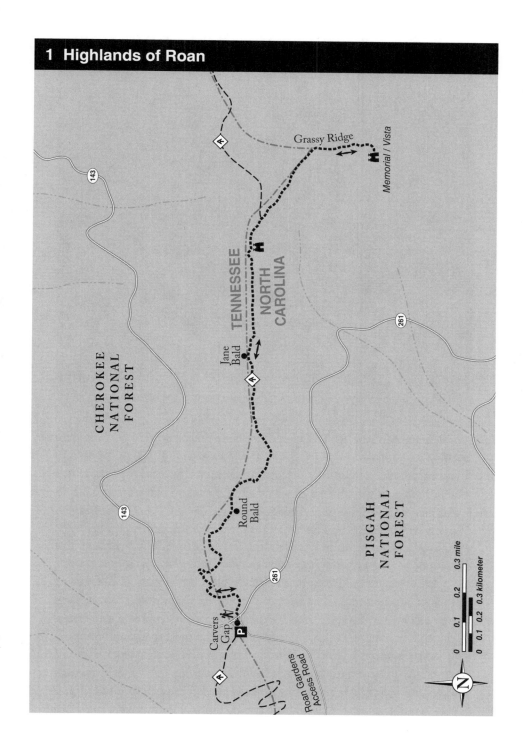

Grassy Ridge

Memorial / Vista

143

TENNESSEE

NORTH CAROLINA

CHEROKEE NATIONAL FOREST

Jane Bald

261

Round Bald

143

PISGAH NATIONAL FOREST

Carvers Gap

P

Roan Gardens Access Road

261

0   0.1   0.2   0.3 mile

0   0.1   0.2   0.3 kilometer

N

As you look out on grassy Jane Bald, Roan Mountain looms in the background.

small evergreen islands. The views just keep on coming. At 2.4 miles the path splits again—stay right, then come to a prominent outcrop where you can see from where you came and points beyond, out to a mosaic of land and vegetation, deserving of its unique place among North Carolina's national forests. A plaque erected by the U.S. Forest Service clings to the loftiest boulder. It is an homage to Cornelius Rex Peake. It states, "A special man who loved God, his country, his fellow men and this land; a legacy from his forefather. Born in the valley below, April 3, 1887, buried near his birthplace March 23, 1964. Because of his love of nature, his long and close association with this mountain, no one was better versed on the Roan and its people." Nothing more to add there. However, you can explore Grassy Ridge beyond the plaque and outcrop. Trails lead along the ridge past more outcrops, along a spruce-cloaked rocky ridge and among grassy swales. Be apprised parts of the ridge are outside the Pisgah National Forest. After walking Grassy Ridge, you will no longer wonder how the highlands of Roan can move a man like Cornelius Rex Peake.

Mileages

0.0 Carvers Gap

0.6 Round Bald

1.1 Engine Gap

1.3 Vista

1.6 Jane Bald

1.8 Trail splits; head right toward Grassy Ridge

2.4 Rock outcrop and plaque

4.8 Carvers Gap

2 • ROAN GARDENS AND HIGH BLUFF

Hike Summary: The natural rhododendron gardens of Roan Mountain have attracted visitors for over 200 years. Today, you can enjoy an all-access sidewalk that wanders among the spruce-fir forest splendor, perched above 6,000 feet on one of the most celebrated peaks of the Southern Appalachians. The half-mile endeavor is complemented by an additional hike to Roan High Bluff, where an observation deck stands on a rock precipice, allowing vistas deep into the Carolina mountains and state line crest dividing the Tar Heel State from Tennessee. Note: The access road for the gardens and Roan High Bluff is open only from mid-May through September.

The gardens of Catawba rhododendron blooming in the highlands of Roan Mountain form one of the most magnificent sights in the Southern Appalachians. Perched at nearly 6,200 feet, the natural gardens of blooming evergreens stretch over 600 acres. During June, with the third week in June being the prime blooming time, visitors flock to this mountaintop. No matter your age or abilities, a half-mile path will take you through this colorful presentation. A small visitor center and picnic area stand at the trailhead. A more elaborate picnic facility stands at the nearby site of the old Cloudland Hotel.

The Gardens Trail, usable by wheelchair-bound visitors, traces a concrete sidewalk under an open sky. Tightly knit, wind-pruned rhododendron borders the trail. Mountain ash, blackberries, and later, evergreens of spruce and fir complement the Catawba.

The all-access loop portion of the hike soon begins, after you pass a spur to a nearby picnic area. This national recreation trail gently eases downhill, then comes to a split. Stay left and follow the narrower outer loop. It is not all-access. Enter a fairyland forest of moss-backed spruce and balsam, ferns and grasses—a green so thick and deep it would make an Irishman pine away for the homeland. The loop dips to reach some crumbling and officially abandoned asphalt paths that stretch farther out the ridge. Hikers still walk these asphalt tracks enough to keep them passable. The official trail begins working its way uphill on a winding trail exhibiting a new high country scene at every turn. It soon rejoins the all-access trail and wanders through a dark spruce-fir thicket. Pass near the picnic area, then complete the loop at .5 mile.

The Cloudland Trail starts across the road from the small trailhead visitor center. A few short steps lead up this path, which started at the nearby picnic area on the site of the Cloudland Hotel. That revamped outdoor dining facility is alluring, with picnic tables, restrooms, and interpretive information, including about the hotel built in 1877. Take the Cloudland Trail left, toward Roan High Bluff. Head out along a ridge, at times tunneling beneath dark evergreens, at other times astride rhododendron. The rocky, natural-surface path stretches southwesterly out a ridge. Shortly pass a spur back to the parking area.

Continue in a green high country forest on a mostly level track. This path is a non-arduous way to savor these spruce-fir woodlands that cloak only the highest mantles of the Southern Appalachians and re-

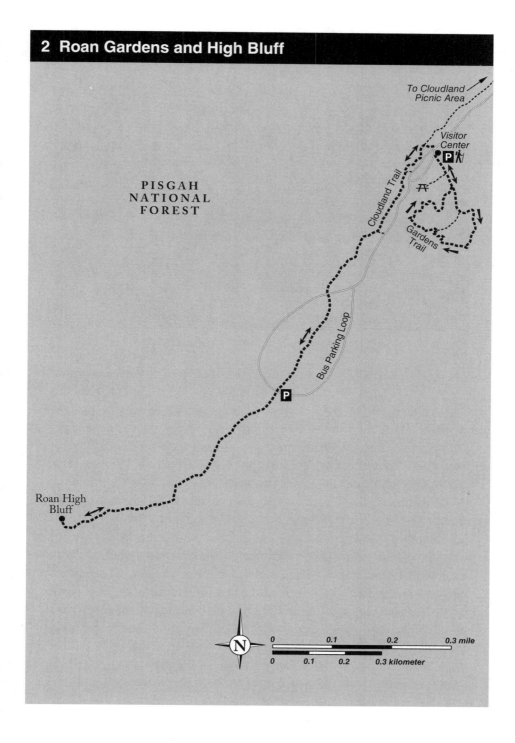

Roan High Bluff provides a panorama of the surrounding countryside.

semble Minnesota's North Woods more than Dixie. Note how thick young spruce grow on the forest floor. These evergreens are replacing their fallen brethren, the full-grown spruce that fall prey to the balsam woolly adelgid, a nonnative insect that has been feeding on these highland forests since the 1950s. The path passes a spur to the bus parking area, then crosses a large loop road for buses. At .6 mile it crosses the bus loop road a final time. You can park here to shorten the hike for less-able trail trekkers. Start an uptick on an old asphalt track. Continue working your way to the ridge's end, passing some stone steps integrated into the rocky landscape. Evergreens continue in thick ranks.

At 1.0 mile from the parking area, open onto Roan High Bluff. A viewing platform extends over the stony precipice. These high-elevation cliffs are home to many a rare plant, and the platform keeps visitors off the cliffs, allowing the vegetation to remain intact. To your right, you can look back along the ridge—see the Cloudland Hotel site picnic area. Sweeping across the panorama, the state line crest dividing North Carolina and Tennessee forms a jagged line to your right. The Appalachian Trail runs along it. Below, the valley of Big Rock Creek drains in multiple tributaries divided by ridges. Across Big Rock Creek, Big Bald rises and Beauty Spot stretches onward. On the far left, Eagle Cliff forms a stony flank, blocking the view farther south. At times, the winds can howl here, limiting the time most visitors can stay. Hopefully the sky will be clear when you visit. And if not, wait a minute and the clouds may lift.

Mileages

0.0   Rhododendron Gardens visitor center
0.5   Return to visitor center and trailhead after loop
1.5   Roan High Bluff, backtrack
2.5   Return to trailhead

3 • HUNT FISH FALLS

Hike Summary: Swimmers and waterfall fans will love this hike, which uses the Mountains-to-Sea Trail (MST) to explore waterfalls and swimming holes on two mountain streams. The trek leads down Gragg Prong, with its impressive waterfalls and slide cascades in an area once proposed as the greater Lost Cove Wilderness. Turn up Lost Cove Creek, enjoying this gorgeous mountain stream. Reach popular Hunt Fish Falls, a two-tier drop with a side-stream falls coming at the same point. However, Hunt Fish Falls's real claim lies in the huge granite-lined swimming hole that is much larger in proportion to the creek where it lies and is widely considered to be the finest backcountry swimming hole in North Carolina's national forests. Elevation changes are less than 500 feet, making the hike fun for everyone.

Hikers can turn this trek into an all-day water extravaganza. Go in the summer, when you can most enjoy the huge pools found along the streams here in the greater Lost Cove area. Kids of all ages will harken back to the fun of swimming and playing around a mountain stream that no artificial swimming pool can mimic.

Join the MST as it crosses a small, clear branch flowing off Bee Mountain above. Immediately, a bluff forces you to Gragg Prong. A campsite and alternate access are across the stream. For now, stay on the right bank of Gragg Prong, at this point a smallish stream with surprisingly large and numerous pools gathering between cascades, gravel bars, and rocky isles. Descend beneath evergreen arbors on the tight valley slope. Ironwood and alder thrive streamside, while holly, black birch, and pines populate the slope.

Make your first rock-hop of Gragg Prong at .4 mile. At normal sum-

3 HUNT FISH FALLS

Distance: 6.0-mile there-and-back

Hiking time: 3.5–4.0 hours

Difficulty: Moderate

Highlights: Three notable waterfalls, huge swimming hole

Cautions: Creek crossings if water is high

Fees/Permits: No fees or permits required

Best seasons: June through September

Other trail users: None

Trail contacts: Pisgah National Forest, Grandfather Ranger District, 109 Lawing Drive, Nebo, NC 28761, (828) 652-2144, www.fs.usda.gov/nfsnc

Finding the trailhead: From Sanford Drive/US 64 on the west side of Morganton, take NC 181 north for 11.5 miles to Brown Mountain Beach Road. Turn right on Brown Mountain Beach Road and follow it 5.0 miles to turn left, as Brown Mountain Beach Road goes left, and the road going straight becomes Adako Road. Look for a national forest sign indicating Mortimer Campground. Follow Brown Mountain Beach Road for 8.5 more miles to a T intersection and gravel NC 90/Edgemont Road. Turn left on NC 90 and follow it past Mortimer Campground for 2.1 miles and the end of NC 90 and a four-way intersection. Turn left here on Roseboro Road/FR 981. Follow FR 981 for 4.1 miles to reach a parking area, then a bridge over Gragg Prong. Cross the bridge, then turn left on a dirt road, passing the Timber Ridge Trail. Ahead, you will see a sign for the Mountains-to-Sea Trail, Trail #440. Start here. Alternate directions: From mile marker 308 on the Blue Ridge Parkway near Linville, take Roseboro Road 4.8 miles to the bridge over Gragg Prong.

GPS trailhead coordinates: N36° 1.890', W81° 48.229'

---

mer flows you can cross dry-shod all the way to Hunt Fish Falls. Trickling tributaries flow across the trail into Gragg Prong. Spur trails lead to alluring pools. At 1.0 and 1.1 miles, rock-hop Gragg Prong again. Campsites are frequent. Then, at 1.2 miles, open onto a gray granite slab and a set of impressive cascades dropping into multiple tiered pools, the lowermost of which is enormous! Open rock slabs lure sunbathers. Some hikers never make it past this locale. The hike continues downstream, coming to a spur leading right to another impressive five-tiered slide cascade at 1.4 miles. This view allows extensive looks down the granite-walled Gragg Prong.

The stream has calmed down, with less rock and more forest, by your crossing at 2.0 miles. At 2.2 miles, meet Lost Cove Creek. Turn right with

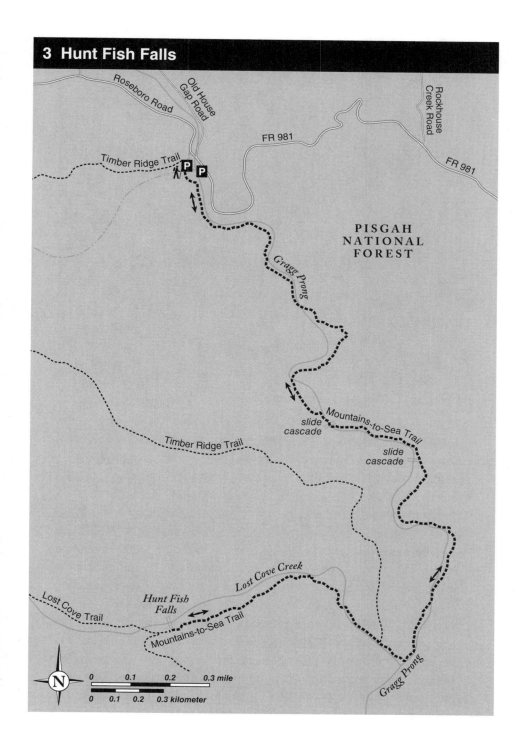

A hiker jumps into one of the many alluring pools along Gragg Prong.

the MST, amid stony stream braids. You are in an easement through private property. At 2.3 miles, the Timber Ridge Trail leaves right. Keep straight in pines, then split left with the MST, rock-hopping Lost Cove Creek at 2.4 miles. The trail opens onto a wide, piney camping flat, then ascends the wooded valley slope. Open onto a rock slab and Hunt Fish Falls at 3.0 miles. The two-tiered falls drops in a sheer curtain followed by a slide, neither of which are high. The first tier drops into an average pool, but the second pool is considered by some to be the best backcountry swimming hole in North Carolina's national forests. Make no mistake: Hunt Fish Falls is about the pool and not the cataracts. The pool is deep, wide, long, and bordered by granite—and worth every step to get here. Ahead, the MST leaves left and climbs .9 mile to Pineola Road and is the most commonly used access for Hunt Fish Falls. The Lost Cove Trail crosses the stream and heads upriver. Expect to spend some time swimming at this fine destination before hiking back past more aquatic beauty of the Pisgah National Forest.

Mileages

0.0   Gragg Prong Bridge trailhead

1.2   First major falls and pools

1.4   Second major falls

2.2   MST turns right up Lost Cove Creek

3.0   Hunt Fish Falls

---

4 • LITTLE LOST CLIFFS LOOP

Hike Summary: Experience highlights both high and low. This hike starts deep in the Pisgah National Forest. First, walk past an old homesite, then find the long and spectacular North Harper Falls, where you can see an extensive 200-foot spilling of water that adds great views to its aquatic beauty. The hike then turns up North Harper Creek in a steep valley. Emerge for a short walk on a quiet forest road, then join the Little Lost Cliffs Trail. This footpath takes you atop Long Ridge, where open crags present spectacular views of other nearby cliffs as well as Grandfather Mountain and the Blue Ridge beyond.

The name of this hike tells only one side of the story. Yes, you will visit the view-laden crags of the Little Lost Cliffs, but that is after stopping by one of the longer and more intriguing falls in the Pisgah–North Harper Falls. It tumbles 200 feet, first as a long slide, then in a more drop-and-pool fashion. As an added bonus, this is one of the few waterfall hikes in the greater Harper Creek area that you can do dry-footed—most others require wet fords. Start your hike on the North Harper Falls Trail, descending. The gated trail to your right is your return route—Little Lost Cliffs Trail. Begin dropping south off Long Ridge on a single-track path overlain on an old forest road. Pines, maples, and oaks shade the wide track. At .1 mile, look left for the standing chimney of an old homesite. Perusal reveals the rock basement and metal relics. A spring is nearby. Imagine scratching out a living in this quiet cove. The trail continues a favorable downgrade, easing in and out of shallow coves. Springs trickle in the hollows divided by drier ridges. In winter you will gain views of Simmons Ridge rising on the far side of North Harper Creek.

Meet the North Harper Creek Trail at 1.0 mile. Turn right here, still on a side slope well above North Harper Creek, and traipse through mountain laurel. Ahead, spur trails lead to parts of North Harper Falls.

4 LITTLE LOST CLIFFS LOOP

Distance: 4.2-mile loop

Hiking time: 2.5–3.0 hours

Difficulty: Moderate

Highlights: Huge waterfalls with mountain views, cliffs with high country vistas

Cautions: Slick bedrock along falls, sheer cliffs

Fees/Permits: No fees or permits required

Best seasons: Year-round

Other trail users: None

Trail contacts: Pisgah National Forest, Grandfather Ranger District, 109 Lawing Drive, Nebo, NC 28761, (828) 652-2144, www.fs.usda.gov/nfsnc

Finding the trailhead: From exit 103 on I-40, take US 64 east for .7 mile, then turn left on US 64 Truck east, also signed as US 64 Bypass. Follow US 64 Truck east for 2.2 miles, then turn left on NC 181 north. Follow NC 181 north for 11.3 miles to Brown Mountain Beach Road, at Smyrna Baptist Church. Turn right on Brown Mountain Beach Road and follow it 5.0 miles to turn left, as Brown Mountain Beach Road goes left, and the road going straight becomes Adako Road. Look for a national forest sign indicating Mortimer Campground. Follow Brown Mountain Beach Road for 8.6 more miles, then turn left on gravel NC 90. Turn left on NC 90 and follow it 1.8 miles, then turn left on Pineola Road/FR 464. Follow FR 464 for 4.9 miles to the Little Lost Cliffs and North Harper Falls trailhead.

GPS trailhead coordinates: N35° 58.651', W81° 45.974'

At 1.2 miles, a well-used spur trail leads left to the top of North Harper Falls. You then gain an understanding of the magnitude of this cataract. Nearby, the stream is beginning an extended downward flow over bedrock, steepening as it descends. The pourover rushes beyond vision. The wide and extensive rock slab opens panoramas of mountains to the east. At normal flows and when it hasn't rained, you can view the remainder of the falls by walking down the bedrock. However, if the water is high or the rock is wet, use the spur trails to access the lower falls. The base of North Harper Falls steepens to a near-sheer drop of 40 feet, ending in a plunge pool.

The North Harper Creek Trail continues beyond the falls, quickly crossing to the left bank of the stream at a campsite. Rock-hop the creek a second time at 1.4 miles. The path steepens and the valley narrows. Cataracts plunge through the shadows of rhododendron, beyond

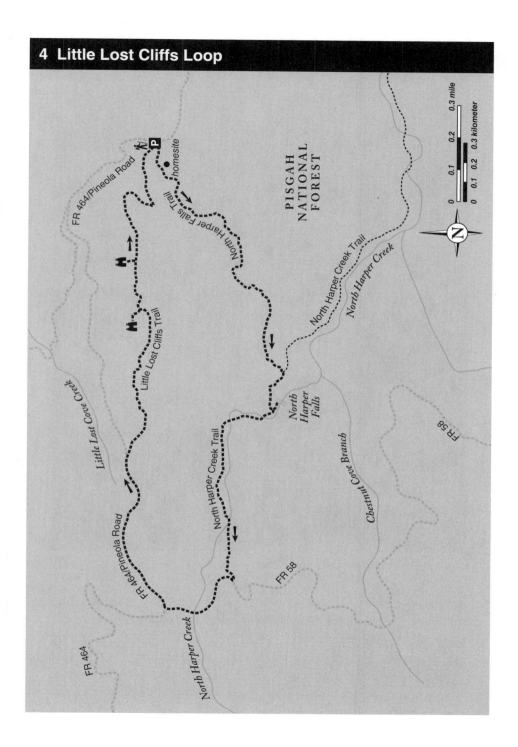

Outcrops along Little Lost Cliffs create dramatic perches.

easy access. Cross an open slab near private property, then rock-hop the creek again at 1.8 miles. The path wanders through a high mountain cove, then emerges onto FR 58 at 2.0 miles. Turn right here, shortly bridging North Harper Creek at 2.2 miles. At 2.3 miles, meet FR 464/ Pineola Road. Turn right here, and begin an easy walk.

Reach the west trailhead of the Little Lost Cliffs Trail at 2.8 miles. Ascend in pine-oak-laurel woods. Level off at 3.0 miles. Make a last jump before the trail splits at 3.2 miles. Head left for the open rock of the Little Lost Cliffs. Magnificent views open before you. The Lost Cove Valley lies in the fore, while a series of ridges rises beyond, culminating in the rocky heights of Grandfather Mountain. Looking right, you can see the other overlook of Little Lost Cliffs. Take time to explore, as other views open. Resume the main trail. Drop to a gap and pass the other vista access at 3.6 miles. From there, the trail wanders through a couple of growing-over wildlife clearings. Note the apple trees hanging on. Wide switchbacks lead you to the trail's end at 4.2 miles.

Mileages

0.0 North Harper Falls/Little Lost Cliffs trailhead
0.9 Right on North Harper Creek Trail
1.2 North Harper Falls
2.0 FR 58
2.3 FR 464/Pineola Road
2.8 Little Lost Cliffs Trail
3.2 First Little Lost Cliffs view
3.6 Second Little Lost Cliffs view
4.2 North Harper Falls/Little Lost Cliffs trailhead

5 • FALLS OF HARPER CREEK LOOP

Hike Summary: Bag two spectacular falls while looping through the wild Harper Creek watershed. First, take a well-trammeled 1.4-mile walk to two-tiered Harper Creek Falls, with its open rock slabs and huge swimming pools. Leave the crowds behind, fording up Harper Creek, passing sand beaches, bald rocks, and grassy islands. Turn up rhododendron-choked South Harper Creek, fording more to reach South Harper Creek Falls, a 200-foot open-rock cascade in a stone gorge. Climb to a top-down view of this cataract, along with a distant mountain vista, before returning to the trailhead through Raider Camp Creek Valley.

This is a great summertime trip in the mountains—swim, fish, and visit cascades to be one with the water. If the mileage seems long, just make the 2.8-mile there-and-back trek to Harper Creek Falls. The way is clear, the hiking easy, and the falls rewarding—and no creek fords required. Beyond there, the creek fords and rougher trail conditions begin. Trailside vegetation can be overgrown along the creeks, but beyond South

Harper Creek Falls, the way clears again. If the streams are high, the respective cascades will be spectacular, but the fords tough. Your best bet is to go when the water is low. Sure, the falls won't be as exciting, but the swimming will be fun and the creek crossings easy.

Leave the trailhead on a single-track path, winding uphill in thick woods. Harper Creek is nowhere to be seen. Top out in a gap at .2 mile. Here, Yellow Buck Mountain Trail leaves right for upper North Harper Creek. The orange-blazed Harper Creek Trail descends straight under white pines and mountain laurel and beside rock ramparts. Meet the Mountains-to-Sea Trail (MST) at 1.1 miles. Stay right, uphill, with the Harper Creek/MST as your return route—Raider Camp Trail—leaves left. Bluffs rise on your right. At 1.3 miles, the trail splits. Stay left with an old logging grade to reach Harper Creek Falls ahead. Hear the roar of the double-dropping watery wonder spilling into a stone cathedral, then falling again into a wide pool. A thick rope allows descent to mid-cataract, where sunbathers hang out and swim. The upper drop is perhaps 30 feet, the second about 15 feet.

Backtrack, rejoining the Harper Creek Trail/MST, deeper into the valley. Any crowds are gone. Holly, white pine, sourwood, and black birch tower over masses of rhododendron, ferns, and doghobble. Along the stream, alder and grasses rise from small islands. Sand beaches gather in places. Gray rock lies slick and smooth. Watch for beaver and their evidence, as well as otters. Make your first ford at 2.3 miles. Continue up the lush, gorgeous gorge. Cross the creek at 2.5 and 2.8 miles. Reach an easy-to-miss trail junction at 3.6 miles. Here, the orange-blazed Harper Creek Trail leaves left, fording Harper Creek, and the blue-blazed North Harper Creek Trail keeps straight along the riverbank. The MST, with its circular white dot, joins North Harper Creek Trail. Leave left, descending to cross Harper Creek at a big pool where North Harper Creek joins Harper Creek. Cross a brushy island, then head upstream in thick rhododendron.

Ford now-smaller, sometimes-canopied Harper Creek at 3.7, 3.9, and 4.0 miles. You are on the right-hand bank. At 4.3 miles, step over an unnamed tributary, then cross over to the left bank of Harper Creek. The next crossing, at 4.5 miles, can be confusing. You must step over several stream braids—which may or may not be flowing—before reaching dry land and the right-hand bank. Shortly cross back over to the left-hand bank. Cruise upstream, passing by an open rock slab where the stream flows down in an S curve, at 4.6 miles.

5 FALLS OF HARPER CREEK LOOP

Distance: 9.4-mile balloon loop

Hiking time: 6.0 hours

Difficulty: Moderate to difficult

Highlights: Two amazing waterfalls, swimming

Cautions: Potentially overgrown trails, stream fords, navigational challenge

Fees/Permits: No fees or permits required

Best seasons: Mid-May through October

Other trail users: Illegal mountain bicyclists along Raider Camp Creek

Trail contacts: Pisgah National Forest, Grandfather Ranger District, 109 Lawing Drive, Nebo, NC 28761, (828) 652-2144, www.fs.usda.gov/nfsnc

Finding the trailhead: From exit 103 on I-40, take the Morganton exit and US 64 east for .7 mile, then turn left on US 64 Truck east, also signed as US 64 Bypass. Follow US 64 Truck East for 2.2 miles, then turn left on NC 181 north. Follow NC 181 north for 11.3 miles to Brown Mountain Beach Road. Turn right on Brown Mountain Beach Road and follow it 5.0 miles to turn left, as Brown Mountain Beach Road goes left, and the road going straight becomes Adako Road. Look for a national forest sign indicating Mortimer Campground. Follow Brown Mountain Beach Road for 7.1 more miles, and the parking area will be on your left.

GPS trailhead coordinates: N35° 58.651', W81° 45.974'

At 4.9 miles, cross to the right-hand bank. You've only climbed 500 feet in nearly 5 miles. That's about to change. The gradient of the trail and creek sharpens. Pass a large pool and beach just before switchbacking uphill. A rock gorge opens. You can hear South Harper Creek Falls. Spur paths leave left to view the cataract from various points along its 200-foot double drop.

Reach the top of the falls and open rock at 5.2 miles. Look back at the stone gorge below. Ahead, the trail splits. Stay left with the Raider Camp Trail, traveling along Harper Creek, then crossing it at a bend. Beyond the crossing, turn left, switchbacking uphill. At 5.5 miles, meet a roadbed and stay left, soon reaching the downhill spur to overlook South Harper Creek Falls. What a view from this piney perch! Below, you can see the two-stage cascade froth white over gray rock. Behind, the distant peaks of Grandfather Mountain and the Blue Ridge rise proudly. Wow! When I think of gorgeous places in North Carolina's national forests, this spot comes to mind.

Resume Raider Camp Trail, traveling southeasterly uphill in pine-oak

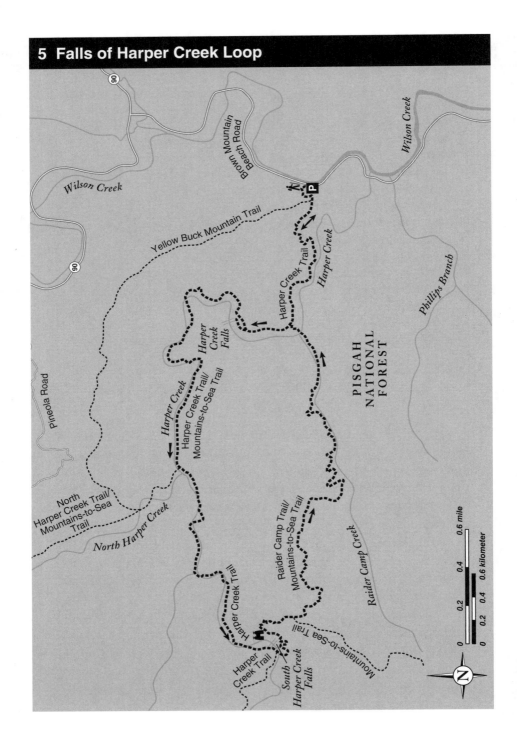

Harper Creek Falls is a dramatic swimming venue.

woods. The absence of water noise is deafening. After the MST joins the Raider Camp Trail, the walking is easy, and you cruise an open ridge with intermittent north views of the Blue Ridge. At 6.5 miles, pass through a gap, and keep straight on an eroded roadbed toward Raider Camp Creek, bisecting tributaries on the decline. The stream comes in sight at 7.4 miles and soon tumbles away in rocky cascades of its own. The sounds of Harper Creek enter your ears. Make your final ford. Work through a jumble of user-created trails and cross a second braid of Harper Creek to reach a trail junction at 8.3 miles. You have completed the loop. Backtrack 1.1 miles to the trailhead.

Mileages

0.0   Harper Creek trailhead
0.2   Yellow Buck Mountain Trail leaves right
1.1   Intersect MST, leave right
1.4   Harper Creek Falls
3.6   Left with Harper Creek Trail, leave MST
5.2   Top of South Harper Creek Falls
5.5   Rock and pine vista of South Harper Creek Falls
5.9   MST comes in from the right, stay left
6.5   Bisect a gap, stay straight
8.2   Ford Harper Creek
8.3   Complete the loop, backtrack
9.4   Reach the trailhead

6 • TABLEROCK LOOP

Hike Summary: *Explore the rim of Linville Gorge on this view-laden trek. Enter Linville Gorge Wilderness amid pines and hardwoods. Hike the inside reaches of the gorge, then climb to Little Tablerock, where warm-up views await. Leave the wilderness. A little more uphill leads to Tablerock summit, where astonishing 360° views expand near and far. It is all downhill back to the trailhead. The overall distance is doable by most hikers. There is one very steep section, but the hike is not too hard relative to other treks in Linville Gorge.*

There's an easier way to reach Tablerock than this one, perhaps too easy. It is not a far walk at all from Tablerock Picnic Area. However, you will savor the view more if you earn it. Moreover, the following hike makes a loop, and you can get a taste of the Linville Gorge Wilderness to boot. Start your hike on the Spence Ridge Trail. Galax, greenbrier, mountain laurel, white pine, and oaks border the mostly level track as it travels westerly. Shortly enter the Linville Gorge Wilderness. Views open of Hawksbill Mountain through the trees. You passed the access trail one mile back on your drive to this hike. It is less than two miles round-trip to its stellar views.

At .4 mile, reach a trail junction. The Spence Ridge Trail turns downhill and to the right, aiming for the Linville River. This hike keeps straight, joining the Little Tablerock Trail, still on the wide, easy roadbed. A light descent bottoms out in a piney gap and campsite at .7 mile. The Little Tablerock Trail curves left and meets a spring branch. Shortly cross a second spring branch. Begin your lung-busting, .5-mile, 800-foot ascent at .9 mile. Since you are within the wilderness, the trails are managed differently. Here, the path will be routed around blowdowns. Brush is not cleared as widely from the path. All of this makes this climb a little bit tougher than it would otherwise be. While you're climbing, be sure to look back at Hawksbill Mountain. Sporadic views can be had of the gorge below. The hike eases upon reaching a rib ridge of Tablerock.

Come to an outcrop and view at 1.5 miles. Step out and take it in. This great vista will seem forgettable in a minute. At 1.6 miles, leave right on a spur for Little Tablerock. User-created trails split off in all directions to rock promontories with stellar views up Linville Gorge and to waves of mountains in the distance. Tablerock is visible behind you through the trees. Across the gorge, Conley Cove Trail can be seen zigzagging up from the Linville River.

Rejoin the Little Tablerock Trail, meeting the Mountains-to-Sea Trail (MST) at 1.7 miles. It has come up a short distance from Tablerock Picnic Area. Keep straight on the MST, and shortly make another intersection. Here, the MST leaves left. For now, keep straight, making the climb to Tablerock, located outside the official delineations of the Linville Gorge Wilderness. The path switchbacks up the stony slopes of Tablerock, dotted with windswept, craggy pines. Watch for sand myrtle, a rare shrub that grows on such outcrops. Interestingly, it thrives on stony peaks like this and along the ocean shore of the Carolinas and a few other states, but nowhere in between. Ahead, an outcrop leads right to a clear view of The Chimneys, a rising formation resembling a smokestack. Continue winding up the peak, avoiding shortcuts of switchbacks. Slip under an

6 TABLEROCK LOOP

Distance: 3.6-mile loop

Hiking time: 2.5 hours

Difficulty: Moderate, but has one steep section

Highlights: Panoramas from Little Tablerock and Tablerock

Cautions: Steep section, wide open rock outcrops

Fees/Permits: Permit required if backpacking inside Linville Gorge Wilderness on May–October weekends

Best seasons: Year-round; winter, spring, and fall for best views

Other trail users: None

Trail contacts: Pisgah National Forest, Grandfather Ranger District, 109 Lawing Drive, Nebo, NC 28761, (828) 652-2144, www.fs.usda.gov/nfsnc

Finding the trailhead: From Sanford Drive/US 64 on the west side of Morganton, take NC 181 north for 23 miles to Gingercake Road (here you will see a sign for Tablerock Picnic Area). Turn left on Gingercake Road and follow it for .2 mile, then veer left on Tablerock Road/SR 1261. After you enter the national forest at .8 mile, the road turns to gravel. Continue following Tablerock Road for a total of 4.3 miles from Gingercake Road to the Spence Ridge trailhead on your right.

GPS trailhead coordinates: N35° 54.216', W81° 52.730'

overhanging rock before cresting out at 2.0 miles. Panoramas open, primarily to the north at first. The Linville River cuts its gorge below, while circular Hawksbill stands out in bold relief. As you walk around the stone- and low-slung-vegetation-covered summit of Tablerock, vistas stretch in other directions. Check out Lake James to the south. The Chimneys and the wall of Shortoff Mountain are easily identified. Rock walls of the other side of the gorge stand out amid the wooded wonderment of the mountain lands around you.

Backtrack to the MST, reaching it at 2.3 miles. Turn right here, keeping downhill on a single-track path. The circular white blazes travel northeast along the base of Tablerock's cliffs. By the way, climbers enjoy the mountain cliffs and have developed several routes. The MST maintains a steady downgrade on a rocky, rooty path, straddling the wilderness boundary. At 2.9 miles, make a big switchback left. Travel beneath rhododendron arbors on the ridge nose.

At 3.2 miles, make a gap. Here, the MST leaves right, but you leave left on an old roadbed bordered in pine. This unnamed trail cruises around the left side of a small knob. Return to the trailhead, completing the loop at 3.6 miles.

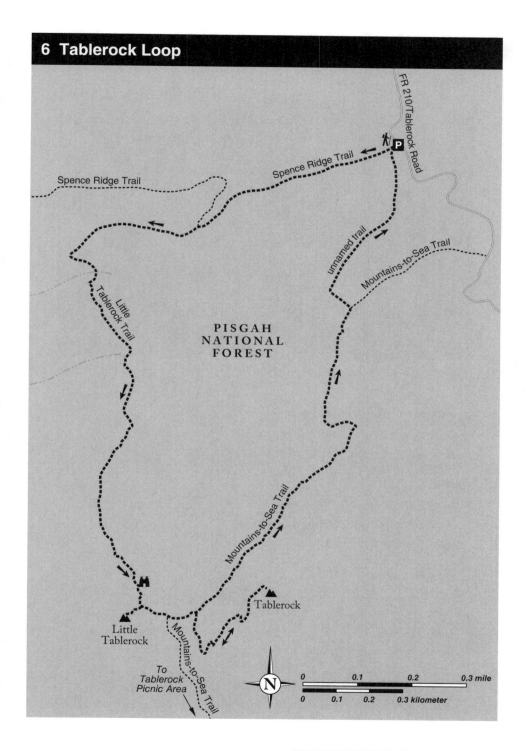

Spence Ridge Trail

FR 210/Tablerock Road

Spence Ridge Trail

P

Spence Ridge Trail

unnamed trail

Mountains-to-Sea Trail

Little Tablerock Trail

PISGAH
NATIONAL
FOREST

Mountains-to-Sea Trail

Tablerock

Little
Tablerock

Mountains-to-Sea Trail

To
Tablerock
Picnic Area

N

| 0 | 0.1 | 0.2 | 0.3 mile |

| 0 | 0.1 | 0.2 | 0.3 kilometer |

Hawksbill Mountain can be seen from Tablerock.

Mileages

- 0.0 Spence Ridge Trail parking area
- 0.4 Stay straight, joining Little Tablerock Trail
- 1.6 Little Tablerock, join MST
- 1.7 Spur trail to Tablerock
- 2.3 Leave Tablerock on MST
- 3.2 MST leaves right in a gap, stay left
- 3.6 Spence Ridge Trail parking area

7 • TOWER OF BABEL AT LINVILLE GORGE

Hike Summary: *This hike explores ultra-rugged upper Linville Gorge. Enter the Linville Gorge Wilderness on a very rocky trail, where you come near the Linville River. A spur leads to the waterway itself, spilling into deep pools after big rapids and chutes. Continuing down the gorge, soak in vistas of the rock-lined valley, ultimately to reach the Tower of Babel, a rock promontory. Grab a view from adjacent outcrops or dare a rock scramble to the tower summit,* *where you can look up and down the gorge, one of the most remarkable places in the entire North Carolina national forest system.*

Time, rock, and water have conspired to craft Linville Gorge, a primitive valley with even more primitive trails. Since this is a wilderness, the trails are maintained at a more rudimentary standard in the uneven, stony terrain. Intersections are signed, however. Expect slow travel and outstanding scenery, both of which will inhibit your hiking speed. Avoid this hike during wet times—slippery rocks will make the path even more hazardous. This is not to say avoid the hike altogether—just be prudent in your endeavor. Remember, permits are required to backpack the wilderness during summer weekends. They can be obtained at the information station on your right, .4 mile before reaching the Pine Gap trailhead.

The hike starts innocuously enough. Pick up the Pine Gap Trail, a single-track path leaving the corner of the parking area. The slender path dips on a stony, rooty trail flanked in dense evergreens. Sidle alongside sheer stone bluffs. Begin switchbacking downhill, coming close to the Linville River at .5 mile. A couple of spur trails lead to the water, where rock slabs border pools and lure in hikers out for brief jaunt into the gorge.

Continue downstream beside rock walls. The path is bisecting a river bend and climbs away from the watercourse. Reach a four-way inter-section deep in evergreens, Pine Gap, at .8 mile. The Bynum Bluff Trail leads right, the Linville Gorge Trail keeps downriver, and a spur leads left down a peninsula. Follow the unnamed trail left down the penin-sula—it's a great place to access the river, on a rocky bar facing a sheer bluff. The peninsular trail travels downward on an ever-narrowing ridge. Views open above the trailside brush. Make the river at 1.0 mile. Explore the waterway and swim if you choose. Otherwise, backtrack to the four-way intersection and pick up the Linville Gorge Trail. Walk be-neath an overhanging bluff at 1.4 miles. At 1.6 miles, come to the edge of a cliff. Upriver panoramas open. Observe pools and cascades of the Linville River, along with vertical waterside walls and more rock forma-tions above.

Switchback down toward the river, meeting it at 1.7 miles. A bluff squeezes the trail to the shore. Climb away, resuming downstream progress. Mosses and ferns thrive in shady, moist locales. More rock walls rise among the dense tree and brush cover. Pick your way through

7 TOWER OF BABEL AT LINVILLE GORGE

Distance: 6.2-mile there-and-back

Hiking time: 4.5–6.5 hours

Difficulty: Difficult due to terrain and primitive trail conditions

Highlights: Gorge vistas and wilderness

Cautions: Lesser-maintained rocky trail, open stone outcrops

Fees/Permits: Permit required if backpacking in wilderness on May–October weekends

Best seasons: Year-round; winter, spring, and fall for best views

Other trail users: None

Trail contacts: Pisgah National Forest, Grandfather Ranger District, 109 Lawing Drive, Nebo, NC 28761, (828) 652-2144, www.fs.usda.gov/nfsnc

Finding the trailhead: From exit 85 on I-40 near Marion, take US 221 north approximately 24 miles to the town of Linville Falls and NC 183. Turn right on NC 183 east and follow it for .7 mile to gravel Kistler Memorial Highway. You will see a sign indicating Linville Falls and Linville Gorge Wilderness. Veer right here and follow the gravel road for .9 mile to the Pine Gap trailhead on your left.

GPS trailhead coordinates: N35° 56.419', W81° 55.812'

irregular footing. Fallen trees become obstacles, and only a foothold is notched in them to aid passage. At 2.3 miles, the trail curves right around a corner. Here, the Cabin Trail leaves right and uphill, headed nearly 1,000 feet up in less than a mile to Kistler Memorial Highway. Stay with the Linville Gorge Trail as it works around a bouldery hollow filled with big rocks. At 2.7 miles, a rock promontory allows a view across the gorge. Ahead, circle around a perennial stream, briefly going downhill. A user-created spur here leads downriver. Don't take it. Instead, stay on the Linville Gorge Trail as it leads uphill over big boulders.

An open rockhouse will come into view on your left just before reaching a four-way trail junction atop a ridge at 3.1 miles. The rockhouse is just off to your left. Here, the Babel Tower Trail comes in from the right; the Linville Gorge Trail keeps straight and drops off the ridge. A wide rock flat is to your left, above the rockhouse. Another trail leads left and downhill. You are in the general Tower of Babel vicinity. Take the left-leading trail toward the tower; a rising rock promontory is visible ahead. Here, spurs circle around the promontory. It you travel the left side of the tower, amid craggy pines and rock aplenty, views open of the gorge below and the river as it bends around the tower. Try to make

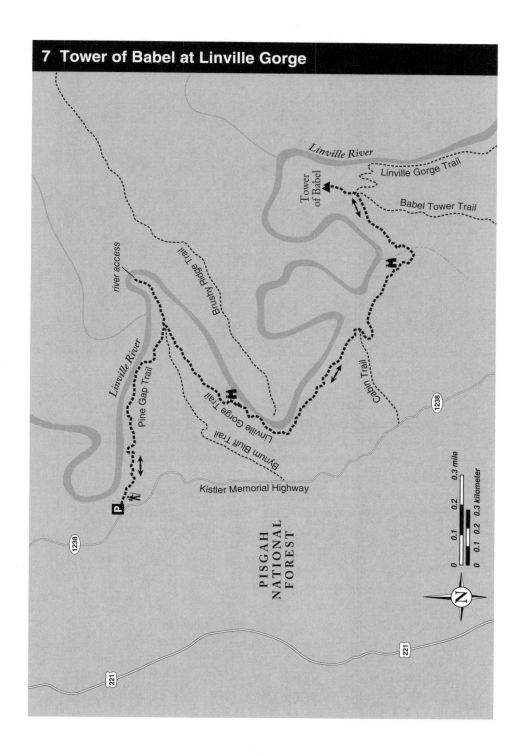

Look downstream into Linville Gorge from the Tower of Babel.

your way up the tower, looking for worn foot- and handholds. If you can make your way atop the tower, likely using all fours, a downriver panorama opens of Linville Gorge. Here, Hawksbill Mountain rises to your left. Tablerock stands in the distance. Cataracts of the river cut a passage through the gorge bottom. Wow!

At this point, you can backtrack to the trailhead. If you have had enough of the gorge, take the Babel Tower Trail 1.2 miles up to Kistler Memorial Highway, then take the dirt road 2 miles back to the trailhead.

Mileages

- 0.0   Pine Gap trailhead
- 0.5   Linville River access left
- 0.8   Pine Gap, four-way intersection, spur left to river
- 1.0   Linville River, backtrack on spur
- 1.6   Cliffside vista
- 2.3   Cabin Trail leads right
- 3.1   Babel Tower area, left to rock scramble with views
- 5.8   Pine Gap trailhead

8 • SHELTON LAUREL BACKCOUNTRY LOOP

Hike Summary: This first-rate circuit offers a waterfall, views, and solitude in a forgotten swath of the Pisgah National Forest. Starting out, the Jerry Miller Trail leads past a 100-foot cascade in a steep hollow. Emerge onto Whiteoak Flats, a former homestead meadow. Climb to a high gap, taking a spur to bold Baxter Cliff. From there, make the Appalachian Trail (AT). Hike a spectacular section of this footpath over the serrated Bald Mountains. Here, a half-mile of continuous outcrops opens multiple views into North Carolina and Tennessee. A steep drop on Fork Ridge returns you to the trailhead.

A memorial to Jerry Miller stands at the trailhead. Mr. Miller was a local who championed the national forests of North Carolina. This hike bridges Big Creek on a wooden span. Turn downstream in a wildflower-filled flat. Begin climbing a ridge, rife with white trillium in spring, dividing Big Creek from Whiteoak Flats Branch. The single-track path turns into Whiteoak Flats Branch watershed at .3 mile. Turn upstream in rhododendron thickets broken with Fraser magnolia, pines, and sourwood.

At .9 mile, the tightening valley nears Whiteoak Flats Branch. Here, a 100-foot slide cascade spills down the hollow. Vegetation blocks a complete view of the froth. The hollow tightens. Step over now-calm Whiteoak Flats Branch at 1.2 miles and a tributary at 1.3 miles. Open onto what remains of Whiteoak Flats meadow. The former homesite is closing in with scrub pines, dogwoods, and tulip trees, but it still offers fall wildflowers and ridge views. This locale is scenic in all seasons.

Leave Whiteoak Flats at 1.6 miles. Open onto a second, smaller clearing at 1.7 miles. Stay with the trail blazes as old roadbeds spur off the main track. Angle upslope, taking a sharp left at 2.1 miles. (An old road goes straight here. Correct routes are evident, and erroneous trails on old roads quickly die out.) Curve onto a dry ridge of gum, mountain laurel, and pine. Turn into Chimney Creek Valley, tunneling beneath rhododendron arbors at 2.8 miles.

Cross trickling branches in upper Chimney Creek. Reach grassy Huckleberry Gap and a four-way intersection at 4.0 miles. To your right is a short path to a campsite. To your left, a trail leads atop a rib ridge then sharply down to the right, making Baxter Cliff after .4 mile. (This mileage is not included in the overall hike mileage.) Stand at the Baxter Cliff precipice, viewing the sheer ramparts of Whiterock Cliff and beyond.

8 SHELTON LAUREL BACKCOUNTRY LOOP

Distance: 10.2-mile loop

Hiking time: 6.5–7.5 hours

Difficulty: Difficult

Highlights: Waterfall, Baxter Cliff, views, good backpacking circuit

Cautions: Steep sections, 2,200-foot elevation gain/loss

Fees/Permits: No fees or permits required

Best seasons: Year-round; spring and fall for wildflowers and views

Other trail users: None

Trail contacts: Pisgah National Forest, Appalachian Ranger District, P.O. Box 128, Burnsville, NC 28714, (828) 682-6146, www.fs.usda.gov/nfsnc

Finding the trailhead: From Asheville, take I-26 west over Sams Gap into Tennessee. Take the first exit in Tennessee, Flag Pond, exit 50. Turn left on Upper Higgins Creek Road, passing under the interstate, traveling .5 mile to TN 23. Turn right onto TN 23 north and follow it for 2.1 miles to TN 352. Turn left on TN 352 west. Reenter North Carolina after 4.1 miles. The road becomes NC 212. Continue for 3.2 miles beyond the state line, then turn right on Big Creek Road, near Carmen Church of God. Follow Big Creek Road for 1.2 miles. The road seems to end near a barn. Here, angle left on FR 111, taking the gravel road over a small creek. Enter the national forest. At .4 mile beyond the barn, veer left onto a short spur road to dead end at Jerry Miller trailhead.

GPS trailhead coordinates: N36° 1.404', W82° 39.177'

The Jerry Miller Trail leaves Huckleberry Gap, angling up rocky tread. Level off just before meeting the AT at 4.5 miles. Turn right, northbound on the AT. Soon come to a trail split. Here, the old AT, now dubbed "Bad Weather Route" stays left, while you stay on the newer AT section. Begin ascending among rock bluffs, boulders, and steps amid northern hardwoods, moss, and doghobble. Make a switchback at 4.7 miles, resuming the state line crest under yellow birch and beech.

Begin the spectacular half-mile at 5.1 miles. Here, a jagged ridge spine rises above the trees. A patchwork quilt of farm and field, framed in mountains, extends into the Volunteer State, with the immediate Pisgah National Forest and layered ridges fading to the Tar Heel State horizon. Interestingly, when the trees are barren, you can see the Jerry Miller Trail climbing toward Huckleberry Gap below.

Stone steps make an irregular course in the rugged geological wonderland. Stunted, windswept trees find purchase in crevices, along with rhododendron, blueberries, mountain laurel, and greenbrier. Your prog-

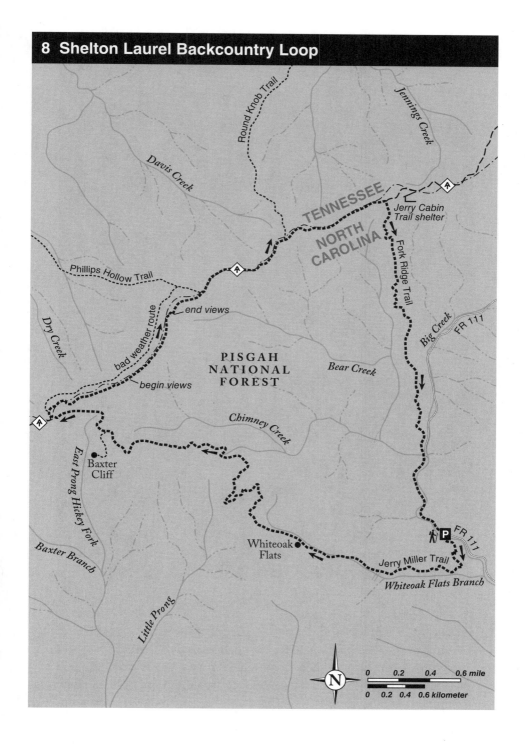

Round Knob Trail

Jennings Creek

Davis Creek

TENNESSEE

NORTH CAROLINA

Jerry Cabin
Trail shelter

Phillips Hollow Trail

Fork Ridge Trail

end views

Dry Creek

begin views

bad weather route

Big Creek

FR 111

PISGAH
NATIONAL
FOREST

Bear Creek

Chimney Creek

Baxter
Cliff

East Prong Hickey Fork

Whiteoak
Flats

FR 111

Baxter Branch

Jerry Miller Trail

Little Prong

Whiteoak Flats Branch

N

| 0 | 0.2 | 0.4 | 0.6 mile |
| 0 | 0.2 | 0.4 | 0.6 kilometer |

Rock inscription greets hikers at the trailhead.

ress is rocky, slow, and remarkable. The trail enters more woods than rock at 5.6 miles. Grab a view of Big Butt on a rock slab, then find one last vista into Greene County, Tennessee, at 5.7 miles. Dip to meet the Bad Weather Route at 6.0 miles. The now foot-friendly AT undulates along the no longer Bald Mountains in hardwoods. (Grazing cattle once kept the ridgecrest open and grassy.) Painted trillium and trout lilies carpet the spring woods. At 6.7 miles, a trail leads left to Tennessee's Round Knob Picnic Area. Bisect a gap at 7.2 miles, then circle right around Andrew Johnson Mountain. At 7.4 miles, turn right and begin free-falling down the Fork Ridge Trail. Drop more than 1,000 feet in the next mile! The pine and rhododendron ridge makes a couple of upticks before descending off the crest to end at FR 111 and Big Creek at 9.4 miles. From here, follow the forest road along trouty, crystalline Big Creek, crossing Chimney Creek at 9.5 miles, then Big Creek at 9.8 miles. Return to the Jerry Miller trailhead at 10.2 miles, completing the hike.

Mileages

0.0   Jerry Miller trailhead
0.9   100-foot waterfall
1.4   Whiteoak Flats
4.0   Huckleberry Gap, spur to Baxter Cliff
4.5   Right on the AT
5.1   Views begin
5.7   Views end
6.0   Meet other end of Bad Weather Route
7.4   Right on Fork Ridge Trail
9.4   Right on FR 111
10.2 Jerry Miller trailhead

9 • LOVERS LEAP LOOP

Hike Summary: *This circuit near the town of Hot Springs travels along a small mountain stream up to a gap and the Appalachian Trail (AT). From there it takes the AT onto Lovers Leap Ridge, a promontory overlooking the French Broad River. Walk a slender rocky crest, gaining glimpses of the French Broad, its rapids and shoals burbling below. Reach an outcrop jutting toward the river lording above the town of Hot Springs and Spring Creek Mountain. Finally, reach the famed Lovers Leap and a stellar view before leaving the AT and returning to the trailhead.*

Purportedly the third-oldest river in the world (only the New River of West Virginia and the Nile River of Egypt are older), the French Broad River is born in the high mountains of western North Carolina near the town of Rosman, traveling a little over 100 miles through the Tar Heel

State before reaching Hot Springs. Here, wooded mountains rise from its banks, hemming in the town formed around warm waters that are among the many area attractions such as rafting, kayaking, camping, and hiking. This hike is certainly an attraction. It isn't too long or too hard, and it is a low-elevation trek by Pisgah National Forest standards, making it a good winter walk. During the shoulder seasons you will see early spring wildflowers on Silvermine Creek. Fall colors will be hanging on into November.

Leave the Silvermine parking area and head up the gravel access road leading to Silvermine Group Camp. Walk the road along Silvermine Creek, rock-hopping Silvermine Creek. Reach the group camp at .3 mile. Pass around a pole gate at the upper end of the camp. Wander amid old forest service junk, and also walk by a pair of concrete dynamite shacks, long in disuse. The Pump Gap Loop Trail then devolves to a single track, piercing the Silvermine Creek Valley under black birch, white pines, striped maple, and rhododendron. The moist, mossy hollow tightens. Wildflowers color the hollow in spring.

At .6 mile, the trail makes a short, abrupt climb as it surmounts an old roadbed, now grown over. To your left, Silvermine Creek is not visible, since it is flowing under a culvert. Soon rejoin the creek, immediately crossing it, then climb away from the water. The hollow alternately widens and tightens as you continue up the diminishing stream. At 1.0 mile, an arm of the Pump Gap Loop Trail leaves left. You can lengthen your loop by taking this spur. It circles back to Pump Gap, where you are headed. This hike stays forward here, climbing sharply. Straight-trunked hardwoods rise from surrounding rhododendron. The ascent eases before reaching Pump Gap and the AT at 1.5 miles.

Turn right on the AT, southbound, climbing a bit. The trail winds in and out of shallow drainages. Top out at 2.1 miles, gaining the crest of Lovers Leap Ridge. Pine, black gum, chestnut oak, and mountain laurel flank the rocky path. The rapids of the French Broad River are audible below, as are sounds of civilization. Partial valley views can be seen through the trees. Undulate on the crest. At 2.4 miles, reach a gap, then slip over to the river side of the ridge. Craggy rocks rise from the pines on this south-facing slope. At 2.8 miles, pass a large campsite on your left. Your descent continues. At 3.1 miles, look for a well-worn trail leading acutely left. Follow the side trail to an incredible tan-colored, rock-rib ridge jutting out toward the French Broad. Be careful as you

9 LOVERS LEAP LOOP

Distance: 3.9-mile loop

Hiking time: 3.0 hours

Difficulty: Moderate

Highlights: Views of French Broad River Valley from Lovers Leap and other outcrops

Cautions: A few steep spots, rock scramble to one view

Fees/Permits: No fees or permits required

Best seasons: Year-round; early spring for wildflowers

Other trail users: None

Trail contacts: Pisgah National Forest, Appalachian Ranger District, P.O. Box 128, Burnsville, NC 28714, (828) 682-6146, www.fs.usda.gov/nfsnc

Finding the trailhead: From exit 19A on US 23/future I-26 north of Asheville, take US 25/US 70 21 miles to Hot Springs. Just before crossing the bridge over the French Broad River, just east of Hot Springs, turn right on River Road. Drive a very short distance to the river and turn left on a paved road, Silvermine Creek Road, following it under the US 25/US 70 bridge. Stay left again as it curves up Silvermine Creek past houses. Reach the signed Silvermine parking area on your left, .3 mile from US 25/US 70.

GPS trailhead coordinates: N35° 53.550', W82° 49.094'

scramble out this narrow outcrop. A forlorn pine stands at the outcrop's end. Clear looks at the river, Hot Springs, and the rising ridges beyond are a just reward for hikers.

Resume the AT southbound, still descending. At 3.4 miles, reach an intersection. Your return route, the Lovers Leap Trail, leaves right. First, follow the AT to two overlooks, the first very near the intersection, and second, follow the AT just a little farther to a switchback and an outcrop. This rock outcrop, with more open views, is Lovers Leap. Here, an Indian princess purportedly leapt to her death after learning of the death of her one and only love at the hands of a rival suitor who wanted the princess for himself.

Begin a steady downgrade on the gravelly Lovers Leap Trail, making a sharp switchback to the left at 3.7 miles, just above the Silvermine Group Camp. Negotiate a steep slope above Silvermine Creek, dropping to creek level before emerging at the trailhead at 3.9 miles, completing the hike.

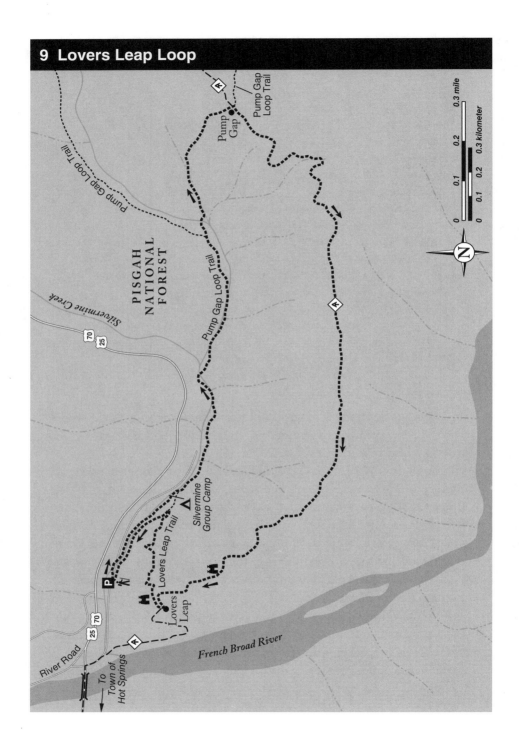

Look into Hot Springs from Lovers Leap.

Mileages

- 0.0   Silvermine trailhead
- 0.3   Silvermine Group camp
- 1.0   Arm of Pump Gap Loop Trail leaves left
- 1.5   Pump Gap
- 3.1   Grand view from rock-rib ridge
- 3.4   Lovers Leap vista, right on Lovers Leap Trail
- 3.9   Silvermine trailhead

10 • MAX PATCH

Hike Summary: *This short loop hike encircles venerated Max Patch, a former mountaintop pasture, now scenic home to stunning views of surrounding highlands. The Max Patch Loop Trail starts along the western slopes, where you can look into Tennessee. Make a short side trip to the 4,629-foot summit of Max Patch, soaking in 360° panoramas. Follow the Appalachian Trail (AT) northbound into woods, skirting past springs. Curve back to the trailhead in a mix of field and forest, taking in more views and high country splendor before the walk is complete.*

10 MAX PATCH

Distance: 2.7-mile loop

Hiking time: 1.5–2.0 hours

Difficulty: Easy to moderate

Highlights: 360° mountain views, blackberries in season

Cautions: Fog obscuring trail, snow in winter

Fees/Permits: No fees or permits required

Best seasons: October through April for best views

Other trail users: None

Trail contacts: Pisgah National Forest, Appalachian Ranger District, P.O. Box 128, Burnsville, NC 28714, (828) 682-6146, www.fs.usda.gov/nfsnc

Finding the trailhead: From exit 7, Harmon Den, on I-40 west of Asheville, Cold Springs Creek Road/FR 148, right for 6.3 miles to reach a T intersection. Turn left here on NC 1182/Max Patch Road. Follow it for 2.0 miles to the Max Patch parking area on your right.

GPS trailhead coordinates: N35° 47.789′, W82° 57.751′

The AT, while passing through North Carolina's national forests, finds many highlights. But some hikers think Max Patch is the best of them all. Known as "the grandstand of the Smokies," this grassy bald presents vistas of that national park, plus views of lands in all four cardinal directions. The grassy slopes reveal more intimate beauty as well: colors of wildflowers in summer, heavy with blackberries in places; tawny brown fields waving in the fall wind; and a blanket of white in winter. And as long as the clouds aren't swirling about, the vistas remain no matter the season. With elevation changes under 500 feet and shortcut options available, this hike is ideal for giving younger and/or less able hikers a taste of the high country.

The most popular path is the one going directly up Max Patch. Instead, head left on the Max Patch Loop Trail, tracing an old roadbed on a grassy track. Vistas open immediately, northwest into the Volunteer State. A few trees and berry bushes begin to border the path. Blackberries will ripen in early August. Enter tree cover, primarily maples, at .2 mile. The main field of Max Patch rises to your right. At .3 mile, a short spur leads left to a spring box, a vestige from the days when cattle roamed the peak, grazing in summer while farmers down in the valleys grew hay for winter.

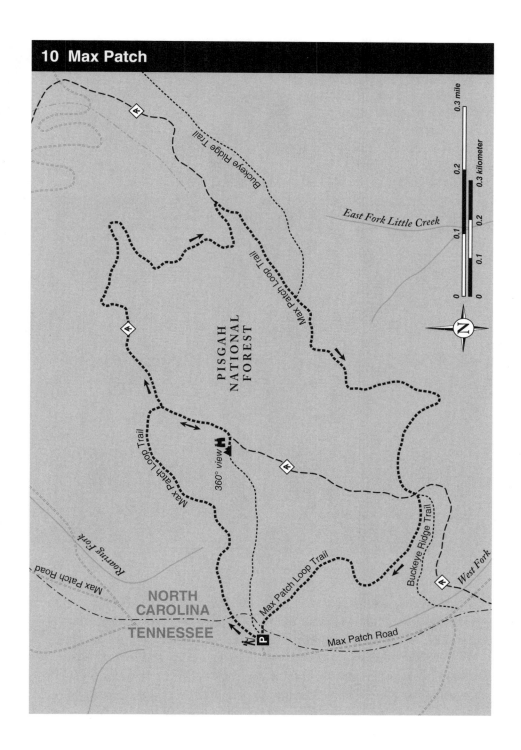

East Fork Little Creek

Buckeye Ridge Trail

Max Patch Loop Trail

PISGAH
NATIONAL
FOREST

Max Patch Loop Trail

360° view

Roaring Fork

Max Patch Road

NORTH
CAROLINA
TENNESSEE

Max Patch Loop Trail

Buckeye Ridge Trail

West Fork

Max Patch Road

0.3 mile

0.3 kilometer

N

A hiker crosses the snow-covered grassy crest of Max Patch.

Open to meadow again at .5 mile. Shortly meet the AT. Turn right here, southbound, aiming for the summit of Max Patch, which you soon reach. A USGS survey marker denotes the spot. You may not notice the marker on a clear day, as your eyes will be drawn southwest to panoramas of yon Smoky Mountains. Mount Cammerer, with its distinct curves, and Mount Sterling, with its metal fire tower, are distinctly visible. Beyond that, swells of ridgelines roll in a sea of highlands. And to the east, Carolina crags extend as far as the clarity of the sky allows.

Nearer, you can see the meadows below and the trail you will soon be walking. This is a truly inspiring panorama.

Turn about, heading northbound on the world's most famous footpath, passing where you were earlier. The wooden trailside posts help hikers find the path in rainy or foggy conditions. The AT descends north, entering woods at 1.0 mile. Reach a fenced-in spring and campsite at 1.4 miles. Travel amid tightly grown rhododendron.

Come to a trail junction at 1.5 miles. Turn right here, back on the loop trail. Enter a mix of meadow, brush, and trees. Buckeye Ridge rises to your left, and views of Max Patch open to your right, above meadows. At 1.7 miles, keep forward as the Buckeye Ridge Trail comes in on your left. Step over a couple of spring branches in woods. At 2.3 miles, come to a four-way intersection. Here, the AT goes right uphill and left downhill, and the Buckeye Ridge Trail follows an old roadbed. You take the grassy path, keeping on a side slope, the loop trail. Wander in a blend of small trees, grasses, and brush. More views open to your left. Return to the trailhead at 2.7 miles, completing the hike.

Mileages

0.0	Max Patch parking area
0.7	Summit of Max Patch
1.5	Leave AT
2.3	Cross AT
2.7	Max Patch parking area

11 • BLACK MOUNTAIN CREST

Hike Summary: *North Carolina's national forests don't get any higher than this. Walk along the rugged crest of the 6,000-foot-plus Black Mountains, soaking in the rare spruce-fir forest community. Begin at esteemed Mount Mitchell State Park to hike a rugged, bouldery track into the Pisgah National Forest, surmounting four named peaks. Favorable weather will treat you to extensive views from outcrops. The hike leads to grassy Deep Gap, with camping potential. The return trip will have more up than down, so allow for plenty of time and energy.*

As the last ice age retreated north, cold-weather plants and animals retreated as well—except for those that survived on the highest peaks

11 BLACK MOUNTAIN CREST

Distance: 7.6-mile there-and-back

Hiking time: 4.5–5.5 hours

Difficulty: Difficult

Highlights: Highest ridge in North Carolina, superlative vistas, rare spruce-fir ecosystem

Cautions: Steep sections, minor rock scrambling

Fees/Permits: Overnight parking permit required if leaving a car at Mount Mitchell State Park

Best seasons: Mid-May through late June, late August through mid-October

Other trail users: None

Trail contacts: Pisgah National Forest, Appalachian Ranger District, P.O. Box 128, Burnsville, NC 28714, (828) 682-6146, www.fs.usda.gov/nfsnc; Mount Mitchell State Park, 2388 State Highway 128, Burnsville, NC 28714, (828) 675-4611, www.ncparks.gov

Finding the trailhead: From Asheville, take the Blue Ridge Parkway north 34 miles to milepost 355. Turn left on NC 128 into Mount Mitchell State Park. Follow the scenic highway nearly to the Mount Mitchell parking area. Very near the top you will be turning right and seeing the state park picnic area on your left. Follow the paved path into the picnic area and beyond as it turns to gravel.

GPS trailhead coordinates: N35° 45.952', W82° 15.905'

down in Dixie. These mountaintops formed cool-climate islands where the northern species comprising what is now known as the spruce-fir community continue to survive in the South. The crest of the Black Mountains forms such an island. You can walk amid this boreal, Canadianesque ecosystem, surmounting the stony peaks that rise from these evergreens. Yet the hike presents other scenes: open grassy locales, ultra-dense woods dark as dusk, and thickets of blooming Catawba rhododendron.

The Black Mountain Crest Trail is also known as the Deep Gap Trail. Start your hike by joining the gravel track leaving the state park picnic area. It immediately enters dense evergreens, primarily Fraser fir, one of the two primary components of this highland forest; the other is red spruce. Mountain ash and yellow birch are two deciduous hardwoods clinging to these heights. Moss grows on anything that doesn't move. The Black Mountains receive more than 80 inches of rain per year, leaving them a very moist, rich locale.

Heavy stone steps make the footing friendly at first. Drop to a gap

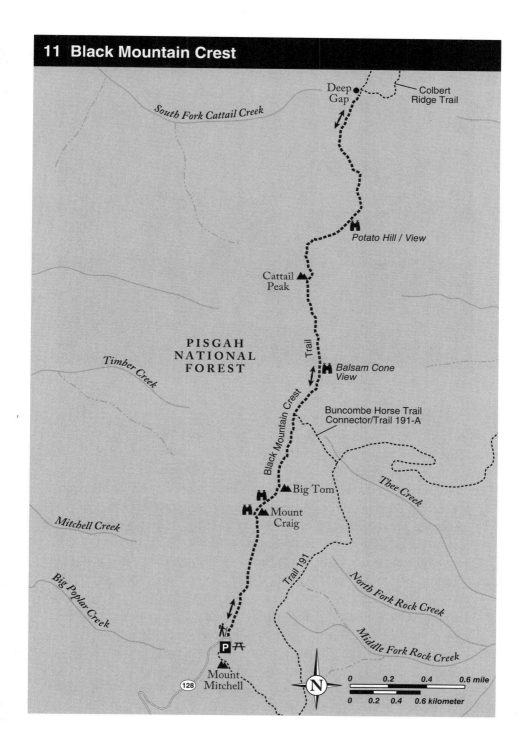

Fraser fir trees rise high as mountains fall away in the distance.

at .4 mile, then begin working uphill. The trail tread turns primitive, and you are working over the first of many irregular rock slabs on the spine of the mountain. Sometimes, hands will be necessary to clamber up or drop down. Sturdy shoes will help with muddy trail sections. Open onto Mount Craig at 0.9 mile. A sign advises to stay on the trail, preserving the fragile plants growing on the adjoining outcrops of the 6,647-foot mountain, second-highest in the East, a mere 37 feet below Mount Mitchell. Views open south to Mount Mitchell, the Blue Ridge Parkway, and points west. While here, thank North Carolina governor Locke Craig for spearheading the establishment of this state park back in 1915. More rocky views open ahead, many to the north, where you are going. Undulate a bit and reach Big Tom at 1.1 miles, a wooded knob named for guide and bear hunter Tom Wilson.

Just ahead, the crest begins dividing the state park on the west side from Pisgah National Forest on the east side. At one point, the drop from Big Tom is steep and slick enough to have ropes aiding your descent. Reach a low point at 1.4 miles. You are still 6,200 feet high. Traverse ever-changing forestscapes to reach a trail junction at 1.6 miles. Here, Trail 191-A, Buncombe Horse Connector Trail, leaves right. The Black Mountain Crest Trail keeps straight, making a solid climb to reach the peak of Balsam Cone at 1.9 miles. Views open on both sides of the 6,611-foot knob. Look below and east for the open slopes of Maple Camp Bald. The rock slab of Potato Hill is visible to the northeast. Scattered communities lie in the valleys below.

Soon, the Black Mountain Crest Trail fully leaves the state park. At 2.4 miles, pass a dry rock overhang on trail left and shortly reach the wooded summit of Cattail Peak. Bronze needles of spruce and fir overspread the level crest, shaded by the evergreens that deposited them. Keep north in dense forest. At 3.0 miles, crest out on Potato Hill. Short spurs lead to views both east and west to spectacular vistas. Look back south at Mount Mitchell and the craggy crest crossed between here and there.

It is mostly downhill to Deep Gap. If the hike has been arduous thus far, consider turning around to avoid the 800-foot return ascent from Deep Gap. However, the only legal camping with water is at Deep Camp, so backpackers must continue. Drop to the right side of the ridge, passing a rock wall. Reach grassy Deep Gap at 3.8 miles. From the clearing, soak in views of stone-pocked Deer Mountain. Camping areas are scattered about. The Colbert Ridge Trail is .1 mile north of the gap. Old Deep Gap Road, an unmaintained track, leaves acutely left from the saddle. If you go far enough down either trail, backpackers will find water. From here, the Black Mountain Crest Trail continues along the ridgecrest to Celo Knob, then descends along Bowlens Creek to its northern trailhead, 8 miles from Deep Gap.

Mileages

0.0   Mount Mitchell State Park picnic area
0.9   Top of Mount Craig, incredible views
1.1   Big Tom
1.9   Balsam Cone, views
3.0   Potato Hill, views
3.8   Deep Gap
7.6   Mount Mitchell State Park picnic area

12 • DOUGLAS FALLS

Hike Summary: Expect solitude on this high country hike featuring two gorgeous yet distinctly different waterfalls. Leave the Craggy Mountains crest on the Mountains-to-Sea Trail (MST) before joining the seldom-trod upper Douglas Falls Trail. Visit Cascade Falls, a long, sliding cataract. Drop past massive boulders to reach 60-foot Douglas Falls, which spills over an overhanging rock cliff. Allow for plenty of time for your 1,300-foot return climb to the trailhead.

This is a great hike when other trails are busy. However, since the hike starts on the Blue Ridge Parkway, you are subject to parkway road closures. By midsummer the trails can be overgrown. Consider wearing long pants. The first two weeks of May are ideal—the streams will be up, the trailside brush down, and the wildflowers showy. Boots will help with the stony footway. The old national forest Halfway Trail once led to Douglas Falls, but the upper part of the Halfway Trail was integrated into North Carolina's master path—the MST—and the lower half renamed Douglas Falls Trail but kept the Halfway Trail's old number, 162. Name and trail aside, Cascade Falls and Douglas Falls continue pouring from the Craggy Mountains, providing scenic rewards for those who take this lesser-used hike.

Leave the southwest corner of the Craggy Gardens visitor center parking area, joining a connector leading to the MST. You are over a mile high. The single-track footpath winds between rock outcrops underneath short, wind-pruned hardwoods of yellow birch, buckeye, and red maple. Ferns, moss, stinging nettle, and hobblebush thicken the understory. At .1 mile, turn right on the MST, heading north, below the Craggy Gardens visitor center. Travel is slow on the rocky, rooty path. Factor this into your hiking time. Shortly enter Pisgah National Forest, undulating north out Big Fork Ridge amid gray boulders and outcrops. Beech trees shade waving grasses. The ridgeline narrows at .7 mile, and the trail descends into the Carter Creek watershed, of which aptly named Waterfall Creek is a tributary. Watch for large but weather-beaten yellow birches on the slope. At 1.0 mile, the hike leaves left on the Douglas Falls Trail, Forest Trail 162. The slender path drops away in numerous switchbacks—don't shortcut them; it only causes erosion. At 1.6 miles, step over a small stream. The watercourse does have a 25-foot slide cascade above the crossing but isn't Cascade Falls.

12 DOUGLAS FALLS

Distance: 6.6-mile there-and-back

Hiking time: 3.5–4.5 hours

Difficulty: Moderate to difficult

Highlights: Two dissimilar yet superlative waterfalls, solitude

Cautions: Irregular, rocky, and sometimes overgrown trail

Fees/Permits: No fees or permits required

Best seasons: May through June

Other trail users: None

Trail contacts: Pisgah National Forest, Appalachian Ranger District, P.O. Box 128, Burnsville, NC 28714, (828) 682-6146, www.fs.usda.gov/nfsnc

Finding the trailhead: From Asheville, take the Blue Ridge Parkway northbound 18 miles to the Craggy Gardens Visitor Center, on your left at milepost 364.6. Do not go to the Craggy Gardens Picnic Area, south of the visitor center. Pick up the Mountains-to-Sea Trail on the southwest corner of the paved parking area.

GPS trailhead coordinates: N35° 41.964', W82° 22.799'

Dip into a rhododendron thicket at 1.9 miles, then reach Cascade Falls. The trail leads you into the middle of an incredibly long rock cascade. It starts way above the trail crossing, then spills over layer after layer of rock, widening and narrowing, dashing across the trail, and then shooting over more rock into a tunnel of vegetation and out of sight. Length? Perhaps 100 feet—or more. The cataract is so long you can't grasp its entirety. Note the metal poles embedded into the rock. A cable connected to the embedded poles once ran across the open rock slab you must traverse. The crossing is a little daunting, since a slip leaves you sliding down Cascade Falls. The crossing could be downright treacherous in icy weather. However, under normal flows you won't even wet your boot tops. Regal, old-growth hemlocks once shaded the stream and following sections of trail. Unfortunately, they have fallen prey to the hemlock woolly adelgid.

Continue working along the western slope of the Craggy Mountains, where the Blue Ridge Parkway snakes northbound. Oaks join the forest as you slowly lose elevation. Cross another stream at 2.2 miles. Work over a rib ridge, then reach yet another stream at 2.6 miles. This unnamed tributary is the creek you will see fall off a cliff face as Douglas Falls. Here, it is simply an alluring mountain rill, spilling in small shoals, in pools, and over rocks. Curve away from the branch, watching for a

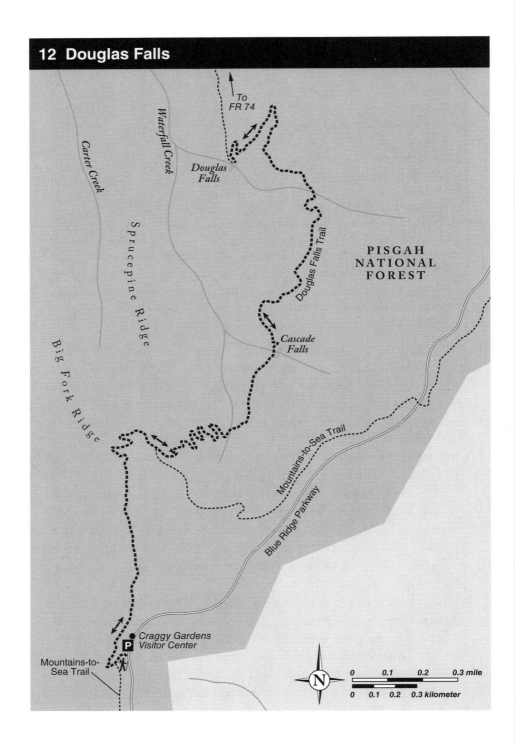

To
FR 74

Waterfall Creek

Carter Creek

Douglas
Falls

Sprucepine Ridge

Douglas Falls Trail

PISGAH
NATIONAL
FOREST

Big Fork Ridge

Cascade
Falls

Mountains-to-Sea Trail

Blue Ridge Parkway

Craggy Gardens
Visitor Center
P

Mountains-to-
Sea Trail

N

| 0 | 0.1 | 0.2 | 0.3 mile |
| 0 | 0.1 | 0.2 | 0.3 kilometer |

Douglas Falls sprays from a stony lip.

huge red oak on trail right at 2.8 miles. Obscured views open as you work around a ridgeline. Drift into a brushy area. A wide, pebbly seep flows across the trail. At 3.0 miles, the path makes a hard switchback left. The abandoned Bullhead Ridge Trail keeps straight at the switchback.

Cross back over the seep, then come to a huge, house-sized boulder. The Douglas Falls Trail descends left around the boulder. Crashing watery noises drift into your ears. Come to a campsite below the huge boulder. Trails go left and right. Walk right, with the official path, as a user-created erosive track dives left for the falls. A short switchback takes you to Douglas Falls at 3.3 miles. The unnamed stream tumbles down an open cliff line into a curved, overhanging stone amphitheater, open to the sky overhead. Go ahead, walk *behind* the ribbonlike chute, enjoying the cataract from multiple vantages. That is one of the highlights of 60-foot Douglas Falls—you can enjoy it in so many ways. Don't be surprised to see more hikers at the falls than you anticipated. Most of them will have come the short, easier way from FR 74.

Mileages

0.0   Mountains-to-Sea trailhead connector at Craggy Gardens visitor center

0.1   Right on MST

1.0   Left on Douglas Falls Trail

1.9   Cascade Falls

3.0   Hard left switchback

3.3   Douglas Falls

6.6   Craggy Gardens visitor center

---

13 • SOUTH MILLS RIVER LOOP

Hike Summary: This loop traverses the lower end of the South Mills River, a trail network that offers day hikes, backpacks, and angling opportunities aplenty. Start at sometimes-busy Turkeypen trailhead, dipping to the South Fork Mills River. Follow the trout haven downstream, making multiple fords in a wildflower-filled vale. Turn up Bradley Creek, which presents more riparian beauty. Surmount Pea Gap, returning to the trailhead. Elevation changes are less than 300 feet, making the stream fords the only challenge to this circuit.

I've hiked the greater South Fork Mills River area in all four seasons. This backcountry trail network is a gem of the Pisgah National Forest. The trails, traveling along the river and its tributaries, as well as ridges dividing them, are well marked and maintained. A look at the Pisgah Ranger District map shows that loop possibilities are limited only by your time. I like this particular circuit because it explores the largest and lowest part of the South Fork, with its big flats, deep pools, and

13 SOUTH MILLS RIVER LOOP

Distance: 7.6-mile figure-8 double loop

Hiking time: 4.5 hours

Difficulty: Moderate, though fords can make it tougher in high water

Highlights: Spring wildflowers, mountain streams, trout fishing, backpacking opportunities

Cautions: Fords at high water

Fees/Permits: No fees or permits required

Best seasons: April through May for wildflowers, June through mid-October for camping and fishing

Other trail users: Mountain bikers, equestrians

Trail contacts: Pisgah Ranger District, 1001 Pisgah Highway, Pisgah Forest, NC 28768, (828) 877-3265, www.fs.usda.gov/nfsnc

Finding the trailhead: From exit 40 on I-26 south of Asheville, take NC 280 west for 10.2 miles to Turkeypen Road, on your right, just after Boylston Creek Church (Turkeypen Road is signed on the highway, but the entrance looks like a gravel driveway). Follow Turkeypen Road for 1.2 miles to dead end at the trailhead.

GPS trailhead coordinates: N35° 20.576', W82° 39.565'

everywhere-you-look beauty, highlighted by spring wildflowers. And it has no steep climbs or descents that characterize much of the Pisgah. Backpackers will find established campsites. Note: You will get your feet wet on this hike, so plan accordingly.

Four trails leave Turkeypen trailhead. As you face north at the signboard, you will have a gated trail to your right, your return route, and a single-track path to your left. Ridge-running trails leave left behind you. Take the footpath descending left on the heavily used gateway South Mills River Trail. Make a junction and South Fork Mills River at .4 mile. A bridge crosses the river here, including the upstream continuation of the South Mills River Trail. You stay right, on this side of the river, heading right, downstream on the Bradley Creek Trail. Just ahead, come to a four-way trail intersection. The road leading right is your return route to the trailhead. A horse ford goes left. You keep straight, still on the Bradley Creek Trail, bordered by ferns, doghobble, and rhododendron. Pines, ironwood, and hardwoods rise overhead. The South Mills is about 30 to 40 feet wide at this point, falling in rocky rapids divided by clear pools.

Make your first ford at .8 mile. If you can get through this one, then

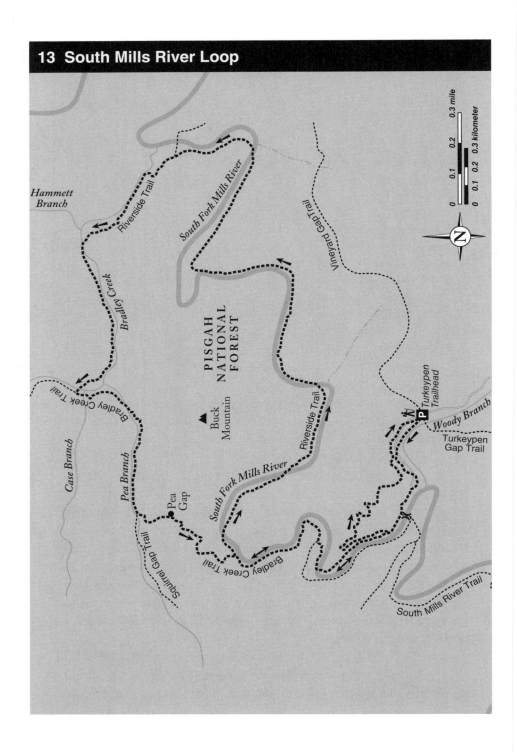

Cool, clear trout streams abound on this hike.

you've got it made. A foot trail leads left from the ford back to the bridge, but you have many crossings ahead, so there is no point avoiding this one ford. Before your hike, you can check USGS water gauge "Mills River near Mills River, NC." This gauge is downstream of the hike but will reveal the likelihood of South Fork being at normal flow levels for any given day.

At 1.3 miles, reach the main loop portion of your hike. Here, the Bradley Creek Trail leaves left (you will return that way). For now, stay right with the Riverside Trail, still following the South Mills past gravel bars, sandbars, and boulders beside the moving water, stilling in pools where sun rays pierce the depths. White oaks, beech, and river birch rise from the forest floor, where fallen trees become cloaked in moss before melding into the soil. Make fords at 1.4, 1.8, and 2.2 miles. Enjoy a long walk on a level track. Bisect a river bend at 2.9 miles.

Cross the South Fork again a final time at 3.4 miles and continue in a widening valley rife with beard cane. The Vineyard Gap Trail comes in on your right at 3.7 miles. Meet Bradley Creek and a ford of it at 3.8 miles. It's a miniature version of the South Fork, smaller yet equal in riverine mountain splendor, but you are going upstream now in a more incised valley. Rhododendron thickets sometimes canopy the path. Ford Bradley Creek at 4.0 and 4.2 miles. At 4.6 miles, the trail enters a meadow, which can be overgrown in summer. Return to woods and a final ford of Bradley Creek at 4.8 miles. The Riverside Trail ends here. Head left on the Bradley Creek Trail, following its namesake downstream before leaving right, up Pea Branch.

Ascend along this branch, your first climb of the hike, meeting the Squirrel Gap Trail at 5.4 miles. Stay left here with the Bradley Creek Trail, stepping over what's left of Pea Branch, then surmounting Pea Gap at 5.6 miles. Savor an easy downhill, winding your way on a wide track to the South Mills River at 5.9 miles, back where you were before. Turn right and head upstream, backtracking to ford the South Fork at 6.3 miles. Reach a four-way intersection at 6.8 miles. This time, pick up the new trail and take the gravel road sharply left, uphill, and make a wide switchback away from the river. Curve in and out of hollows before emerging at the Turkeypen trailhead at 7.6 miles, completing the hike.

Mileages

0.0   Turkeypen trailhead
0.4   Right on Bradley Creek Trail
1.3   Right on Riverside Trail, multiple fords of South Fork Mills River
3.8   Ford Bradley Creek, turn upstream
4.8   Left on Bradley Creek Trail
5.6   Pea Gap
5.9   Right at Mills River
6.8   Acute left on wide gravel roadbed
7.6   Turkeypen trailhead

14 • PINK BEDS LOOP

Hike Summary: *On this hike, you can walk a historic section of Pisgah National Forest near what is known as the Cradle of Forestry. Travel a perched valley, walking along a ridge-rimmed wetland with rich plant life. Head down the upper South Fork Mills River Valley. The return trip takes you through*

14 PINK BEDS LOOP

Distance: 5.3-mile loop

Hiking time: 2.5–3.5 hours

Difficulty: Easy to moderate

Highlights: High-altitude wetland, laurel and rhododendron blooms

Cautions: Wet trail from beaver dams

Fees/Permits: No fees or permits required

Best seasons: March through November; summer for programs at nearby Forest Discovery Center, fall for driest trail

Other trail users: Mountain bikers on second half of loop

Trail contacts: Pisgah Ranger District, 1001 Pisgah Highway, Pisgah Forest, NC 28768, (828) 877-3265, www.fs.usda.gov/nfsnc

Finding the trailhead: From the intersection of NC 280 and US 276 in Brevard, take US 276 north for 11.3 miles to the Pink Beds Picnic Area, on your right, .2 mile beyond the right turn to the Forest Discovery Center.

GPS trailhead coordinates: N35° 21.212', W82° 46.728'

thickets of mountain laurel and rhododendron, the Pink Beds, while crossing streams. Finally, explore numerous meadows where you might see wildlife on your return trip. Elevations changes along the hike are less than 200 feet, nearly unheard of in these highlands.

The Pink Beds harbor the headsprings and uppermost tributaries of South Fork Mills River. Nestled within Pisgah Ridge and Soapstone Ridge, the perched valley of approximately 1,500 acres stands around 3,200 feet, creating a rare, large upland bog, and is a significant property within North Carolina's national forest system. Rare bog plants such as swamp pink thrive in the ferny wetlands bordering the South Fork Mills River and its tributaries. Boardwalks and bridges help you explore these areas while preserving the resource. Flowering plants brighten the wetlands throughout the warm season.

Once the home of hardscrabble farmers, then part of Vanderbilt's Biltmore properties, the Pink Beds lie adjacent to the Cradle of Forestry, where forest management began in the United States. A forestry school opened in 1898, and now the buildings and adjacent acreage are a natural national historic site. Today, you can hike this upland bog and visit the historic and informative place now known as the Forest Discovery Center.

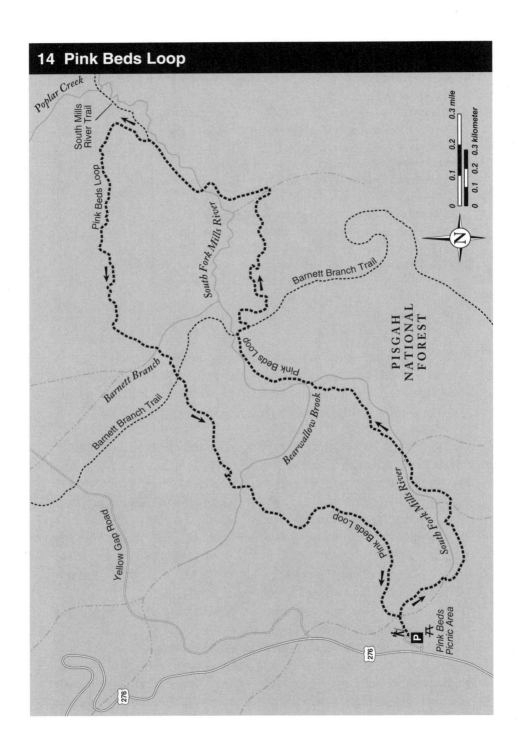

A log bridge provides dry passage across the South Mills River.

Forest management is going on here still. A prescribed burn was undertaken in 2011 in the Pink Beds to educate the public about prescribed burns, to improve habitat diversity, and to reduce ground-level forest litter to safeguard nearby historic buildings at the Cradle of Forestry. Expect more burns in the future.

The Pink Beds Picnic Area has several tables in a variety of sun and shade, picnic shelters, water, and restrooms in season. Leave the upper end of the picnic area parking lot around a pole gate and immediately dip to bridge Pigeon Branch. At .1 mile, reach the orange-blazed loop. Head right, away from a meadow into woods. Towering white pines rise over the wide trail. This is a rich wildflower area. Come along South Fork and cross an unnamed tributary footbridge at .3 mile and another at .6 mile. Mountain laurel and rhododendron flourish in thickets. The demise of the hemlock is leaving this forest in transition, though some are still hanging on. Hike wet flats on boardwalks. Moss-covered tree trunks and doghobble stand beside the path. Unnamed rills stream across the trail, adding more "wet" to the wetlands. Fern fields stretch beneath the forest.

Don't be surprised if a stretch of trail may be underwater. Beavers are active in the area and have been known to flood the path. Of course, their dams make the vale even wetter, sometimes flooding standing trees and killing them in droves. Cruise the nexus of hillside to your right and wooded wetland to your left. Bridge a small tributary, then South Fork Mills River at .9 mile. Note the goldish color of the stream. At 1.3 miles, cross the South Fork on an unusual bridge. The first half is standard lumber and the second half is a fallen tree trunk. You are now on the right-hand bank, descending nearly imperceptibly.

Pass a sandy campsite on your left at 1.4 miles. At 1.6 miles, meet the Barnett Branch Trail. It shortcuts the loop. Go ahead and walk the impressive boardwalk over adjacent wetland and to the bridge spanning South Fork Mills River. This is a great opportunity to observe these biologically important wetlands.

Continuing the main loop hike, you reach another junction. Here, the Barnett Branch Trail leaves south for Rich Mountain, while the Pink Beds Loop heads left, eventually gaining the slope of Soapstone Ridge. At 1.8 miles, bridge a trickling tributary on a substantial bridge. Cross more feeder streams between views northwest of Mount Pisgah. Return to the South Fork in a flat, bridging the river at 2.5 miles. Continue downriver, reaching a trail junction at 2.8 miles. Here the Pink Beds Loop leaves left and keeps downriver.

Ahead, turn left. The path now undulates some over small hills nestled between streamlets. Drier species such as oak and sourwood predominate on the hills. Step over Barnett Branch at 3.8 miles. Tunnel under sinewy branches of laurel. Bridge another stream at 3.9 miles. Ahead, intersect the Barnett Branch Trail. Keep straight on the Pink Beds Loop, passing through a meadow. Cross Bearwallow Branch at 4.4 miles. Travel along and through a multitude of meadows, where you may see deer browsing. Complete the loop portion of the hike, then backtrack over Pigeon Branch, completing your circuit at 5.3 miles.

Mileages

0.0   Pink Beds Picnic Area

1.3   Span South Fork Mills River on a log bridge

1.6   Barnett Branch Trail leaves left on boardwalk

2.8   Pink Beds Loop leaves left at junction with South Fork Mills
River Trail

3.9   Intersect Barnett Branch Trail again

5.3   Pink Beds Picnic Area

15 • SHINING ROCK WILDERNESS LOOP

Hike Summary: Start high and climb higher on this challenging hike. Enter Shining Rock Wilderness, traveling Shining Creek Valley past slide cascades beneath remote forests. Hike into spruce-fir highlands atop Shining Rock Ledge. Visit the quartz outcrop of Shining Rock before joining seldom-trod Old Butt Knob Trail, hiking by views in a mix of evergreens and highland hardwoods. Pass outcrops with unobscured vistas of the surrounding Pisgah National Forest before dropping 1,500 feet in a mile and concluding the trek.

This is a big hike—big woods, big ridges, big views, big climbs, and big descents, all in a big wilderness that avails big rewards to those big enough to take on the trek. There is a combined ascent and descent of nearly a mile on this hike, so be prepared. Furthermore, you will use your map, compass, GPS, and maybe tarot cards in working through the myriad trails around Shining Rock Gap. Or you could just ask some other hiker for help with directions, but that can be tough, especially if you are a man.

Pass around boulders and beside a trailhead kiosk on the wide Shining Creek Trail. Blasted rock walls rise to your right. Big East Fork crashes to your left. Step over flowing Dry Branch, then wander away from Big East Fork. At .3 mile, the grade keeps forward as an unofficial trail to Big East Fork, but you veer right and uphill on a narrower track. Shining Creek Trail climbs along a rhododendron-shrouded creeklet, then switchbacks to Shining Creek Gap at .7 mile. Look right for the Old Butt Knob Trail. This is your return route. For now, keep straight, delving deeply into the lush watershed where towering buckeye, maple, birch, and tulip trees shade Shining Creek, which you reach at 1.0 mile, rushing among gray and white boulders in chutes and drops, swirls and curls.

Continue up the right bank of the precipitous valley, littered with boulders and scattered in wildflowers later in spring. At 1.9 miles, curve around a tributary flowing from Daniels Cove. The Shining Creek Valley narrows. At 2.3 miles, look for camping flats below as the Shining Creek Trail now follows North Prong Shining Creek. Watch for slide cascades up here. The understory becomes grassy in places. Spruce and fir begin intermingling with the hardwoods.

At 3.0 miles, cross a tributary flowing from Birch Spring Gap, then trace uppermost North Prong. Keep uphill, making switchbacks and

15 SHINING ROCK WILDERNESS LOOP

Distance: 8.3-mile balloon loop

Hiking time: 5.5–8.0 hours

Difficulty: Difficult

Highlights: Shining Rock Wilderness, cascades, views from Shining Rock and other outcrops

Cautions: Steep trail, unmarked intersections, remoteness on Old Butt Knob

Fees/Permits: No fees or permits required

Best seasons: Year-round, though winter could be snowy up high

Other trail users: None

Trail contacts: Pisgah Ranger District, 1001 Pisgah Highway, Pisgah Forest, NC 28768, (828) 877-3265, www.fs.usda.gov/nfsnc

Finding the trailhead: From the intersection of NC 280 and US 276 in Brevard, take US 276 north 15 miles to the Blue Ridge Parkway at Wagon Road Gap. Set your odometer and stay straight on US 276 north. Follow it for 2.9 more miles to the signed East Fork trailhead on your left. You will see a parking area on your left just before reaching the official East Fork trailhead. (The upper parking accesses the Big East Fork Trail, not a part of this hike.) Alternate directions: From exit 31 on I-40 near Canton, take NC 215 south. Stay with 215 south as it winds through Canton for 2.3 miles to NC 110. Turn right, following NC 110 south for 5.4 miles to US 276. Turn left and take US 276 south for 11.6 miles to the trailhead on your right.

GPS trailhead coordinates: N35° 21.953', W82° 49.082'

stepping over stony streamlets amid brush and wildflowers such as Joe Pye weed, bee balm, and yellow daisies. Bisect spruce thickets before reaching Art Loeb Trail and Shining Creek Ledge at 4.0 miles. Turn right here, shortly reaching small, grassy Shining Rock Gap. Ivestor Gap Trail comes in from your left. Keep forward, trying to stay with the Art Loeb Trail. Watch right for a trail with wooden erosion bars leading uphill in brush at 4.1 miles. (False or user-created trails will not have the wooden water-erosion bars.) The path leads into a spruce thicket, then climbs into brush and reaches a small clearing atop a knob at 4.3 miles. Here, a clear trail leads left and downhill to Shining Rock. (This trail also leads up from Art Loeb Trail to Shining Rock, adding to the confusion.) It isn't long before the spur comes to the base of Shining Rock and its unmistakable white quartz. Scramble to clearings atop the white linear outcrop, then soak in views of the western Shining Rock Wilderness and

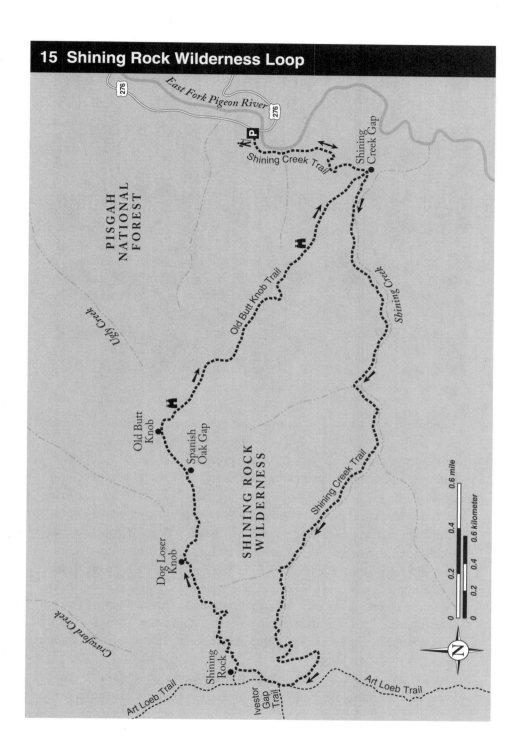

Wildernesses are filled with wonders large and small.

points west. I've never seen more naturally occurring quartz in any one place in my life. Backtrack to where you were at 4.3 miles. Here, a trail leads left to a grassy campsite. The trail going right is the Old Butt Knob Trail. This maintained path leads southeast, then northeast, dropping off the knob in open brush. (It might take a try or two to get on the correct trail. False trails peter out.) Descend under multitrunked mountain laurel bushes, then among beech trees, meeting Beech Spring Gap at 4.9 miles. Gently ascend to spruce-pocked Dog Loser Knob (an all-time great Southern Appalachian name). Your downgrade leads past views and through spruce copses before coming to gorgeous Spanish Oak Gap at 5.6 miles. Here, stout oaks and other hardwoods idyllically meld with spruce and fir. This is a place to linger. A scant climb leads to Old Butt Knob at 5.9 miles, then it's all downhill from here, as you join a narrow and rocky Chestnut Ridge.

At 6.0 miles, look for a trail leading right to an outcrop with great views. Spy Shining Rock Ledge and Flower Knob in the distance, Bearpen Ridge nearby, and Daniels Cove below. Wander the ridgeline in mixed woods until 6.8 miles. Here, the Old Butt Knob Trail begins switchbacking steeply in pines, laurel, and chestnut oaks. Woe to those going uphill. The declivitous descent is relentless! Views open across the East Fork at the Blue Ridge Parkway. A brief level spell in pines avails a view to your right at 7.2 miles. Resume a foot-pounding decline on the slender edge, meeting the Shining Creek Trail at 7.6 miles. Turn left here and backtrack to the trailhead, completing the hike.

Mileages

0.0   Big East Fork trailhead
0.7   Shining Creek Gap
4.0   Shining Rock Gap
4.3   Knob above Shining Rock
5.6   Spanish Oak Gap
6.0   View on right
7.2   View on right
7.6   Shining Creek Gap
8.3   Big East Fork trailhead

16 • SHINING ROCK HIGH COUNTRY HIKE

Hike Summary: This hike is as spectacular as it is busy. Start your trek at nearly 6,000 feet, then take a level railroad grade for miles along Shining Rock Ledge, enjoying stellar panoramas and forests recalling New England. After an easy 4 miles, join the ridge-running Art Loeb Trail. Make a series of moderate climbs and descents, passing view after view on open slopes, grassy meadows, and rock outcrops. A clear day will be a photographer's dream. Be apprised the trails can be crowded on summer and fall weekends and moderately busy any day during July and August. If the mileage is a little long, you can turn this trek into shorter loops, or simply take the old railroad grade out and back as far as you please.

The open country that is Shining Rock is an accidental—and scenic—byproduct of timber extraction in the western North Carolina highlands. Starting in the early 1900s, what became Shining Rock Wilderness was logged. The complete takedown of an almost contiguous stand of red spruce and Fraser fir up high, and hemlocks and hardwoods down low, left the mountainsides barren, save for dried-out, unwanted cuttings left behind. These cuttings caught fire and burned the ground to bedrock in places, leaving a sterile landscape open to the sky overhead where formerly stood dark, damp evergreen forests so dim that noon seemed like dusk. More fires burned later. Nearly a century has passed since the logger's day, yet vast stretches of the highlands remain treeless. However, these open areas, now covered in grass, brush, and some tree stands, harbor open terrain and a series of rocky ridges and valleys draining more than 18,000 acres of designated wilderness lands, along with mountains stretching to distant horizons.

Pass around the pole gate and join the Ivestor Gap Trail, tracing a wide railroad grade left over from the logging days. Views open down the Little East Fork Pigeon River to your left and up to Shining Rock Ledge on your right. Immediately pass a spring on your right. More upwellings deposit water over the trail ahead. This path can be partially iced over in winter. Rhododendron, willow, pin cherry, and brush border the trail. Keep on the west side of Shining Rock Ledge, northbound. At 1.2 miles, a spur trail leads right to the Art Loeb Trail in a gap between Tennent Mountain and Black Balsam Knob. At 1.4 miles, cut through a ridge between stands of exotic red pine. Ahead, at 1.7 miles, you may

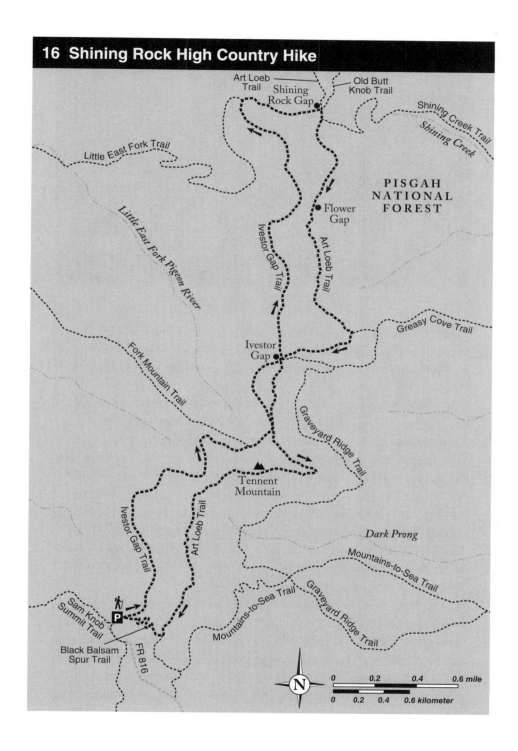

Art Loeb Trail

Old Butt Knob Trail

Shining Rock Gap

Shining Creek Trail

Shining Creek

Little East Fork Trail

PISGAH NATIONAL FOREST

Flower Gap

Little East Fork Pigeon River

Ivestor Gap Trail

Art Loeb Trail

Greasy Cove Trail

Ivestor Gap

Fork Mountain Trail

Graveyard Ridge Trail

Tennent Mountain

Ivestor Gap Trail

Art Loeb Trail

Dark Prong

Mountains-to-Sea Trail

Sam Knob Summit Trail

P

Mountains-to-Sea Trail

Graveyard Ridge Trail

Black Balsam Spur Trail

FR 816

N

| 0 | 0.2 | 0.4 | 0.6 mile |

| 0 | 0.2 | 0.4 | 0.6 kilometer |

Ridges roll away in this vista from atop Tennent Mountain.

miss the Fork Mountain Trail going left for Sunburst Campground. Reach a gap at 1.8 miles. This is not Ivestor Gap. The loop stays left on the wide railroad grade and stays on the west side of Shining Rock Ledge.

Curve into Ivestor Gap and a five-way trail junction at 2.2 miles. Here you will see a sign designating Shining Rock Wilderness. This is another chance to shortcut your loop by joining the single-track Art Loeb Trail back to the parking area. For the whole loop, stay left here with the railroad bed, but now the trail is much narrower. If the wind isn't blowing, you can hear crashing mountain streams below. The views are still coming and the path remains easy as you traverse evergreen thickets and beech copses. Headsprings continue flowing over the trail. At 3.9 miles, Little East Fork Trail leaves left. Stay right, curving for Shining Rock Gap. Come to the small grassy flat of Shining Rock Gap at 4.3 miles.

Meet the Art Loeb Trail and turn right here, lest you get trapped in the confusion of user-created trails and real trails. Since this is a wilderness, no trails are signed. (You can hike about a quarter-mile on the Old Butt Knob Trail to reach Shining Rock on your left, but at your own peril.) Stay on a wide railroad grade, now southbound. Watch for log steps on your left just below the trail. This is where the Shining Creek Trail comes in. Also, pass a spring. Wind around the east side of Flower

Knob and ease into grassy Flower Gap at 4.9 miles. The easy walking on a level grade is over. The Art Loeb Trail becomes a narrow, eroded footpath heading over the crest of Shining Rock Ledge. Watch for wind-flagged trees rising above the brush. Look back north at the quartz outcrop of Shining Rock. Top out at 5.2 miles. Views remain extensive. The Art Loeb Trail slips over to the left side of the ridge, then reaches an intersection at 5.7 miles. Here, a spur leads left to the Greasy Cove Trail.

At 6.1 miles, return to Ivestor Gap. Take a right, then a quick left as the Art Loeb Trail cuts through a wooden stile, crosses a grassy clearing, and climbs into a stand of red pines. Open to views ahead of Tennent Mountain, which you are fixing to climb. Drop to a gap at 6.5 miles, then, as you start uphill again briefly on the wide Ivestor Trail, look left for the Art Loeb Trail making a rutted, narrow ascent. Work up the east side of Tennent Mountain, opening to incredible views. Top out at 6,046 feet at 7.2 miles. Soak in 360° panoramas. You can see where you came from, including Shining Rock, and where you are going, and waves of mountains in the distance. Also, look for the trails wandering through the land around you. Drop to a gap at 7.5 miles, where a spur dips right to Ivestor Gap Trail. Climb through wind-sculpted brush of Black Balsam with its spectacular 6,000-plus-foot views to the west. Be wary, as trails split here to views, to campsites, and over the top of Black Balsam. The actual trail has water-erosion bars and slips over to the right side of the summit. At 8.4 miles, take the marked Black Balsam Spur leading right. Grab some final panoramas of Sam Knob, Fork Ridge, and ample mountains and valleys. A series of switchbacks eases the descent, then you emerge at the trailhead at 8.8 miles, completing the hike.

Mileages

0.0   Black Balsam trailhead
1.2   Spur leads right to gap near Tennent Mountain—
      shortcut opportunity
1.8   Gap before Ivestor Gap
2.2   Ivestor Gap, Shining Rock Wilderness; stay left on grade
3.9   Little East Fork Trail leaves left; stay right
4.3   Small grassy Shining Rock Gap; right on Art Loeb Trail
4.9   Flower Gap
6.1   Ivestor Gap
7.2   Summit of Tennent Mountain

---

17 • SAM KNOB LOOP

Hike Summary: *This highland trek, pushing 6,000 feet in the Pisgah high country, takes you from one high point to another, with stunning vistas, followed by a jaunt along one of the highest streams in North Carolina. Start just south of Shining Rock Wilderness. Soak in immediate views as you descend to a more-than-mile-high meadow. Climb to Sam Knob, where rocky panoramas stretch in all directions. Next, walk down to Flat Laurel Creek, with its numerous cascades, meadows, and campsites. Hike up the stream, then circle around the upper Flat Laurel Creek Valley, taking in more scenes of this ultra-high land and the peaks that encircle it.*

The greater Shining Rock high country extends north from the Blue Ridge Parkway, covering not only the Shining Rock Wilderness but also that parcel around Black Balsam Knob drained by Flat Laurel Creek, outside the wilderness. That is where this hike takes place, in a land more open than not—a land of highland meadows, wind-pruned trees rising among rocky crags, dark spruce dotting the grassy hills, tan streams spilling chilly water from upland bogs, and dense tree stands where noon is as dark as dawn.

Make this hike on a clear day and you will be manifestly rewarded. And plan on taking your time, as there are multiple contemplation spots, places for soaking in the ambiance of this distinctive acreage in mountain Carolina. First, start on the correct trail, as numerous paths emanate from the large and often busy Black Balsam trailhead. From the parking area, as you face the restrooms, look just right of the restrooms for a path leading west on a level grade. This is the Sam Knob Summit Trail. The path immediately splits—a short path goes left to a campsite. Stay right in a mix of trees—mountain ash, Fraser fir, and birch—dotting meadowland. At .3 mile, the level trail opens to a field, with a gap lying between you and Sam Knob, standing due west. Ignore user-created trails leading left and stay with Sam Knob Trail, descending toward the gap and Sam Knob.

Open looks extend left into the Flat Laurel Valley, Little Sam Knob,

17 SAM KNOB LOOP

Distance: 3.9-mile loop with spur

Hiking time: 2.0–3.0 hours

Difficulty: Moderate

Highlights: Miles of mountain views, highland knob, high country stream

Cautions: None

Fees/Permits: No fees or permits required

Best seasons: Year-round, as long as Blue Ridge Parkway is open

Other trail users: Bicyclists and equestrians on Flat Laurel Creek Trail

Trail contacts: Pisgah Ranger District, 1001 Pisgah Highway, Pisgah Forest, NC 28768, (828) 877-3265, www.fs.usda.gov/nfsnc

Finding the trailhead: From the intersection of NC 280 and US 276 in Brevard, take US 276 north for 15 miles to the Blue Ridge Parkway. Follow the Blue Ridge Parkway southbound 8.4 miles to FR 816, on your right. Turn right on FR 816 and follow it for 1.2 miles to dead end at the Black Balsam trailhead.

GPS trailhead coordinates: N35° 19.565', W82° 52.882'

and Pisgah Ridge, where the Blue Ridge Parkway runs, and Fork Ridge, in the Middle Prong Wilderness, as you wander through the meadow, which is thick with tawny grasses in summer and a wind-blown, icy field in winter. Reach a trail intersection. Turn right with the Sam Knob Summit Trail. You will return here later.

Start working your way up the mostly wooded dome, toiling upward via switchbacks on a rocky tread. As you rise, the yellow birches, red maples, and other trees bend and cower to the relentless winds. In summer, blackberries and blueberries find their place. At 1.0 mile, a prominent outcrop extends west from the trail. Stop and rake the horizon. Flat Laurel Creek flows below. A keen eye will be able to spot hikers walking through the open areas. Little Sam Knob and a host of mountains border the watershed. Climb higher, reaching the knob crest and a trail split at 1.2 miles. Trails to views go left and right through scrubby vegetation and outcrops. Head right to the first view. It features a prominent look to the east, where the open grasses and evergreen stands of Black Balsam Knob and Shining Rock Ledge form a walled fortification, with the meadow through which you walked acting as an easel. Backtrack to the other overlook, passing a white quartz outcrop. Gaze deep into the West Fork Pigeon River Valley, among other views.

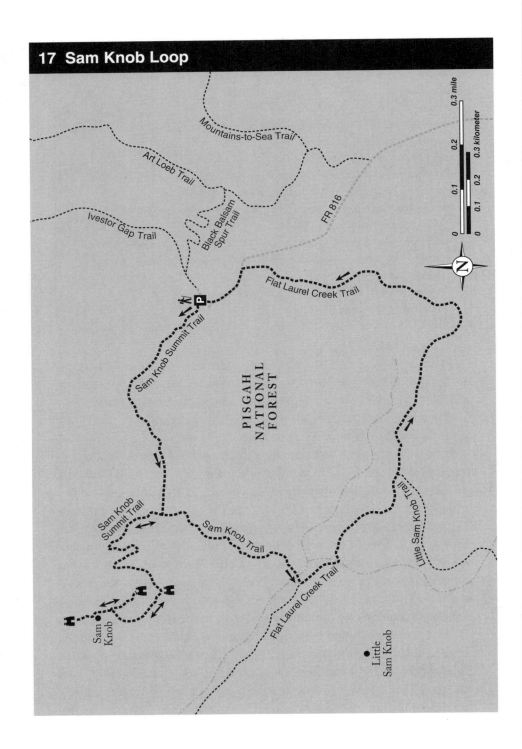

Mountains-to-Sea Trail

Art Loeb Trail

Ivestor Gap Trail

Black Balsam Spur Trail

FR 816

Flat Laurel Creek Trail

Sam Knob Summit Trail

PISGAH NATIONAL FOREST

Sam Knob Summit Trail

Sam Knob Trail

Little Sam Knob Trail

Flat Laurel Creek Trail

Sam Knob

Little Sam Knob

N

0.3 mile

0.3 kilometer

Sam Knob forms a backdrop for this flowery meadow.

Perhaps the most notable vista is of the distant white quartz that is Shining Rock, to the northeast. The clearer the day, the more layers of mountains stretch to the back of beyond.

Continue the next part of the hike at 2.0 miles, after dropping off Sam Knob. Take the Sam Knob Trail down toward Flat Laurel Creek, straddling the nexus of field and forest. Brush and fire cherry indicate the clearings are closing in. Boardwalks and stones allow dry passage over spring seeps. Drift through meadows and woods. Be watchful, as user-created spurs split to campsites. At 2.4 miles, rock-hop Flat Laurel Creek. Note the surprisingly big plunge pools, here at the hike's low point of 5,400 feet.

Reach a trail junction on the other side. Head left with the Flat Laurel Creek Trail, ascending along the deeply forested creek. Cross a tributary at 2.5 miles. Continue past the intersection with the Little Sam Knob Trail at 2.8 miles. Begin making a wide arc around the headwaters of Flat Laurel Creek. Views commence of the ridges encircling Flat Laurel Creek—and Sam Knob. The path turns north toward the parking area as you step over rills that gather to make Flat Laurel Creek. Roam through more evergreens, then reach the trailhead at 3.9 miles, completing the hike.

Mileages

0.0 Black Balsam trailhead
0.6 Begin climbing Sam Knob on Sam Knob Summit Trail
1.2 Top of Sam Knob; view spurs go left and right
2.0 Begin downgrade to Flat Laurel Creek on Sam Knob Trail
2.4 Cross Flat Laurel Creek; left on Flat Laurel Creek Trail
2.8 Little Sam Knob Trail leaves right
3.9 Black Balsam trailhead

18 • MIDDLE PRONG WILDERNESS LOOP

Hike Summary: Start a mile high, traveling rare spruce-fir forest on the Mountains-to-Sea Trail (MST). Easy walking traces a level rail grade where occasional views open of adjacent highland ridges. Join the little-used Buckeye Gap Trail dropping past a waterfall. Explore Middle Prong, an incised mountain valley, rich in trees, centered with a spectacular pool-and-drop stream that deserves its wilderness status. You'll trace the creek up to its spring-born origins, then complete the circuit back in cool, spruce-fir woods.

The Middle Prong Wilderness, as its name suggests, protects the uppermost basin of Middle Prong West Fork Pigeon River. This 7,460-acre area was logged from 1906 to 1926. The forest has recovered nicely in the ensuing decades. The trail system mostly follows the old logging grades left behind. Along the way you may spot relics of this logging—

old steel cables, bits of coal, and pieces of metal machinery. You won't miss the works of Mother Nature—regal spruce trees shading the path, wildflowers from stem to stern, and rock outcroppings amid botanically rich plant life. Perhaps most of all you will remember the crystalline streams reflecting the sunlight as they bound down mountainsides and through the Middle Prong Valley.

From the Blue Ridge Parkway, trace a single-track path into thick woods. Step over a highland stream to reach a trail junction at .1 mile. Here, pick up the MST leaving right on a narrow path overlain upon a railroad grade. Look for old railroad ties embedded in wet areas. The walking is easy under northern hardwoods of yellow birch and cherry along with copious red spruce and Fraser fir; you are over 5,400 feet. A trail sign officially welcomes you to Middle Prong Wilderness. Begin crossing clear tributaries steeply falling from the Blue Ridge, all feeding Middle Prong. At .8 mile, the MST leaves right suddenly off the railroad, climbing a bit, then rejoins the railroad grade. Note the blasted rocks astride the old track. Rock-hop upper Buckeye Creek and a second prong at 1.1 miles. At 1.2 miles, the MST splits right and uphill, while you stay left, joining the Buckeye Gap Trail, Forest Trail 104, still tracing

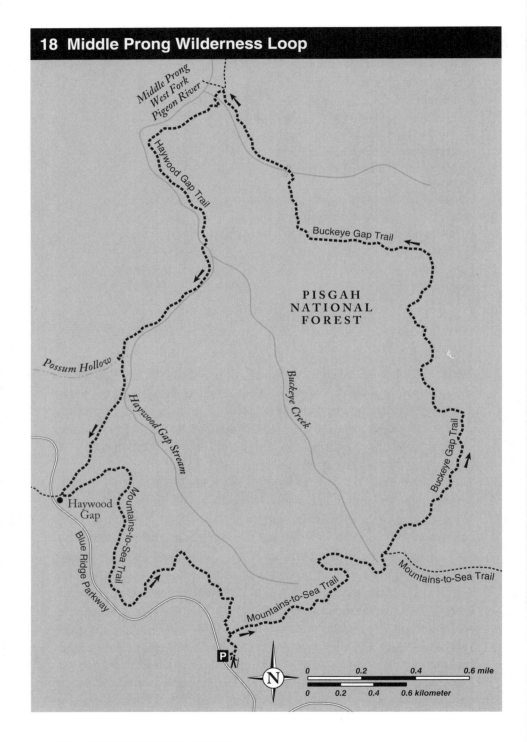

Middle Prong
West Fork
Pigeon River

Haywood Gap Trail

Buckeye Gap Trail

PISGAH
NATIONAL
FOREST

Possum Hollow

Buckeye Creek

Haywood Gap Stream

Buckeye Gap Trail

Haywood
Gap

Mountains-to-Sea Trail

Blue Ridge Parkway

Mountains-to-Sea Trail

Mountains-to-Sea Trail

P

N

| 0 | 0.2 | 0.4 | 0.6 mile |
| 0 | 0.2 | 0.4 | 0.6 kilometer |

A rustic sign greets those who enter Middle Prong Wilderness.

the railroad grade. Since this is a designated wilderness, the intersection will likely not be signed.

The walking remains easy on the northbound track. Blackberries will crowd open parcels of the path. Ferns carpet shadier areas under red maple, cherry, and buckeye. Fragrant evergreens still rise strong, dropping their needles and bronzing the trailbed. Occasional seeps dribble down from Fork Ridge above. Partial views open across Middle Prong toward the Blue Ridge Parkway. At 2.5 miles, the trail abruptly drops to a stream and rises back to the railroad grade. At 2.8 miles, leave the grade left, beginning your descent. The evergreens are left behind. At 3.1 miles, briefly level off, bisecting a disappearing clearing. Level off again before resuming a descent at 3.3 miles. The slim path dives to cross Grassy Ridge Branch just above a waterfall at 3.6 miles. The cataract spills out of sight. Ahead, a steep, irregular slope makes for a challenging descent.

The wicked drop ends at 4.0 miles in a four-way unmarked intersection. To your right, the Haywood Gap Trail leads right toward Sunburst Campground. Ahead, a user-created trail leads to a campsite and Middle Prong. You turn left on the Haywood Gap Trail, heading into the maw of the valley. Cross Grassy Ridge Branch at 4.1 miles. Continue uphill shaded by northern hardwoods. Middle Prong roars and crashes in chutes and flumes below, stilling in boulder-bordered pools before moving on downstream. At 4.6 miles, look right for a two-tiered cascade tumbling into a huge pool. A campsite lies on the far bank. At 4.8 miles, the trail becomes squeezed by a bluff on the left and the watercourse on the right. Ease your way past this washed-out slope. Tunnel beneath rhododendron, rock-hopping Middle Prong at 4.9 miles. Doghobble borders the trail. At 5.0 miles, you stay right on a much smaller Middle Prong, as Buckeye Creek leaves left.

The trail and stream gradient both steepen. The valley tapers. At 5.3 miles, pass a campsite beside the creek. Red spruce reappear. Boulders and bluffs pinch in the trail on the irregular climb. At 5.5 miles, turn right up Possum Hollow along a steep stream, then cross the watercourse. The Haywood Gap Trail keeps aiming for its namesake, crossing an old log bridge. Rise to buckeye forest before coming to a trail intersection at 6.2 miles, just below Haywood Gap. Turn left here, rejoining the MST. The hard part is over as you circle around Parker Knob, back in spruce-fir evergreens. Red squirrels scold your presence while ruffed grouse blast away from your feet, startling the weary hiker. Come near Horsebone Gap at 7.1 miles. Make a hard right turn at 7.5 miles, then reach the spur to the Blue Ridge Parkway. Backtrack, completing your loop at 8.1 miles.

Mileages

0.0   Rough Butt Bald Overlook, milepost 425.4
0.1   Right on MST
1.2   Left on Buckeye Gap Trail
3.6   Cross Grassy Ridge branch, waterfall
4.0   Left on Haywood Gap Trail
4.9   Cross Middle Prong
6.2   Left on MST
8.1   Rough Butt Bald Overlook, milepost 425.4

---

19 • FALLS OF GRAVEYARD FIELDS

Hike Summary: *This hike combines high country vistas with highland waterfalls, an alluring amalgamation. Yellowstone Prong, nestled among three mile-high ridges, presents two cataracts as it descends this perched valley.*

Between visits to these cascades you will hike a montage of meadow and forest, allowing views beyond the stream. First, visit Lower Falls, traveling a multi-stair boardwalk. Turn upstream, hiking through an upland meadow where towering mountains rise in the distance. Reach Upper Falls, a white froth tumbling over a wall. Your return trip tunnels through rhododendron before returning to the trailhead.

It is hard to find such a combination of high country and high falls. Since you access this national forest land from the Blue Ridge Parkway, the hike is very popular during the summertime. To avoid the crowds, simply hike this trail during the shoulder seasons or, in summer, early in the morning and late in the evening. In winter you will be subject to Blue Ridge Parkway closures.

Leave the overlook on stone steps, descending to an asphalt trail. Enter Pisgah National Forest, winding through rhododendron thickets, black birch, and pin cherry. At .1 mile, bridge Yellowstone Prong, a stony stream channeling in flumes and chutes, then gathering in pools. Leave right from the bridge, toward Lower Falls. Boardwalks take you over tributaries. At .2 mile, a spur leads left to access the Mountains-to-Sea Trail. It isn't long before you encounter the hazard of this hike: user-created trails that make trail junctions potentially confusing. Continue downstream closer to the river and shortly come upon a multitiered, twisting boardwalk leading to the base of Lower Falls, also known as Second Falls. This cataract spills about 50 feet in four tiers, each tier angled differently. A massive boulder jumble lies at the base of the falls. These boulders provide seats for visitors. This is the low point of your hike, and you are still above 5,000 feet!

From here, backtrack toward the trailhead, joining new trail where you see a sign heading toward Upper Falls. Leave most other hikers now and enter a fluctuating landscape, sometimes meadows, sometimes forest, sometimes upland bogs, sometimes creekside gravel bars. At .5 mile, the trail opens to views of the upper stream basin, bordered by Graveyard Ridge on your right, 6,214-foot Black Balsam Knob rising in the foreground, and Pisgah Ridge, where the Blue Ridge Parkway runs, to your left.

At .6 mile, reach a trail intersection. A user-created trail leads left to Yellowstone Prong, but you turn right and immediately come to another intersection, this one signed. Go left here, toward Upper Falls, as the Graveyard Ridge Connector Trail keeps straight.

19 FALLS OF GRAVEYARD FIELDS

Distance: 3.2-mile loop

Hiking time: 2.0 hours

Difficulty: Easy to moderate

Highlights: High-elevation falls, views from meadows, highland stream

Cautions: Unofficial, potentially confusing side trails

Fees/Permits: No fees or permits required

Best seasons: May through mid-October; winter can be iffy with potential closing of Blue Ridge Parkway

Other trail users: None

Trail contacts: Pisgah Ranger District, 1001 Pisgah Highway, Pisgah Forest, NC 28768, (828) 877-3265, www.fs.usda.gov/nfsnc

Finding the trailhead: From the intersection of NC 280 and US 276 in Brevard, take US 276 north for 15 miles to the Blue Ridge Parkway. Follow the Blue Ridge Parkway 7 miles south to the Graveyard Fields Overlook, on your right at milepost 418.8.

GPS trailhead coordinates: N35° 19.220', W82° 50.821'

Continue deeper up Yellowstone Prong, crossing a boardwalk spanning a ferny meadow. The trailside flora in this highland vale continues changing—blackberry patches, shady multitrunked maples and yellow birch, grassy meadow, and deep laurel thickets. Elevation change is minimal thus far. At .9 mile, reach another intersection. Stay right, still aiming for Upper Falls. The other way is your return route to the overlook.

The Graveyard Fields Trail crosses another tributary. The name comes from now-unseen upturned spruce stumps resembling graves in the level valley that was formerly covered in forest. Note the thick brush bordering the wetlands. Stunning views of the surrounding ridges continue. It is simple to pick out Pisgah Ridge. You can even look back at the Graveyard Fields Overlook, and perhaps even your car. Stay with the most heavily used trail while occasionally passing through or near campsites. Rock-hop the main tributary to Yellowstone Prong at 1.3 miles. Note the quartz scattered among the streamside rocks.

By 1.5 miles, you have joined a slope covered in yellow birches rising over bright green grasses. The trail does its only real climbing. Twist among rocks on the slope. The path splits at 1.7 miles. Most hikers go left, down to a slide cascade flowing over a rock face, located below the

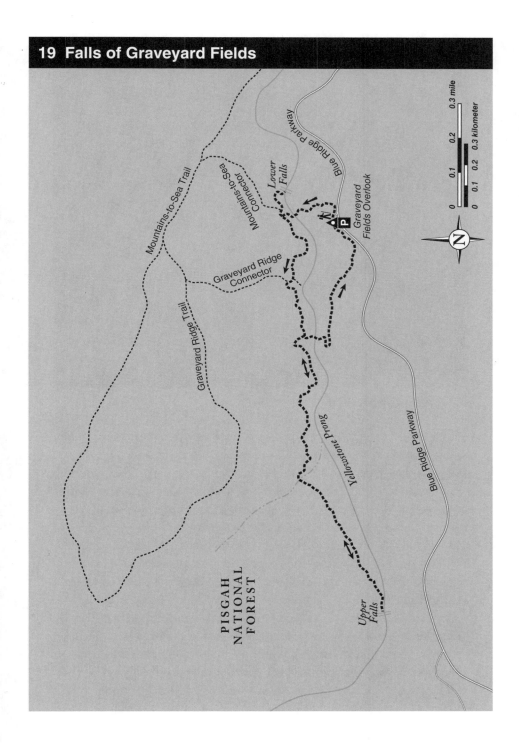

Lower Falls tumbles in stages over barren rock.

actual Upper Falls. This cataract runs over an open rock slab, usually along a channel to the right. Continue to Upper Falls, at 1.8 miles. It starts narrow, then spills about 45 feet over a tan rock base, widening out as a fan would. Then it tumbles into a short, sheer drop and continues over a wide rock slab, briefly slowing at an impromptu stony viewing spot before it pushes onward. Upper Falls is the more impressive of the two falls, in my opinion. However, the whole high-altitude valley of Yellowstone Prong is a nonstop highlight reel. No wonder the area is so popular. But this is one of those "must-do" popular hikes, even for a solitude-seeker.

Backtrack .9 mile from Upper Falls, then resume the loop. Shortly bridge Yellowstone Prong, enjoying the willow-and-rhododendron-lined stream framed in Carolina highlands. Begin working your way through evergreen copses roofing the trail. Make a big curve to the east, then reach stone steps just below the overlook, completing the hike at 3.2 miles.

Mileages

0.0   Graveyard Fields Overlook, milepost 418.8, Blue Ridge Parkway

0.3   Lower Falls

0.6   Graveyard Ridge Connector Trail splits away

0.9   Stay right toward Upper Falls; loop leads left

1.8   Upper Falls; backtrack

2.7   Right at loop; cross Yellowstone Prong

3.2   Graveyard Fields Overlook, milepost 418.8 Blue Ridge Parkway

---

20 • LOOKING GLASS ROCK

Hike Summary: Hike to the top of North Carolina's iconic summits, where inspiring views await from a granite dome rising from the Davidson River Valley. From the trailhead, a well-graded trail leads up a tributary of the Davidson before scaling Looking Glass Rock using what seem like innumerable switchbacks. Rock slabs scattered in the woods tease you en route to the peak. Just after cresting out, open onto a huge stone slab revealing incredible views of the Blue Ridge above and woodlands beyond.

Looking Glass Rock is one of the most recognizable features in North Carolina's national forests. This monolith rises nearly 2,000 feet above the surrounding forest floor to an elevation of 3,969 feet. Sheer granite walls curve around the peak on three sides, lending an unmistakable appearance. Not only does the summit provide wonderful views of the surrounding Blue Ridge and other mountains of the greater Davidson River area, but you should also take the time to look upon Looking Glass Rock from the Blue Ridge Parkway or from other mountains, especially from nearby John Rock or Pilot Mountain on Art Loeb Trail. Perhaps you may see the sun reflecting off the rock face that gave Looking Glass Rock its name.

The hike is a nearly continuous climb from the trailhead to the top. However, the trail has been redone and uses enough switchbacks to make a hiker dizzy on the ascent. The switchbacks ease the gradient, making the hike very manageable. The only word of caution is to use care along the granite slopes, since water seeps over the rock face in

20 LOOKING GLASS ROCK

Distance: 5.6-mile there-and-back

Hiking time: 3.5–4.5 hours

Difficulty: Moderate to difficult

Highlights: Grand views from notable granite dome

Cautions: Water seeps over dome slab at viewing point

Fees/Permits: No fees or permits required

Best seasons: Year-round; spring, fall, and winter for clearest skies

Other trail users: None

Trail contacts: Pisgah Ranger District, 1001 Pisgah Highway, Pisgah Forest, NC 28768, (828) 877-3265, www.fs.usda.gov/nfsnc

Finding the trailhead: From the intersection of NC 280 and US 276 in Brevard, take US 276 north for 5.2 miles, then turn left on FR 475 toward the Pisgah Center for Wildlife Education. Follow FR 475 for .3 mile, and the trailhead will be on your right.

GPS trailhead coordinates: N35° 17.445', W82° 46.580'

places. These seeps can be especially hazardous in subfreezing conditions.

A wider-than-average, hiker-only trail leads past a trailhead kiosk, then bridges a small creek. Ferns, mosses, stinging nettle, and doghobble thrive under magnolia, black birch, and tulip trees. Curve along a side slope, then enter a streamshed you will be following for a while. Look for signs of old trails working more steeply up to the crest. Avoid user-created erosive shortcuts. The unnamed stream noisily drops below.

Make the first of many switchbacks at .5 mile. At first, the trail turns come infrequently, but the higher you rise, the shorter the stretches between turns. At .8 mile, the Looking Glass Rock Trail leaves the streamshed and enters a drier forest of pine, black gum, sourwood, mountain laurel, and Carolina hemlock. Fragrant galax lines the trailbed. Reach the nose of the ridge at 1.0 mile. Grab southerly views through the trees, where the Art Loeb Trail traces the far ridge over Pilot Mountain among other peaks. The grade remains steady.

At 1.5 miles, come along a dribbling trickle, then turn away. The steepness of the mountain has eased, but the gradient of the trail remains the same. By 1.9 miles, a few rock slabs can be seen. At 2.1 miles, come to a wide-open rock slab on your left. Walk out here and look for

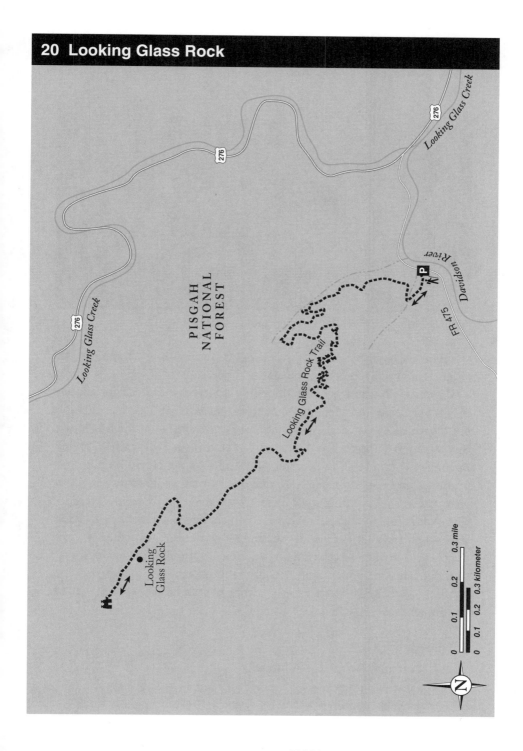

Enjoy the view of Looking Glass Rock from the Blue Ridge Parkway.

the painted H on the slab. This is a helicopter landing. The main trail keeps straight beyond the open slab.

Continue on a rooty, sandy track interspersed with occasional open rock slabs. Stone and log steps aid your passage. At 2.4 miles, a short spur leads right to a large open slab. Turn northwest atop the ridgecrest. Spurs lead to campsites and harder-to-reach vistas. Top out at 2.7 miles. Begin a downgrade, still in woods. At 2.8 miles, open onto a huge sloped granite slab—the main vista. Craggy pines and cedars cling to crevices where soil accumulates. Water seeps over the rock in channels. The granite slope sharpens below, to an incline down which no hiker walks. Before you, the crest of the Blue Ridge rises majestically, stretching end-to-end across the horizon. Parkway overlooks are visible. Waves of mountains roll southwest. This is the most accessible open view on Looking Glass Rock, but there are other overlooks to explore. Just be careful while doing it.

Mileages

0.0   Looking Glass Rock trailhead

0.5   First switchback

2.1   Helicopter pad rock slab to left

21 • JOHN ROCK

Hike Summary: *Hike to a granite dome rising from the banks of the David-son River. At John Rock you can gaze on Looking Glass Rock, backed by the summit of the Blue Ridge. Start out at a wildlife center and fish hatchery, then cruise along the Davidson River. A steady climb leads to the granite face of John Rock, where an upgrade of 800 feet delivers a stunning panorama. From there, work your way downhill, coming alongside Cedar Rock Creek, which presents cascades aplenty. Before or after your hike, consider visiting the hatchery and wildlife education center.*

John Rock is located near the famed Looking Glass Rock. This has its good points and bad points. John Rock doesn't receive near the recognition as does Looking Glass Rock. Nor does it receive as much visitation. But John Rock does function as the grandstand to view not only Looking Glass Rock but also the crest of the Blue Ridge, rising to the north beyond the valley of the Davidson River. Also enjoy visiting the adjacent fish hatchery and wildlife education center, generally open during the warm season.

Leave the large trailhead parking area, heading east on the Cat Gap Loop. Walk through an area popular with fishermen astride a picket fence. Ahead, the official trail veers right and bridges Cedar Rock Creek. Stay left, continuing in wooded flats along the Davidson River. The hemlocks are dead and the forest is transitioning. A sea of rhododendron and doghobble carpets the floor. Pass several large campsites. Bridge trickling branches.

At .5 mile, the wide path turns up Horse Cove, cut by an unnamed tributary of the Davidson River, flowing loud as it pushes downstream. The wildflower-rich valley narrows, and you step over the stream at .9 mile, in the shade of tulip trees. The trail crosses an old forest road and keeps ascending. Bridge a tributary at 1.1 miles. At 1.2 miles, meet the John Rock Trail. Turn right here and curve around a mountain cove. Meanwhile, the Cat Gap Loop keeps straight. You will rejoin it later.

21 JOHN ROCK

Distance: 5.4-mile loop

Hiking time: 3.0–4.0 hours

Difficulty: Moderate

Highlights: Sweeping vistas from granite face

Cautions: Water seeps over dome slab at viewing point

Fees/Permits: No fees or permits required

Best seasons: Year-round; spring, fall, and winter for clearest skies

Other trail users: Bikers on last part of loop

Trail contacts: Pisgah Ranger District, 1001 Pisgah Highway, Pisgah Forest, NC 28768, (828) 877-3265, www.fs.usda.gov/nfsnc

Finding the trailhead: From the intersection of NC 280 and US 276 in Brevard, take US 276 north for 5.2 miles, then turn left on FR 475 toward the Pisgah Center for Wildlife Education. Follow FR 475 for 1.4 miles to cross the bridge over the Davidson River at the wildlife center and fish hatchery. The hike starts at the lower end of the parking area, away from the wildlife center.

GPS trailhead coordinates: N35° 17.054', W82° 47.436'

For now, alternate between dry oak woods and small flowing streams, cloaked in rhododendron.

By 1.9 miles, the trail levels out on John Rock, among flanks of mountain laurel and dense tree growth. Step over a small spring branch, soon making the north side of John Rock, the side of the granite face. Here, the trail angles left and rises among blueberry bushes topped with xeric hardwoods. At 2.1 miles, a spur trail leads right to the open granite. Incredible panoramas open before you. Below, in the Davidson River Valley, the fish hatchery is clearly visible. Looking Glass Rock stretches north, pointing toward the crest of the Blue Ridge, where mile-high mountains majestically unfold across the skyline. Nearer, stunted pines and mosses cling to crevices in the granite. Seeps trickle over the rock. At this point, dog owners should have their pets leashed. Several dogs have fallen from John Rock to their death. I can attest to the potential danger, having slipped one cold winter day on an iced-over seep here.

Ahead, a second spur leads to another vista on John Rock, your grandstand for viewing this parcel of the Blue Ridge, with its deep wooded valleys, granite outcrops, and evergreen-cloaked peaks. The path turns south from the face of John Rock, climbing among sourwood and chest-

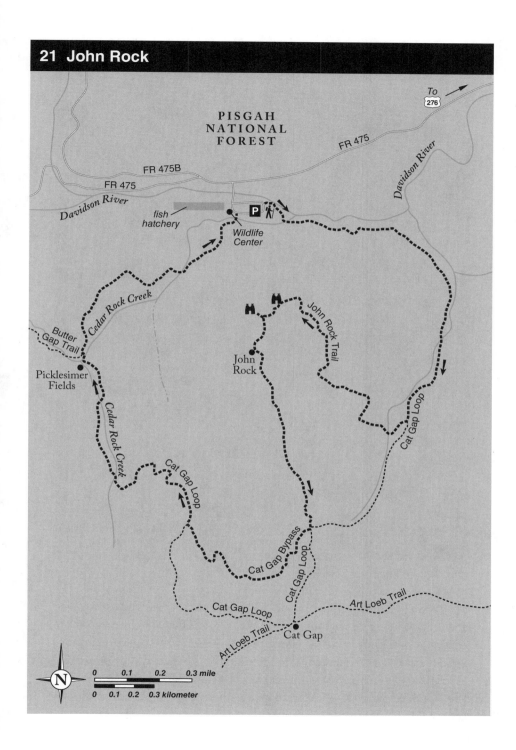

PISGAH
NATIONAL
FOREST

To 276

FR 475

FR 475B

FR 475

Davidson River

Davidson River

fish
hatchery

P

Wildlife
Center

Cedar Rock Creek

Butter
Gap Trail

Picklesimer
Fields

Cedar Rock Creek

John Rock Trail

John
Rock

Cat Gap Loop

Cat Gap Loop

Cat Gap Bypass

Cat Gap Loop

Cat Gap Loop

Art Loeb Trail

Art Loeb Trail

Cat Gap

N

| 0 | 0.1 | 0.2 | 0.3 mile |
| 0 | 0.1 | 0.2 | 0.3 kilometer |

Aquatic seeps can freeze in winter atop John Rock.

nut oaks. Reach a high point of 1,000 feet above the Davidson River, then dip to a gap. Make one more climb, mercifully working around the east side of a knob, reaching your high point of 3,270 feet at 2.8 miles. Put the brakes on for a steep drop to reach a four-way trail intersection at 2.9 miles. Turn right here, joining the Cat Gap Bypass Trail. You will do less climbing than if you were to go all the way to Cat Gap and the Art Loeb Trail.

Glide through north-facing coves on a slender track. Step over headwaters of John Rock Branch to meet the Cat Gap Loop at 3.6 miles. Stay right, back on Cat Gap Loop. It soon drops quickly by switchback. Step over Cedar Rock Creek at 4.1 miles. Turn downstream in pines, bronze needles spread gold at your feet. Ahead, cut through a planted pine grove and campsites. Cross back over to the right-hand bank of the creek at 4.3 miles.

Enter the growing-over Picklesimer Fields, then reach a bridge over now-bigger Cedar Rock Creek at 4.5 miles. Grogan Creek has added much volume. Big boulders enhance the wooded scenery. This is a good break spot. Stay right, still with the Cat Gap Loop. To your right, Cedar Rock Creek is crashing in one cascade after another. Rough spur trails lead down to pools and shoals. The path then works past fences of the fish hatchery, staying outside its bounds. Bridge Cedar Rock Creek another time at 5.1 miles. Continue descending to bridge Cedar Rock Creek one last time, then emerge at the rear of the wildlife center, completing the hike.

Mileages

0.0   Fish Hatchery & Wildlife Education Center trailhead
1.2   John Rock Trail
2.1   John Rock
2.9   Cat Gap Bypass Trail
3.6   Cat Gap Loop
5.4   Fish Hatchery & Wildlife Education Center trailhead

Nantahala National Forest Hikes

Nantahala National Forest Hike Locator Guide

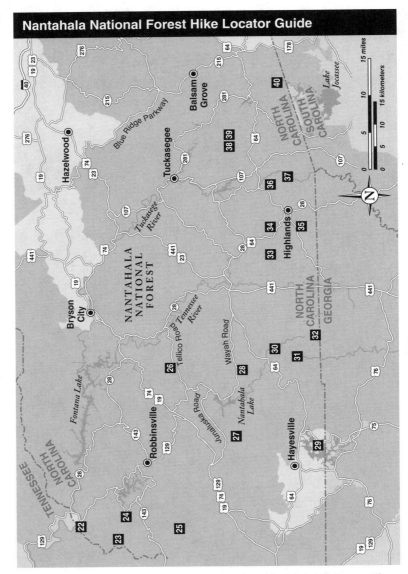

22 Lower Falls Loop
23 The Hangover
24 Joyce Kilmer Memorial Forest
25 Falls of Snowbird Creek
26 Wesser Bald Tower
27 Fires Creek Rim Loop
28 Siler Bald
29 Jackrabbit Mountain Loop
30 Park Creek Loop
31 Standing Indian

32 Southern Nantahala Wilderness Hike
33 Jones Knob via the Bartram Trail
34 Cliffside Lake Double Loop
35 Glen Falls
36 Whiteside Mountain
37 Chattooga Wild and Scenic River Hike
38 Panthertown Backcountry Loop
39 Schoolhouse Falls Loop at
   Panthertown
40 Whitewater Falls

Hike Summary: This is a great national forest alternative to the Smoky Mountains. The scenery is more similar than not. Make a wilderness loop in the Slickrock Creek drainage, a wild mountain watercourse framed in wooded beauty. First walk above serpentine Calderwood Lake, then turn into the Smokies-esque Slickrock Creek. The first of two fords leads to Lower Falls, with its huge pool, a draw for summertime swimmers. Finally, climb away from the stream to traverse lonely ridges and hollows back to Calderwood Lake.

This hike takes place within Joyce Kilmer–Slickrock Wilderness, a federally designated preserve laced with a stellar trail network, encompassing parts of North Carolina's Nantahala National Forest and Tennessee's Cherokee National Forest. Pick up an old roadbed, Slickrock Creek Trail, with Calderwood Lake to your right. The clear, clean impoundment of the Little Tennessee River silently snakes between high ridges. A steep wooded hillside rises to your left. Lush hardwoods of birch, beech, tulip trees, and maples rise on the stony hillside. At 0.5 mile, the trail devolves to a single track. At 0.6 mile, the Ike Branch Trail leaves left. This is your return route.

Keep forward on the Slickrock Creek Trail. Rock-hop Ike Branch. The path works around rock promontories and bluffs on a declivitous slope. Occasional wooden bridges help you negotiate the steepest bluffs. Curve into Slickrock Creek embayment. Views open to the north of the lake.

The watery intimations of Slickrock Creek drift to your ears. Drop to reach the stream at 1.8 miles. For the entire time you are following Slickrock Creek, it actually forms the boundary between the Volunteer State and the Tar Heel State. Walk a primitive wilderness-grade trail along bluffs and through rocky stream braids. The beauty of Slickrock Creek roars as loud as its rapids—crystalline water flowing over grayback boulders, rich vegetation growing on anything that doesn't move, mountain slopes rising to the sky, trout-filled pools, tree-covered islands, and waterside gravel bars. An overabundance of campsites is the valley's only downside. Anglers might want to bring a fishing pole.

Keep upstream as the trail alternately passes through thickly wooded stream flats and along riverside bluffs that make passage challenging. Trace the bends of the creek, going on and off an old railroad bed. At

22 LOWER FALLS LOOP

Distance: 6.4-mile loop

Hiking time: 3.5–4.5 hours

Difficulty: Moderate

Highlights: Mountain lake, wilderness, Lower Falls, swimming, fishing

Cautions: Sloped rocky trail in parts, two fords

Fees/Permits: No fees or permits required

Best seasons: April through November

Other trail users: None

Trail contacts: Nantahala National Forest, Cheoah Ranger District, 1070 Massey Branch Road, Robbinsville, NC 28771, (828) 479-6431, www.fs.usda.gov/nfsnc

Finding the trailhead: From Robbinsville, take US 129 north for 16 miles. Turn left on the road just before crossing the bridge over the Little Tennessee River just below Calderwood Dam at the North Carolina-@Tennessee state line. Follow the road just a short distance to dead end at the trailhead.

GPS trailhead coordinates: N35° 26.961′, W83° 56.520′

2.7 miles, reach your first ford of Slickrock Creek. The stream bottom is relatively shallow and even. Cross over to the Tennessee side of the watercourse, keeping upstream. At 2.9 miles, pass below at a tributary forming a small trailside waterfall. Reach Lower Falls at 3.0 miles. Here, Slickrock Creek pours over a wide stone lip about 15 feet into one of the larger pools in the Southern Appalachians, a mountain swimming hole if there ever was one. In summer, give the pool a test swim. The width of the stream allows ample sunlight at the falls. Large flat boulders provide sunning spots beside the cataract.

Leave the roaring tumbler behind, continuing upriver. The plethora of campsites sometimes makes the route confusing, as spur paths will lead to the camps. Join a south-facing piney bluff before dropping to meet the second ford at 3.5 miles. This ford is a little more challenging, as it is deeper with an irregular stream bottom. A stout stick helps here. Cross back over to North Carolina, continuing upstream among doghobble and rhododendron. Fight your way around a gnarly curved bluff, then reach a campsite and trail junction at 3.7 miles. Look left as the somewhat-dim-yet-signed Ike Branch Trail leaves left away from Slickrock Creek and uphill. Step over a small branch. The path climbs under yellow birch, black birch, and buckeye. Circle up the hollow to reach

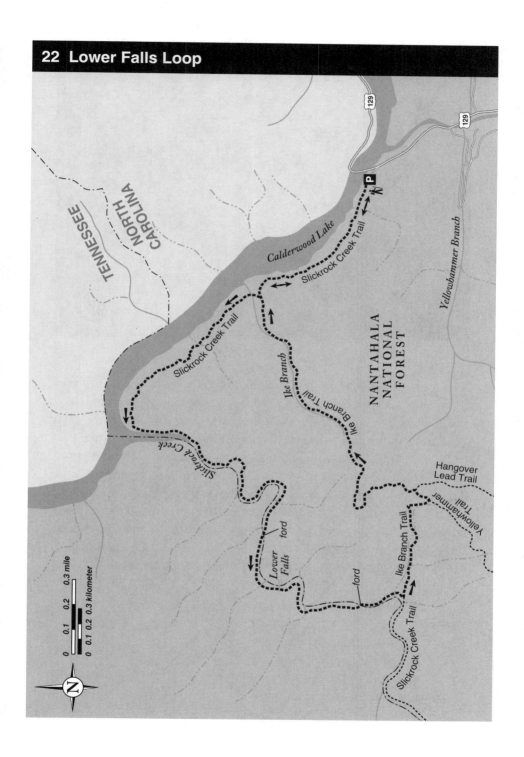

Lower Falls is impressive in flow and the size of its pool.

a trail intersection at 4.2 miles. Here, the Yellowhammer Trail leaves right. Stay left with the Ike Branch Trail, wandering the mountainside on a ribbon of trail. The northbound path meets the Hangover Lead Trail at 4.3 miles, just below Yellowhammer Gap. Continue straight on Ike Branch Trail beneath mid-slope dogwoods, oaks, and white pines. Pass through gaps at 4.6 miles and 5.0 miles. Dip into the intimate Ike Branch hollow. Cross Ike Branch a few times, then pass an improbable homesite on your right. Piled rocks are all that remain of Ike's highland homestead. The path steepens before opening into the Little Tennessee River Valley. Come to the Slickrock Creek Trail at 5.8 miles, completing the loop portion of the hike. Backtrack .6 mile to the trailhead.

Mileages

0.0 Slickrock Creek trailhead near US 129
0.6 Ike Branch Trail leaves left
1.8 Reach Slickrock Creek
2.7 First ford of Slickrock Creek
3.0 Lower Falls
3.5 Second ford of Slickrock Creek

3.7 Left on Ike Branch Trail
4.2 Yellowhammer Trail leaves right
4.3 Hangover Lead Trail leaves right
5.8 Right on Slickrock Creek Trail
6.4 Slickrock Creek trailhead near US 129

23 • THE HANGOVER

Hike Summary: This wilderness overlook is a Southern Appalachian high-light. Start in an elevated, remote section of the Nantahala National Forest. Join a mile-high ridgeline. Enter the Joyce Kilmer–Slickrock Wilderness, dropping to historic Naked Ground. Continue on a rocky spine amid boulders and northern hardwoods. End at a declivitous stone precipice so steep it seems to be hanging over. The views here stretch northeasterly into the Smoky Mountains and beyond. The lack of extreme elevation changes adds appeal to this high country ramble.

The Hangover is one of those places you go to, become enamored of, then bring someone else to the next time. There are several approaches to the rewarding overlook, most of them very steep. However, this approach is the least painful, and the scenery is fine along the way. The trailhead drive can be a bit tedious, but you end up starting your trek at more than 4,500 feet!

From the trailhead, do not take the closed grassy forest road; rather, take the single-track Wolf Laurel Trail leading uphill into northern hardwoods of cherry and beech. At .2 mile, turn left onto the Stratton Bald Trail. Resume your climb among lichen-covered boulders scattered in the forest. Level off at .5 mile, enjoying a highland ridge walk. Grasses wave under the scattered tree cover, a relic from when this area was meadow grazed by cattle. Intermittent views open through the trees to your right, into the Little Santeetlah Creek watershed. The ascent resumes, and you reach a mile-high trail intersection at 1.2 miles. Here, turn right, joining the Haoe Lead Trail. Immediately lose the elevation gain, working your way through brushy, thin forest toward Naked Ground. Briars can be troublesome here in summer.

Make Naked Ground at 1.8 miles. Cherokee Indians named this gap. It was treeless during their time. Now-wooded Naked Ground is an

23 THE HANGOVER

Distance: 6.2-mile there-and-back

Hiking time: 3.5–4.5 hours

Difficulty: Moderate

Highlights: Joyce Kilmer–Slickrock Wilderness, views

Cautions: Potentially overgrown trails during late summer

Fees/Permits: No fees or permits required

Best seasons: Late March–mid-May, late September through November

Other trail users: None

Trail contacts: Nantahala National Forest, Cheoah Ranger District, 1070 Massey Branch Road, Robbinsville, NC 28771, (828) 479-6431, www.fs.usda.gov/nfsnc

Finding the trailhead: From Robbinsville, take US 129 north 1.1 miles to Massey Branch Road/NC 143. Turn left on Massey Branch Road and follow it 3.4 miles to a T intersection. Turn right on Snowbird Road, still NC 143. Follow it 6.8 miles to NC 1127/Rattler Ford Campground Road (the road to Joyce Kilmer Memorial Forest). Between Rattler Ford Road on your right and NC 143/Cherohala Skyway on your left, you will see a paved road, FR 81. Turn left onto FR 81. The road soon becomes gravel. It descends to cross Santeetlah Creek. Continue up Santeetlah Creek for 6.8 miles to FR 81-F. Turn right here, following it past a side road to the Swan Cabin to dead end at the Wolf Laurel trailhead at 4.8 miles.

GPS trailhead coordinates: N35° 21.843', W83° 58.705'

important trail intersection in Joyce Kilmer–Slickrock Wilderness and has a heavily used campsite. Pass an overlook on your right at the gap. Stay straight, rising on the Haoe Lead Trail in beeches with a grass and boulder understory. Roller-coaster atop a knife-edge ridge. At 2.5 miles, make a short but steady ascent to reach the summit of Haoe Mountain and a trail junction at 2.8 miles. Stay left with the Hangover Lead Trail, as the Haoe Lead Trail leaves right. Descend to another intersection at 2.9 miles. Here, the Hangover Lead Trail drops left to Big Fat Gap. This is the steepest way up to the Hangover. Its alternate name contains expletives unsuitable for a University of North Carolina Press book.

Keep straight on the main ridgeline, coming to yet another trail intersection at 3.0 miles. Here, the Deep Creek Trail leaves right for the lowlands. Keep straight again, opening onto a grassy area cleared as a temporary helicopter landing pad. The controversial clearing is regenerating. Continue beyond the mini-meadow, then rise a bit. Soon open

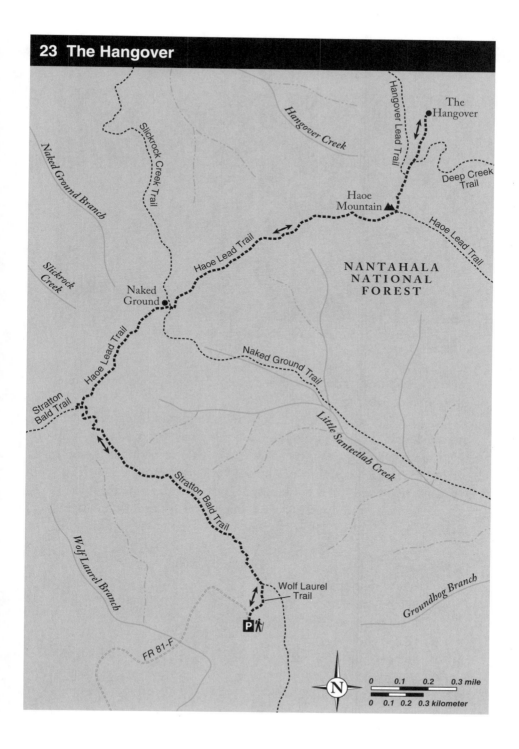

The Hangover

Hangover Creek

Hangover Lead Trail

Deep Creek Trail

Slickrock Creek Trail

Naked Ground Branch

Haoe Mountain

Haoe Lead Trail

Slickrock Creek

Naked Ground

NANTAHALA NATIONAL FOREST

Haoe Lead Trail

Haoe Lead Trail

Stratton Bald Trail

Naked Ground Trail

Little Santeetlah Creek

Stratton Bald Trail

Wolf Laurel Branch

Wolf Laurel Trail

Groundhog Branch

FR 81-F

| 0 | 0.1 | 0.2 | 0.3 mile |
| 0 | 0.1 | 0.2 | 0.3 kilometer |

N

This view looks back at the rampart of Bobs Bald from the Hangover (photo by Bryan Delay).

onto a rock spine and the Hangover. Work your way among the boulders to the end of the crag.

The rock outcrop, 5,180 feet, bordered in stunted evergreens, falls steeply below. The views from the Hangover on a clear day can be simply stupendous. The peaks and valleys of the wilderness are in the near, while the Smoky Mountains rise across the Little Tennessee River Valley. Wave upon wave of mountain rolls in the far Carolina distance. It is simply one of the finest places to be in North Carolina's national forests.

Mileages

- 0.0 Wolf Laurel trailhead
- 0.2 Left on Stratton Bald Trail
- 1.3 Right on Haoe Lead Trail
- 1.8 Naked Ground
- 2.8 Top of Haoe Mountain, 5,249 feet
- 3.0 Hangover Lead Trail
- 3.1 Hangover Lead, backtrack
- 6.2 Wolf Laurel trailhead

Hike Summary: The preserved tree grove at Joyce Kilmer truly is impressive. Your walk among the giants, primarily tulip trees, centers on Little Santeetlah Creek and an unnamed tributary flowing from Poplar Cove. First, bridge Little Santeetlah Creek, then work your way up to Poplar Cove. Here, make a mini-loop in a concentration of old-growth forest that will leave you revering Mother Nature. Saunter back to Little Santeetlah Creek, following this scenic watercourse through lush woods to the trailhead.

Most of western North Carolina's national forest lands were logged. But we can be thankful that a swath of woodland in the Little Santeetlah Creek Valley was spared. Here, trees exceeding 450 years in age tower over a rich cove. Some trees exceed 20 feet in circumference. This land of the giants was purchased and protected by the U.S. Forest Service in 1936. Later, the area was named for the journalist and poet Joyce Kilmer (1886–1918). The New Jersey native was killed in World War I. He wrote a poem titled "Trees" with the famous opening lines, "I think that I shall never see / A poem lovely as a tree." Today, you can walk among these trees and consider the words of Kilmer. You will likely be inspired to come up with your own prose.

The hike takes place within the boundaries of the Joyce Kilmer–Slickrock Wilderness, designated in 1975 by Congress. Most trails within the wilderness are primitive, but this nature trail is easy to follow. The walk does have a little bit of vertical variation. The stone shelter with interpretive information greets you at the trailhead, which also has picnic tables and a restroom for your convenience. Begin walking up a wide path, immediately crossing Little Santeetlah Creek on a sturdy footbridge. Angle up the mountainside in rhododendron tangles, then make a quick switchback. Much of the forest is open due to adelgid-infested dead hemlocks falling and taking other trees with them. However, the tree growth cycle is starting anew, and perhaps some of these young trees will reach the size of the colossi currently standing in Joyce Kilmer Memorial Forest.

A wide trail along with wood and earth steps makes this path user-friendly. Reach your first big trees—beeches and yellow birches—after a quarter-mile. Joyce Kilmer is also a rich wildflower destination, as well as a great place for herbaceous plants and ferns. The upper loop,

24 JOYCE KILMER MEMORIAL FOREST

Distance: 2.0-mile double loop

Hiking time: 1.5 hours

Difficulty: Easy

Highlights: Old-growth forest, huge trees

Cautions: None

Fees/Permits: No fees or permits required

Best seasons: Year-round

Other trail users: None

Trail contacts: Nantahala National Forest, Cheoah Ranger District, 1070 Massey Branch Road, Robbinsville, NC 28771, (828) 479-6431, www.fs.usda.gov/nfsnc

Finding the trailhead: From Robbinsville, take US 129 north 1.1 miles to Massey Branch Road/NC 143. Turn left on Massey Branch Road and follow it 3.4 miles to a T intersection. Turn right on Snowbird Road, still NC 143. Follow it 6.8 miles to NC 1127. Turn right on NC 1127/Rattler Ford Campground Road and follow it 2.2 miles. Turn left on Joyce Kilmer Road and follow it .4 mile to dead end at the trailhead.

GPS trailhead coordinates: N35° 21.531', W83° 55.731'

though, is the heart of the old-growth zone. At .5 mile, come to a plaque memorializing Joyce Kilmer and the beginning of the upper loop. Ironically, just as Joyce Kilmer's life was suddenly shortened in one moment during World War I, the giant tree behind the Kilmer Memorial is now dead, broken off, likely from a lightning strike.

Stay left, beginning the upper loop. You are climbing higher into Poplar Cove. The conditions here are nearly ideal for tulip trees, cool with moist, well-drained soils. Look around and take inventory of the grove. Before you imagine a continuous stand of giant trees, realize authentic old-growth woodland is not an agglomeration of even-aged trees. On the contrary, even-aged trees are a sign of disturbance. An old-growth forest will have many big trees, along with younger trees that grow when they get the chance. A growth opportunity happens when a big tree falls, creating a light gap. Young trees sprout in this light gap, and other, already somewhat grown trees thrive in the additional sun. Trees are continually growing and dying, as older trees succumb to lightning strikes, disease, or old age, creating a healthy mosaic of trees of all ages.

After this hike, you'll need a neck brace from craning up at the massive tulip trees here. In times past, tulip trees were commonly known

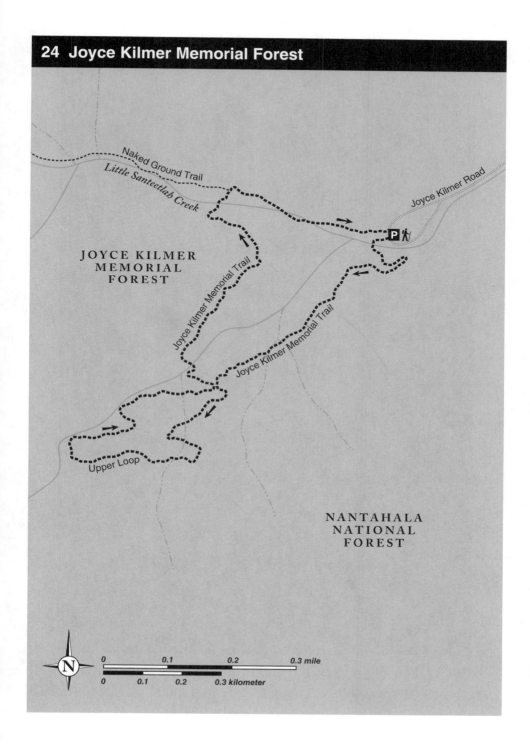

Naked Ground Trail

Little Santeetlah Creek

Joyce Kilmer Road

JOYCE KILMER
MEMORIAL
FOREST

Joyce Kilmer Memorial Trail

Joyce Kilmer Memorial Trail

Upper Loop

NANTAHALA
NATIONAL
FOREST

N

| 0 | 0.1 | 0.2 | 0.3 mile |
| 0 | 0.1 | 0.2 | 0.3 kilometer |

The mass of the tulip trees at Joyce Kilmer will amaze.

as poplars; hence the name Poplar Cove. There are also large red oaks, basswood, Carolina silverbells, and more. Reach the top of Poplar Cove at .9 mile. Pass more impressive trees, the largest living things in North Carolina's national forests. Complete the upper loop at 1.2 miles. Stay left, wandering downhill toward Little Santeetlah Creek. Step over the stream flowing through Poplar Cove. The path steepens. Soon you are near Santeetlah Creek, bridging it at 1.7 miles. Here, the Naked Ground Trail leaves left. Stay right, turning downstream along Little Santeetlah Creek as it crashes downstream between boulders. An easy downhill takes you back to the trailhead and the hike's end.

Mileages

0.0 Joyce Kilmer trailhead
0.5 Begin upper loop
1.2 Complete upper loop
1.7 Bridge Little Santeetlah Creek
2.0 Joyce Kilmer trailhead

25 • FALLS OF SNOWBIRD CREEK

Hike Summary: *The Snowbird watershed is a wooded wildland with several notable waterfalls. This hike visits three of them. Walk an old railroad grade to Big Falls. The going gets tougher as you make several fords to reach brawling Middle Falls. Inexperienced hikers should turn around here, as the loop joins faint Burntrock Ridge Trail, fighting over a hilltop to Sassafras Creek. Follow Sassafras Creek Trail past high and inspiring Sassafras Falls. Work down to Snowbird Creek, then backtrack to the trailhead.*

What a wild and beautiful valley is Snowbird Creek! The trail system is primitive, but don't let that deter you. On this hike, the first 4 miles are clear and easy. Two trails emanate from the upper parking area. Stay left with the Big Snowbird Trail—the King Meadows Trail leaves right. Join a wide railroad grade bordered by rhododendron thickets. Snowbird Creek roars to your right, enshrouded in rhododendron. Northern hardwoods, primarily yellow birch, rise from evergreen tangles. Ferns, doghobble, and wildflowers find their places. You'll probably miss the faint intersection after a quarter-mile where the Snowbird Mountain Trail leaves left.

25 FALLS OF SNOWBIRD CREEK

Distance: 10.6-mile balloon loop

Hiking time: 6.0–7.5 hours

Difficulty: Difficult

Highlights: Three waterfalls, each different in size, shape, and flow; remote setting

Cautions: Challenging, overgrown, and poorly marked trail sections

Fees/Permits: No fees or permits required

Best seasons: April through November

Other trail users: Anglers closer to the trailhead

Trail contacts: Nantahala National Forest, Cheoah Ranger District, 1070 Massey Branch Road, Robbinsville, NC 28771, (828) 479-6431, www.fs.usda.gov/nfsnc

Finding the trailhead: From Robbinsville, take US 129 north for 1.1 miles to Massey Branch Road/NC 143. Follow it for 3.4 miles to a T intersection. Turn right here on Snowbird Road, still on NC 143. Follow Snowbird Road for 2.1 miles, then turn left on NC 1115. Follow NC 1115 for 2.0 miles, still on Snowbird Road. Make an acute left on NC 1127, after passing Robinson's Grocery. Follow NC 1127 for .9 mile, then turn right on Big Snowbird Road/NC 1120. NC 1120 turns gravel after 2 miles, then becomes FR 75, where it dead-ends at the trailhead 4 miles beyond the blacktop.

GPS trailhead coordinates: N35° 15.866', W83° 56.285'

The Big Snowbird Trail mimics the curves of Snowbird Creek, penetrating the mountain fastness. Trickling branches spill over the gently climbing logging railroad grade, left over from a 1930s harvesting operation. At 2.5 miles, reach Sassafras Creek. To your right stands a bullet-riddled old jalopy, nicknamed the "getaway car." Rock-hop Sassafras Creek, passing a campsite. Keep upcreek, intersecting the lesser-used Sassafras Creek Trail, your return route at 2.8 miles. For now, keep upstream, well above Snowbird Creek. At 3.6 miles, a spur trail drops precipitously to Big Falls. Carefully descend to a rock slab in mid-fall. Here, Snowbird Creek charges over a ledge below, narrowing into a chute. Another ledge falls above you.

More cascades tumble just uptrail. At 3.9 miles, the trail crosses Snowbird Creek on a big log bridge with handrails, erected in 2011, replacing an older footbridge. You are now on the right stream bank. Keep upstream, quickly opening onto a campsite. Here, the Middle Falls Trail, #64A, leaves right, uphill. It continues about a mile, then returns to Snowbird Creek upstream of Middle Falls, though a flagged spur cuts

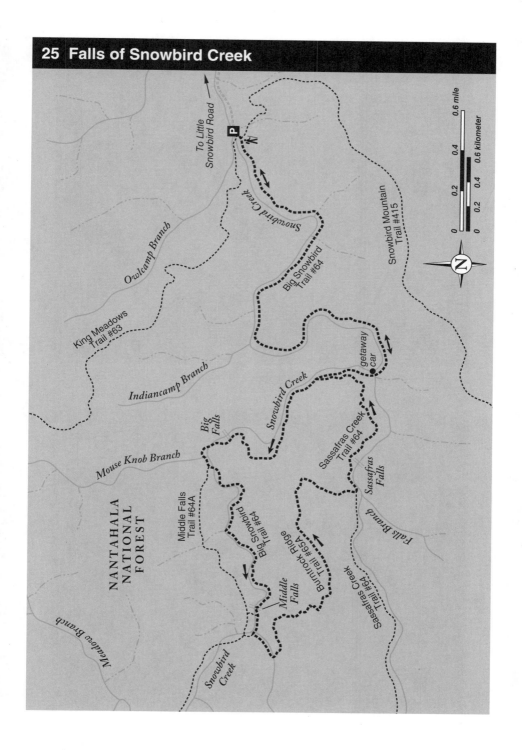

Brawling Middle Falls can be heard from a ways downtrail.

The getaway car lies dormant near Sassafras Creek.

directly to the falls. This path avoids the ensuing eight fords of Snowbird Creek. However, it also misses the intimate beauty of the creek.

This hike leaves the campsite and makes the first of those eight fords about 60 yards upstream of the log bridge. The trail can be faint here. You will be one with the crystalline stream, the mosses, the gravel bars, and the greenery. Your eighth ford is over after 4.7 miles, and you are on the right bank, rejoining the railroad grade. The roar of Middle Falls calls at 4.9 miles. A path leads left to what I think is the most impressive tumbler on Snowbird Creek. Middle Falls is a 60-foot-wide ledge that spills in a massive curtain into a more massive pool. It feels wild and remote beside this brawling torrent, here in the heart of the Snowbird Mountains.

If navigation and faint trail tracking aren't your thing, consider returning to the trailhead from Middle Falls. If you have time, an adventurous soul, experience, and maybe a map-loaded GPS, continue beyond Middle Falls. Just ahead, the faint spur from Middle Falls Trail enters on your right. Ford Snowbird Creek a final time at 5.1 miles. Littleflat Branch flows in here. Come to a trail junction. To make the loop, turn left up Littleflat Branch on the likely overgrown Burntrock Ridge Trail, #65A.

Turn left away from Littleflat Branch at 5.3 miles, then cross some rivulets before working your way up Burntrock Ridge. Expect blowndown trees and hope for flagging tape left by previous hikers. Crest out atop the ridge at 5.8 miles. Trace the crest easterly in oaks. At 6.5 miles, in a gap, the trail dives right off the ridge, down a draw, dropping 350 feet in .3 mile.

At 6.8 miles, turn left on the Sassafras Creek Trail, rejoining a railroad grade in yellow birch woods. Sassafras Creek gurgles nearby. At 7.0 miles, pass a sign indicating Sassafras Falls. A short spur leads to the cataract top. Keep going to reach a second sign ahead, then follow a winding spur to the fall's base. From the bottom, peer up at the tall, multitiered, multifaced waterfall. What a contrast! Middle Falls is a wide ledge with a single curtain dropping into a big pool, while Sassafras Falls is tall and multistaged and crashes into a rock jumble! The Sassafras Creek Trail turns away from the stream, angling into Snowbird Creek. Its follows a railroad grade, but the path gets tough at points where bridges spanned hollows, leaving no trailbed. Make Big Snowbird Trail at 7.8 miles, completing the loop. From here, backtrack to the trailhead, concluding the hike after 10.6 miles.

Mileages

0.0   Snowbird trailhead

2.5   Sassafras Creek and getaway car

2.8   Sassafras Trail leaves acutely left

3.6   Big Falls

3.9   Bridge Snowbird Creek, begin fords

4.9   Middle Falls

5.1   Left on Burntrock Ridge Trail

5.8   Crest of Burntrock Ridge

6.5   Dive right off ridge

6.8   Left on Sassafras Creek Trail

7.0   Sassafras Falls

7.8   Big Snowbird Trail, backtrack

10.6   Snowbird trailhead

---

26 • WESSER BALD TOWER

Hike Summary: When it comes to views in North Carolina's national forests, Wesser Bald may be hard to beat. No longer an open meadow, the mountain peak is topped with a viewing tower that leaves nothing between you and the surrounding mountainscape. This turret was once a standard metal fire observation tower. It was topped with a box and manned by a ranger during the fire season. The tower was cut down, however, and an open observation deck was placed above the trees, allowing for unobstructed 360° views. You will take the Appalachian Trail (AT) to the tower, an easy uptick from Tellico Gap. Your return route traces the road used to build the tower, making for a short and easy return trip.

For approximately 40 years, from the 1930s through the 1970s, fire towers were used to observe the wooded landscapes of the Carolinas and beyond, as rangers watched for emerging conflagrations. This development of fire towers followed the establishment of the American national forest system, of which the Pisgah, Nantahala, Uwharrie, and Croatan are part. These towers were primarily used in the mountainous western part of the state. Some were the metal towers like the one that used to be on Wesser Bald. Yet others were built of stone, such as the one atop Wayah Bald, or on Mount Cammerer in Great Smoky Moun-

26 WESSER BALD TOWER

Distance: 2.2-mile loop

Hiking time: 1.5 hours

Difficulty: Easy

Highlights: 360° panoramas from viewing tower

Cautions: None

Fees/Permits: No fees or permits required

Best seasons: Year-round; fall and winter for best views

Other trail users: None

Trail contacts: Nantahala National Forest, Nantahala Ranger District, 90 Sloan Road, Franklin, NC 28734, (828) 524-6441, www.fs.usda.gov/nfsnc

Finding the trailhead: From Andrews, North Carolina, take US 19/US 129 north for a little over 6 miles to the point where US 129 turns left toward Robbinsville. At this point, keep forward on US 19 for 2.3 miles to NC 1310/Wayah Road. Turn right on Wayah Road and follow it 5.0 miles to Otter Creek Road. Turn left on Otter Creek Road and follow it 4.0 miles to Tellico Gap, situated under a transmission line clearing. There are several parking spots here. Alternate directions from Franklin: Take NC 28 north 12 miles to Tellico Road. Turn left on Tellico Road and follow it 8.2 miles to Tellico Gap.

GPS trailhead coordinates: N35° 16.090', W83° 34.322'

tains National Park. Hired rangers would live on-site at these towers, and many towers had adjacent outbuildings in which the rangers quartered. In the 1970s, fire management began to change. National forests and other interested parties began using airplanes to watch for fires. Many towers were dismantled, but luckily for us, some were restored and are open for our viewing pleasure.

Wesser Bald Tower was built in 1936 and included living quarters at the base of the lookout, but the quarters were destroyed by fire in 1979. In the early 1990s, the forest service converted the tower to what you see today. Though the tower is lower, the views remain as striking as ever—and the climb is a lot less scary for most folk. Ascending those old-time, ever-narrowing, slender aluminum structures, flight after flight, step after step, gets to hikers with a fear of heights. No problem here at Wesser Bald Tower.

Leave Tellico Gap, northbound on the AT. It briefly follows your return route, the gated road leading directly to Wesser Bald Tower. Stay left on the single-track AT, in maples, black birch, and rhododendron.

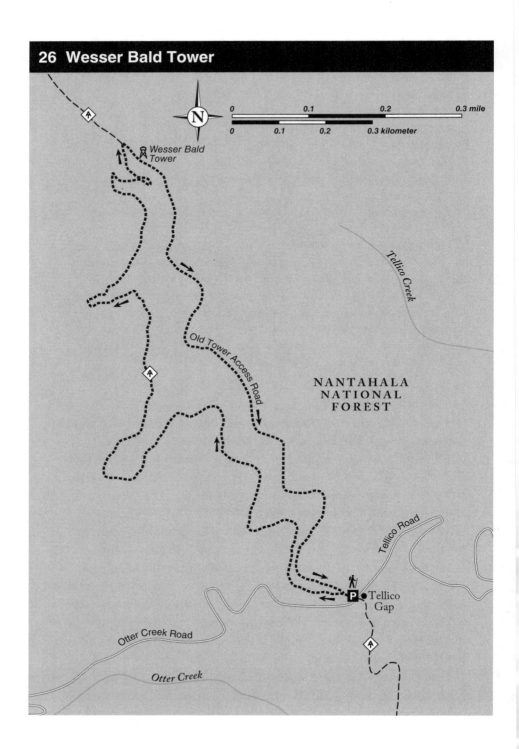

Wesser Bald
Tower

Tellico Creek

Old Tower Access Road

NANTAHALA
NATIONAL
FOREST

Tellico Road

P • Tellico
     Gap

Otter Creek Road

Otter Creek

A hiker looks out from Wesser Bald Tower on a glorious fall day.

Curve into a cove, and the forest ecotone changes to sourwood, mountain laurel, and oaks. Continue gently upslope. Curve out to a rib ridge at .7 mile. Turn back northeast. The hiking remains easy as the well-graded path turns into another cove, then joins another rib ridge. Make a couple of switchbacks to reach the slender crest of Wesser Bald and a trail junction at 1.4 miles. Here, the AT heads left, but you take the spur leading right.

A little farther up, and you are at the tower. Steps lead to the open observation area. Unobstructed panoramas stretch in every direction. You don't even know where to look first! Try the north. The dark crest of the Great Smoky Mountains forms a backdrop in that direction. Look for the tower on Clingmans Dome. Beyond the crest of the Smokies stand the three peaks of Tennessee's Mount LeConte. Below that, the winding embayment of the Nantahala River forms a serpentine arm of Fontana Lake, pointing north. And the east-west portion of Fontana Lake marks the southern boundary of the Great Smoky Mountains National Park. The transmission towers of Wine Spring Bald stand south. Cheoah Bald rises to the west, on the far side of the Nantahala Gorge. What a feast of mountains!

Your return trip is easy. Simply follow the old tower road south from the peak. The trail is well worn but can be overgrown in areas open to the sun. Imagine trucks and men rumbling on the track, bringing tools and supplies to construct the tower during the 1930s. Back then, Wesser Bald was the back of beyond. Soon you are back at Tellico Gap, having completed the loop.

Mileages

0.0 Tellico Gap trailhead
1.4 Spur right to Wesser Bald Tower
2.2 Tellico Gap trailhead

---

27 • FIRES CREEK RIM LOOP

Hike Summary: *Want to hike a remote ridgetop with views? The Fires Creek Rim Trail makes a highland circuit around a scenic watershed. On this hike, you will climb steeply to the rim, walking a serrated rock and forest crest, opening to views of Carolina mountainlands in the distance. Ramble past grown-over balds and stunted forest of yellow birch and other northern hardwoods. Drop from the rim on the Shinbone Ridge Trail, returning to Fires Creek. Expect solitude any time of year. Winter could be cold atop the rim, but spring and fall present wildflowers and autumn colors. Summer will be pleasant, save for afternoon storms.*

This loop is but one possibility in the solitude-laden greater Fires Creek trail network. The Rim Trail itself makes a 25-mile loop around the Fires Creek watershed. Several spur trails emanate from forest roads along Fires Creek. Furthermore, the Chunky Gal Trail leaves the Fires Creek rim and travels east to meet the Appalachian Trail and the trail network of the Standing Indian backcountry and the Southern Nantahala Wilderness, expanding the hiking possibilities to multiple miles and multiple days.

Other hikes in Fires Creek backcountry may be longer, but you certainly won't be hiking trails with better names. Your climb to the crest begins on the Far Bald Springs Trail. After cruising on the Rim Trail, you will make your descent on the Shinbone Ridge Trail, another entrant in the all-time Southern Appalachian name contest.

27 FIRES CREEK RIM LOOP

Distance: 5.8-mile loop

Hiking time: 3.5–5.0 hours

Difficulty: Difficult

Highlights: Solitude, views, northern hardwood forest

Cautions: Steep trail sections

Fees/Permits: No fees or permits required

Best seasons: Mid-April through October

Other trail users: None

Trail contacts: Nantahala National Forest, Tusquitee Ranger District, 123 Woodland Drive, Murphy, NC 28906, (828) 837-5152, www.fs.usda.gov/nfsnc

Finding the trailhead: From the intersection of US 64 Bypass and US 64 on the west side of Hayesville, take US 64 west for 4.2 miles to SR 1300/Fires Creek Road. Turn right on SR 1300 at a three-way intersection with a small store on one corner, just after Lance Cove Road. You will soon pass Sweetwater Baptist Church. Drive for 3.8 miles to reach Fires Creek Wildlife Road/SR 1344. There will be a national forest sign indicating Fires Creek recreational facilities. At 1.7 miles, SR 1344 becomes gravel FR 340. Keep straight on FR 340. At 8.1 miles, make sure and stay right on FR 340, bridging Fires Creek, as FR 340-C leaves left. The road becomes more primitive here. Continue driving for a total of 11.6 miles on SR 1344/FR 340 to reach the trailhead on a sharp left curve. There is parking for a couple of cars here.

GPS trailhead coordinates: N35° 8.574′, W83° 45.038′

Far Bald Springs, trail #389, leaves FR 340 around a pole gate to enter a meadow offering views up to Shinbone Ridge. Step over uppermost Fires Creek, then enter a second meadow. Reenter woods at .3 mile, then cross Far Bald Springs Branch. Maples, oaks, and tulip trees dominate the lower end of the wildflower-rich hollow you are now ascending. By .5 mile, the rocky trail steepens, and a streamlet trickles to your right. It isn't long before you break the 4,000-foot barrier. Yellow birches become more numerous. Switchback steeply from the hollow at .8 mile. The climb eases at 1.2 miles. You just climbed 1,000 feet in 1 mile! Join a southwest-facing slope amid galax, oaks, and sourwood. Grasses on the forest floor are the only remaining relics of an open field. Hop a running stream at 1.5 miles. Ascend sharply beneath red oak and beech trees before topping out at 1.7 miles, meeting the Rim Trail.

Turn left on the Rim Trail, reveling in the mixed woods of the level

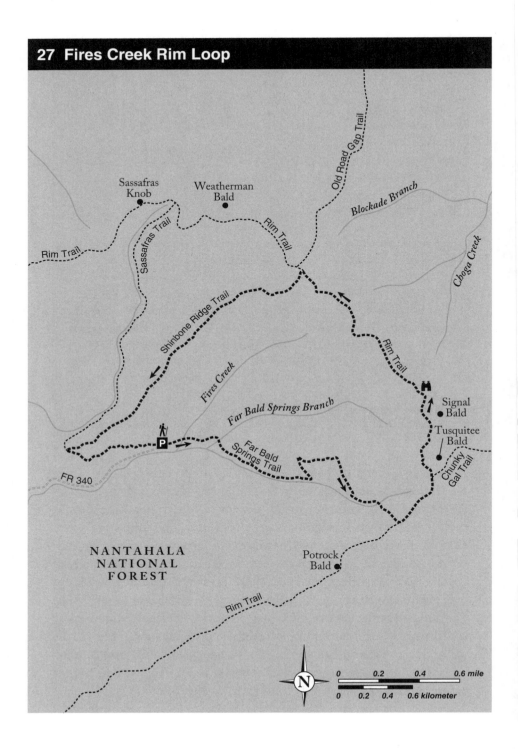

Sassafras
Knob

Weatherman
Bald

Old Road Gap Trail

Blockade Branch

Choga Creek

Rim Trail

Sassafras Trail

Rim Trail

Shinbone Ridge Trail

Rim Trail

Fires Creek

Far Bald Springs Branch

Signal
Bald

Tusquitee
Bald

P

Far Bald
Springs Trail

Chunky
Gal Trail

FR 340

NANTAHALA
NATIONAL
FOREST

Potrock
Bald

Rim Trail

N

| 0 | 0.2 | 0.4 | 0.6 mile |
| 0 | 0.2 | 0.4 | 0.6 kilometer |

Fires Creek Rim presents solitude aplenty and views like this.

ridgetop, nearly a mile high. Winter views open to the east. At 2.0 miles, under rhododendron, the Chunky Gal Trail leaves right. Stay left on the Rim Trail, making a slight uptick. At 2.1 miles, level out in rhododendron. Here, a spur trail leads right and fades into what is left of Tusquitee Bald. The Rim Trail descends, rejoining the crest at 2.5 miles. Here, on a jagged rock upthrust, views open from an outcrop rising above craggy evergreens. The Nantahala Mountains form a rampart in the distant east. Closer, the Nantahala River and its tributaries flow below. The Cheoah Mountains rise in the north. And the Tusquitee Mountains, upon which you walk, undulate northwest.

The Rim Trail slaloms the meager crest betwixt laurel thickets, craggy rocks, and stunted trees. Swing around the west side of a knob at 3.0 miles. Ahead, you can see Shinbone Ridge stretching out to your left. At 3.5 miles, meet the Shinbone Ridge Trail. A small campsite lies just ahead on the Rim Trail, and the Old Road Gap Trail leaves right. The Rim Trail continues along the crest, passing the upper Sassafras Trail. (You could extend your hike by about a mile by staying on the Rim Trail, then descending on the Sassafras Trail to FR 340 and the trailhead.) However, this hike turns left on the Shinbone Ridge Trail. Shortly, a trickling spring crosses the slender trail. Stay below the top of Shinbone Ridge in a mixture of and hardwoods and evergreens. Gain the ridgecrest at 3.9 miles. Enjoy a brief level stretch before resuming your downgrade in oaks.

At 4.4 miles, the trail dives downhill on an ever-narrowing edge. At 5.2 miles, come to the lower Shinbone Ridge trailhead and the end of FR 340. The Sassafras Trail leaves right from this trailhead. From here, this loop turns left onto FR 340. Follow the double track downhill. The sounds of Fires Creek drift into your ears. At 5.8 miles, reach the Far Bald Springs trailhead, completing the circuit.

Mileages

0.0 Far Springs Bald trailhead on FR 340
0.8 Switchback left in steep section
1.5 Stream
1.7 Left on Rim Trail
2.5 Great views from outcrop
3.5 Left on Shinbone Ridge trail
5.2 Left on FR 340
5.8 Far Springs Bald trailhead on FR 340

28 • SILER BALD

Hike Summary: *The Appalachian Trail (AT), as it travels through North Carolina's national forests, visits many special places. Siler Bald is widely regarded to be among the best of these distinctive destinations. The restored meadow of Siler Bald, with unknown origins like so many other Southern Appalachian mountaintop fields, offers extensive views. From Siler Bald's nearly mile-high perch, mountains stretch in all directions: the Smokies to the west, the Blue Ridge to the south, the Nantahala Mountains to the north, and the Fishhawk Mountains to the east. The climb from Wayah Gap is gradual and well worth what you'll see from atop Siler Bald.*

Save this hike for a clear day. You will be amply rewarded with extensive vistas. Balds, or open meadows, such as Siler Bald's are one of the mysteries of the Southern Appalachians. Many balds lie within the North Carolina national forest system. The origin of these fields is not

28 SILER BALD

Distance: 3.6-mile there-and-back

Hiking time: 2.0–3.0 hours

Difficulty: Moderate

Highlights: Nearly 360° views, restored bald

Cautions: None

Fees/Permits: No fees or permits required

Best seasons: Year-round; fall and winter for best views

Other trail users: None

Trail contacts: Nantahala National Forest, Nantahala Ranger District, 90 Sloan Road, Franklin, NC 28734, (828) 524-6441, www.fs.usda.gov/nfsnc

Finding the trailhead: From the intersection of US 23/441 and US 64 in Franklin, take US 64 west for 3.8 miles to turn right on Old Murphy Road. Drive for .2 mile, then turn left on Wayah Road/NC 1310. Follow NC 1310 for 9.2 miles to Wayah Gap. There are parking spots on both side of the road. FR 69 leaves right from the gap, and you can also park along its shoulder.

GPS trailhead coordinates: N35° 9.244', W83° 34.804'

known, although natural fires, clearing by Indians, and grazing cattle possibly kept the fields open. Balds once stretched along many ridges throughout the Southern Appalachians. In summer, residents of the nearby lowlands would drive their cattle upon the meadows to graze for the summer while using fields to grow winter hay. Grazing certainly helped keep the balds open, for when the practice ceased, trees began reclaiming the meadows. Now, only names recall many balds. Siler Bald is being kept open by mowing.

Those who want to restore the Southern Appalachians to their "original" state find the question of preserving the balds a vexing one. Are the historic vistas worth keeping, or should the balds be maintained for their natural qualities? Or should the balds be allowed to disappear? Hikers are lured to places like Siler Bald. On a clear day its views are phenomenal.

Leave south from Wayah Gap, southbound on the AT. Wood and earth steps lead into maple-dominated hardwoods. Shortly cross a very rough road used as an access to mow Siler Bald. The AT stays a single-track path, slipping over to the west side of a ridge spurring off Siler Bald. Turn into a rich cove, then reach a spring at .5 mile. AT thru-hikers

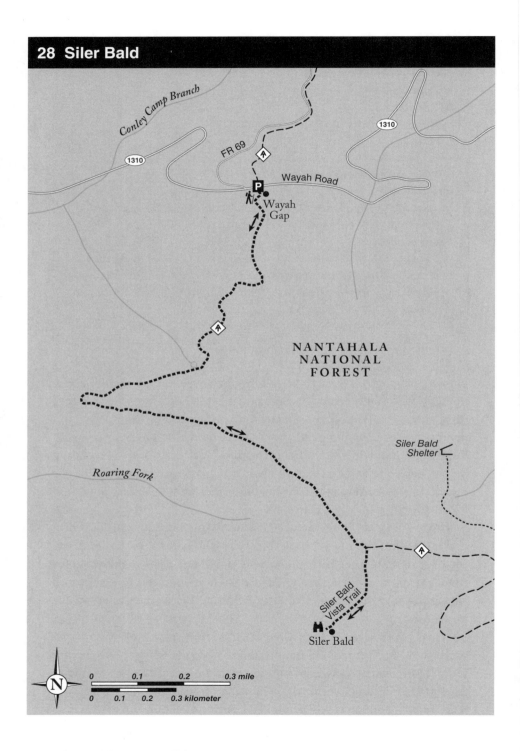

The open meadow of Siler Bald allows panoramas limited only by the clarity of the sky.

use springs such as these to obtain their drinking water. Most treat the mountain aqua in some way, whether by filtering or chemically rendering it harmless and drinkable. I am in the minority—those who drink it straight from the source without treating it. Treat your water. Consider this do as I say, not as I do, advice.

At .9 mile, join the crest of the ridge. Travel south in oaks, ascending gradually. By 1.2 miles, you have slipped over to the west side of Siler Bald, on a nearly level trail. At 1.6 miles, the AT opens onto the lower end of Siler Bald. Turn right here on the Siler Bald Vista Trail. A single-track path cuts up the middle of the mown meadow, which rises along the nose of a ridge. Top out at 1.8 miles. A marble marker delineates the high point, 5,210 feet. You have climbed 1,000 feet. So many mountain places detailed in this guidebook open up before you. The Snowbird Mountains, Fires Creek Rim and the Tusquitee Mountains, and Nantahala Lake are to the west. Standing Indian, the tower of Albert Mountain, and the Blue Ridge rise to the south. Farther in the Georgia distance is that state's highest point—Brasstown Bald. The rocky faces of the Fishhawk Mountains stand to the east but are partially blocked by the few trees up here. To the north rise the transmission towers on Wine Spring Bald. On a clear day you can see northwest into Tennessee and the western edge of the Great Smoky Mountains. The main crest of the Smokies stands farther north. Look for the dark balsams along its tops.

While you're here, consider driving FR 69 4.5 miles from Wayah Gap up to the restored Wayah Bald Tower. (The low stone tower is difficult to see from Siler Bald.) The stone structure not only provides great views; it is a scenic spot where you can picnic, hike, and further enjoy nature.

Mileages

0.0	Wayah Gap
0.5	Trailside spring
0.9	Join rib ridge
1.6	Spur to Siler Bald
1.8	Siler Bald summit, backtrack
3.6	Wayah Gap

29 • JACKRABBIT MOUNTAIN LOOP

Hike Summary: This shorter hike explores the shores of Lake Chatuge, a gorgeous mountain impoundment near the Georgia state line. Start your trek near Jackrabbit Mountain campground, making the walk up Jackrabbit Mountain. Drop to the shore of Lake Chatuge, enjoying aquatic and mountain views. A spur heads to a pine-studded point on the lake, before the loop is completed. Consider adding adjacent national forest recreation options, including camping, boating, fishing, and swimming, to your hike.

This is a fun hike and is suitable for everyone from families to hardcore trekkers. Originally designed as a nature trail to complement the adjacent Jackrabbit Mountain Campground, the path can be enjoyed as a stand-alone activity. But if you're going to come this way, why not try to incorporate camping, picnicking, swimming, canoeing, fishing, or boating into your adventure? Chatuge Lake is a gorgeous impoundment of the Hiwassee River stretching from North Carolina into Georgia. Verdant mountains rise in the distance in all directions. The climb to Jackrabbit Mountain's summit is less than 300 feet. Parts of the trail travel along the shoreline, making it a varied and not too difficult experience.

Walk from the boater access parking area back toward the campground access road, then pick up the Jackrabbit Mountain Trail. The

29 JACKRABBIT MOUNTAIN LOOP

Distance: 2.8-mile loop

Hiking time: 1.5–2.0 hours

Difficulty: Easy

Highlights: Mountain and lake views, adjacent recreation opportunities

Cautions: None

Fees/Permits: No fees or permits required

Best seasons: May through September for water recreation, rest of year for solitude

Other trail users: None

Trail contacts: Nantahala National Forest, Tusquitee Ranger District, 123 Woodland Drive, Murphy, NC 28906, (828) 837-5152, www.fs.usda.gov/nfsnc

Finding the trailhead: From the intersection of US 64 Bypass and NC 69 in Hayesville, take US 64 east for 4.7 miles to turn right on NC 175 south. At .8 mile, stay right with NC 175 south as it bridges Shooting Creek embayment of Lake Chatuge. Travel a total of 3.3 miles, then turn right on Jackrabbit Road. Follow Jackrabbit Road. (At .5 mile you will pass the Jackrabbit Mountain trailhead. This is not the stop for this hike, though the network offers 14 miles of mountain bike–oriented interconnected loops that are open to hikers). At 1.2 miles, Jackrabbit Road splits. The left fork goes to Jackrabbit Mountain Campground. The hike begins at this split, but you keep forward to the boat ramp, then turn right into the boating access parking area. Do not park at the boat ramp or campground.

GPS trailhead coordinates: N35° 0.569', W83° 46.058'

single-track, hiker-only trail enters an oak-dominated woodland slope mixed with shortleaf pines, dogwoods, and sourwood rising from red clay soil. At .1 mile, the Short Loop leaves left. Continue climbing up the west slope of Jackrabbit Mountain. Notice the black scars at the base of trees here. The forest service practices fire ecology on a regular basis to keep the forest as it would be under natural conditions instead of as a managed recreation area.

Informative interpretive plaques are scattered along the trail. Continue working up the shoulder of Jackrabbit Mountain amid hickories, sassafras, and holly. Switchback up the mountainside, topping out at .6 mile. Turn north along the ridgecrest. Reach the north end of the Short Loop at .8 mile. Stay right, descending Jackrabbit Mountain. Note the abundance of dogwoods here. The short tree with scaly brown bark and widespread crown is easy to identify. The dogwood is widely regarded as one of the most beautiful trees in the Southeast. It ranges from east

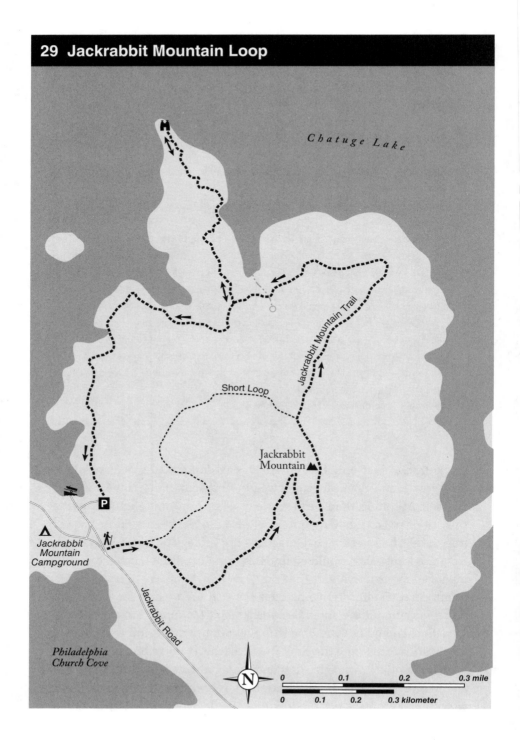

Chatuge Lake

Jackrabbit Mountain Trail

Short Loop

Jackrabbit
Mountain

P

Jackrabbit
Mountain
Campground

Jackrabbit Road

Philadelphia
Church Cove

N

| 0 | 0.1 | 0.2 | 0.3 mile |
| 0 | 0.1 | 0.2 | 0.3 kilometer |

Majestic mountains rise from the shores of Lake Chatuge.

Texas north to Michigan, east to Massachusetts, and south to Florida. Dogwoods grow in both moist and dry soils at lower elevations in the North Carolina mountains. In the spring, dogwoods display showy white blooms that can also be pinkish. Dogwoods produce a shiny red fruit in fall. These small, berrylike fruits are bitter to humans but are an important food for birds. Dogwood is extremely hard and is used to make mallet heads, jeweler's blocks, and spools.

As you descend, lake views open through the trees. At 1.3 miles, the trail curves past a small embayment. Look left for a small spring box near a footbridge, indicating that a home stood here long before this lake was dammed. At 1.4 miles, look right for a spur trail. Pick up this path as it wanders north, curving near the lakeshore before emerging on a piney point overlooking Lake Chatuge at 1.8 miles. Look for a Tennessee Valley Authority survey marker. Incredible views open once you reach the point. Here, Garland Ridge rises to the east, and the Tusquitee Mountains form a northerly wall beyond the shore of the lake. Islands rise from the impoundment. Since only part of the shoreline is owned by the forest service, you will see plenty of houses, too. The point is an ideal place to picnic, swim, or fish. Backtrack to the main loop after you have enjoyed your time here.

The trail continues circling Lake Chatuge. At 2.4 miles, the path emerges along the shoreline near an attractive wooded island just off-shore. In fall and winter, when the lake levels are lower, you can actually walk to this island without wetting your feet. More lake and fishing accesses lie ahead, amid sourwood, mountain laurel, and pines. Other shoreline woods harbor river birches. Turn away from the shoreline to emerge at the boating access parking area at 2.8 miles, completing the hike.

Mileages

0.0 Jackrabbit Mountain trailhead
0.1 Short Loop leaves left
0.6 Crest of Jackrabbit Mountain
0.8 Other end of Short Loop
1.2 Spring box and footbridge
1.4 Spur leads right to piney point
1.8 Piney point
2.4 Come near wooded island
2.8 Boater access parking area

30 • PARK CREEK LOOP

Hike Summary: This excellent hike displays much of what the Standing Indian backcountry has to offer. After passing through Standing Indian Campground, the hike joins the gorgeous Nantahala River as it courses through its uppermost valley. The hike then turns into wildflower-rich Park Creek, a trouty tributary. Work your way up this junglesque valley to reach Park Gap. From here the Park Ridge Trail takes you along a slender mountain crest before returning to the rugged Nantahala River Valley, completing the circuit. This makes for a rewarding full day hike or an overnight backpack.

Some loop hikes are too rough, rugged, and remote. Others can be too busy or too short. Even Goldilocks would like this loop—it is just right. All the trails are hiker-only. They are well marked, signed, and blazed, but not paved. The trailhead is simple to find, and the parking is good.

30 PARK CREEK LOOP

Distance: 8.8-mile loop

Hiking time: 5.0–6.5 hours

Difficulty: Difficult

Highlights: Nantahala River, wildflowers, backcountry

Cautions: None

Fees/Permits: No fees or permits required

Best seasons: Summer and fall for mild weather conditions, winter for solitude

Other trail users: None

Trail contacts: Nantahala National Forest, Nantahala Ranger District, 90 Sloan Road, Franklin, NC 28734, (828) 524-6441, www.fs.usda.gov/nfsnc

Finding the trailhead: From the crossing of US 23/441 and US 64 in Franklin, take US 64 west for 12 miles to West Old Murphy Road. There will be signs for Standing Indian Campground here. Turn left on West Old Murphy Road and follow it for 1.9 miles to the right turn onto FR 67. Follow FR 67 for 2.0 miles to the Backcountry Information Center on your right.

GPS trailhead coordinates: N35° 4.488', W83° 31.645'

And one more thing—there's Southern Appalachian mountain beauty everywhere you look. What more could you ask for? Perhaps good weather . . .

Leave the Backcountry Information Center on a natural surface path. Descend to reach Long Creek, crossing on a footbridge, then emerge onto a paved portion of the Standing Indian Campground. Turn left here, crossing the Nantahala River on a road bridge. Just after the crossing, look right for the Park Creek Trail heading downstream along the Nantahala. Trace an old railroad grade alongside this coursing river. Campsites stand on the far bank. The walking is easy amid lush, junglesque forest, with flora battling for sunlight in deep woodland. Look for steel cables from logging days. Intersect the Kimsey Creek Trail at .3 mile. Stay straight on the grade, absorbing views of the wild valley. At .5 mile, pass the intersection with the Park Ridge Trail. This is your return route. For now, stay straight, still on Park Creek Trail. At .6 mile, an outcrop allows easy access to the Nantahala River in a deep pool. Just past there, the official Park Creek Trail leaves left as a single-track path, while the railroad grade runs straight, often passing through mucky, overgrown spots. Rejoin the grade at 1.6 miles. Shortly leave the Nan-

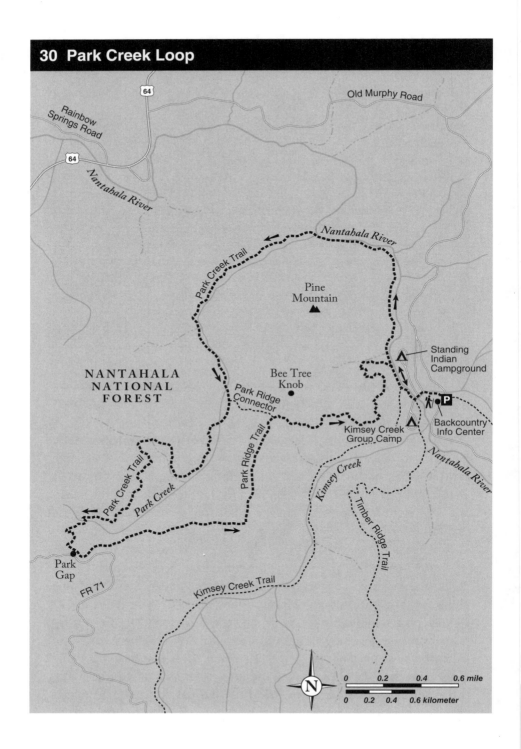

The Nantahala River flows beneath a green canopy on a summer morn.

tahala River, then turn left into Park Creek, quickly bridging it. Head up beneath black and yellow birches, beeches, ample rhododendron and doghobble, and wildflowers galore in season.

The trail goes off and on an old road grade while penetrating the Park Creek watershed. In flats, the stream divides into braids. Additionally, feeder branches course across the path, making the entire watershed a moist place. The trail continues circling around Pine Mountain. At 3.0 miles, make an unbridged crossing of Park Creek. Open to a flat and meet the Park Ridge Connector. If you want to shortcut this loop, here is your chance. The connector leads .3 mile up to a gap and the Park Ridge Trail. Keep straight here, crossing back over to the right bank of now-small Park Creek. Note the remains of an old bridge here.

At 3.7 miles, the path turns up a tributary, crisscrossing it a few times. Bisect a closed forest road at 4.1 miles. Traipse a drier slope with many recurring young chestnut trees and larger oaks. At 4.9 miles, step over the remains of Park Creek, now at 4,200 feet. Drift into Park Gap and meet FR 71 at 5.2 miles. Immediately join single-track Park Ridge Trail. Oddly enough, area topographical maps don't show a Park Ridge, but the trail does follow Middle Ridge. But first, curve around a high-elevation cove, circling headsprings of Park Creek. Bisect another closed forest road at 5.5 miles, in Penland Gap. The trail then joins a narrow linear crest dividing Kimsey Creek from Park Creek, clothed in oaks, galax, mountain laurel, and emergent rocks. Drive up a ridgeline and the hike's high point at 6.1 miles, elevation 4,300 feet. Mercifully curve around the next knob. The Park Ridge Trail then dives north and headlong, dropping 300 feet in .3 mile, a relic from the old school of trail construction.

Undulate among chestnut oaks and mountain laurel to meet the Park Ridge Connector in a grassy gap at 6.9 miles. Three closed forest roads gather here. Stay right with the single-track, signed Park Ridge Trail. Work around an irregular side slope below Bee Tree Knob. Kimsey Creek flows far below. The slender path is rough in places here as you drift lower, looking for an easy way down to the Nantahala River. The trail finally turns down a small tributary, then meets the Park Creek Trail at 8.3 miles. From here, it is a simple backtrack to the trailhead.

Mileages

0.0   Backcountry Information Center trailhead
0.5   Pass the Park Ridge Trail
1.7   Turn up Park Creek
3.1   Park Ridge Connector leaves left
5.2   Park Gap
6.1   Hike high point
6.9   Meet Park Ridge Connector
8.3   Right with Park Creek Trail, backtrack
8.8   Backcountry Information Center trailhead

31 • STANDING INDIAN

Hike Summary: *Take a hike on the Appalachian Trail (AT), reaching the most southerly mile-high mountain in the Appalachians. Leave Deep Gap, enter the Southern Nantahala Wilderness. Gently climb to a ridgeline. Pass an AT shelter. Continue an uptick on many a switchback. Pick up a spur trail to the summit and a line of craggy cliffs. Here, eye-popping views open into Georgia as far as the clarity of the sky allows. Since you start high, the climb isn't bad, and it's well graded, never steep, rising approximately 1,150 feet in 2.5 miles.*

31 STANDING INDIAN

Distance: 5.0-mile there-and-back

Hiking time: 3.0–4.0 hours

Difficulty: Moderate

Highlights: Great views from atop Standing Indian, Southern Nantahala Wilderness

Cautions: None

Fees/Permits: No fees or permits required

Best seasons: Year-round, though drive to trailhead could be hairy in winter

Other trail users: None

Trail contacts: Nantahala National Forest, Nantahala Ranger District, 90 Sloan Road, Franklin, NC 28734, (828) 524-6441, www.fs.usda.gov/nfsnc

Finding the trailhead: From the intersection of US 23/441 and US 64 in Franklin, take US 64 west for 14.5 miles FR 71/Deep Gap Road (there will be a sign for Deep Gap). Turn left on FR 71. It starts out paved, then turns to gravel as it turns away from US 64. Stay with FR 71, driving a total of 5.9 miles to dead end at Deep Gap.

GPS trailhead coordinates: N35° 2.378', W83° 33.148'

Standing Indian, elevation 5,499 feet, is the first significant mountain in the Tar Heel State for northbound AT thru-hikers. It is also the first mile-high mountain of the AT. Regardless of its intersection with the AT, Standing Indian is still a significant peak. It is part of the Tennessee Valley Divide. Waters flowing off its south slope make their way to the Gulf of Mexico via Georgia, while its north side drains through North Carolina into Tennessee and beyond to the Mississippi River and thence to the Gulf. Its south face falls steep and sheer, with open rock slabs and wind-sculpted trees and diminutive brushes clinging to its surface.

To ensure the passing on of an oft-repeated Cherokee legend, here's how Standing Indian Mountain purportedly got its name: A village child was carried away by a great winged monster. The stunned tribe prayed for the recovery of the child and the slaying of the monster. Subsequently, a giant lightning bolt struck the mountaintop, killing the winged monster, clearing the peak of vegetation, and simultaneously transforming a Cherokee sentry posted atop the peak, turning him to stone—the "Standing Indian." To this day, the tip-top of the summit is grassy, and a rock slab opens to a fantastic view.

At Deep Gap, take the AT northbound. Sugar maple, yellow birch, and buckeye shade the path. You are angling up the west shoulder of Stand-

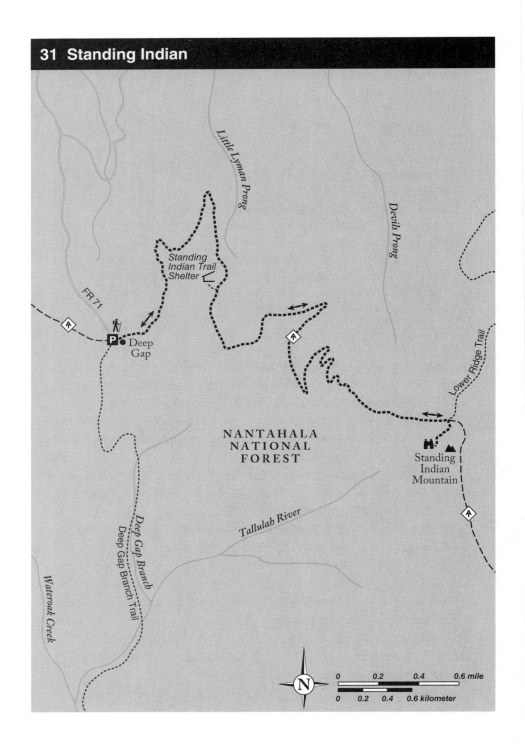

Little Lyman Prong

Devils Prong

Standing
Indian Trail
Shelter

FR 71

Deep
Gap

Lower Ridge Trail

NANTAHALA
NATIONAL
FOREST

Standing
Indian
Mountain

Deep Gap Branch
Deep Gap Branch Trail

Tallulah River

Wateroak Creek

| 0 | 0.2 | 0.4 | 0.6 mile |
| 0 | 0.2 | 0.4 | 0.6 kilometer |

Standing Indian is the most southerly mile-high mountain in the Southern Appalachians.

ing Indian Mountain. Thousands of boots have rendered the single-track trail rocky and rooty. At .5 mile, the path circles around the point of a rib ridge, turning sharply south. A sign welcomes you to the Southern Nantahala Wilderness at .6 mile. At .7 mile, the AT comes alongside a spring branch to your left, then picks up an old roadbed. The path widens. At .8 mile, a spur trail leads right to the Standing Indian trail shelter. The three-sided, open-fronted wooden structure stands atop a small knob covered in hickory and oak. These shelters are strung out along the AT for the entirety of its 2,100-plus mile length. They also serve as a refuge for day hikers in storms but are primarily used by backpackers overnighting it, whether for a weekend or the customary six months that people take to thru-hike the entire AT.

Continue along the now less-rocky AT. The old roadbed you are now following leads to the top of Standing Indian, and the AT follows the road, originally constructed to build a fire tower that once sat atop Standing Indian. It was removed when the tower on nearby Albert Mountain was constructed. Pass through a highland flat before resuming your ascent via long, loping switchbacks. Standing Indian continues looming overhead despite your elevation gains. Winter views open to the west beyond the chasm of Deep Gap. Rhododendron cloaks portions of the mountainside. The switchbacks tighten as you climb. Reach the spine of the mountain at 2.1 miles. Level off in low yellow birches with an understory of ferns. At 2.3 miles, the Lower Ridge Trail leaves left for the lowlands. Stay with the AT just a short distance, then you will see a wide trail heading right and uphill. This is the access to the summit of Standing Indian. Leave the AT and begin working upslope, passing a few campsites. Keep climbing and reach the level grassy peak at 2.5 miles. Here, you will immediately notice the outcrop to your right and the views it provides. Look south from the open stone. Below, the Tallulah River Valley opens and leads into Georgia. The Blue Ridge stretches off to your right, as does Chatuge Lake. On a clear day, it seems you can see all the way to Atlanta. Notice how declivitous is the south slope of Standing Indian. If you walk around, there are more stone overlooks, less obvious than the mountaintop outcrop, that present other views. To your south there is nothing higher until you reach the island peaks of the Caribbean.

Mileages

- 0.0   Deep Gap trailhead, FR 71
- 0.8   Spur to Standing Indian trail shelter
- 2.3   Lower Ridge trail leaves left; spur leads right to Standing Indian summit
- 2.5   Standing Indian summit, 5,499 feet, great views
- 5.0   Deep Gap trailhead, FR 71

32 • SOUTHERN NANTAHALA WILDERNESS HIKE

Hike Summary: *This hike encapsulates much of the greater Southern Nantahala Wilderness experience. Start by visiting Big Laurel Falls, an attractive cascade tumbling through a wildflower-laden vale. Climb through deep woods to meet the Appalachian Trail (AT), walking through backwoods on a ridge that circles the Nantahala River headwaters. Reach eye-pleasing Beech Gap, a great place to camp or picnic, then undulate along Indian Ridge. Finally, cross the Nantahala River on a footbridge to complete the circuit.*

The AT forms a horseshoe within the greater Standing Indian trail system. This particular hike explores the trail system's most southerly

32 SOUTHERN NANTAHALA WILDERNESS HIKE

Distance: 8.8-mile loop

Hiking time: 5.0–7.0 hours

Difficulty: Difficult

Highlights: Big Laurel Falls, Southern Nantahala Wilderness

Cautions: Couple of small, unbridged stream crossings

Fees/Permits: No fees or permits required

Best seasons: Summer and fall for mild weather conditions, winter for solitude

Other trail users: None

Trail contacts: Nantahala National Forest, Nantahala Ranger District, 90 Sloan Road, Franklin, NC 28734, (828) 524-6441, www.fs.usda.gov/nfsnc

Finding the trailhead: From the crossing of US 23/441 and US 64 in Franklin, take US 64 west for 12 miles to West Old Murphy Road. There will be signs for Standing Indian Campground here. Turn left on West Old Murphy Road and follow it for 1.9 miles to the right turn onto FR 67. Follow FR 67 for 6.8 miles to the Timber Ridge and Laurel Falls trailhead, on a left curve, passing Standing Indian Campground and the Backcountry Information Center on the way.

GPS trailhead coordinates: N35° 1.315', W83° 30.206"

reaches, mostly inside the confines of the Southern Nantahala Wilderness. To explore the entire Standing Indian backcountry would take days, and I hope this hike will inspire you to see more of this trail haven. The Standing Indian Campground makes an excellent base camp from which to hike.

Leave the parking area on FR 67, already at 3,700 feet in elevation. Immediately descend to Mooney Creek on wood-and-earth stairs. This mountain rill noisily courses among mossy boulders. Span the stream on a bridge to immediately reach a trail junction. Turn right here toward Big Laurel Falls. Go to the falls now instead of waiting until after you do your loop—you may be too tired then. Travel downstream on an old railroad grade, then turn up Big Laurel Branch on a narrow footpath through tunnels of laurel, from which rise gnarled birches and cherry. The spring wildflower hollow closes tighter before you come to Big Laurel Falls at .5 mile. Here, the multitiered cataract makes a drop, then spills over an expanding rock slide into a reflecting pool. What a start! Less able hikers make Big Laurel Falls an out-and-back proposition. Our loop backtracks almost to the trailhead, then picks up the Timber Ridge

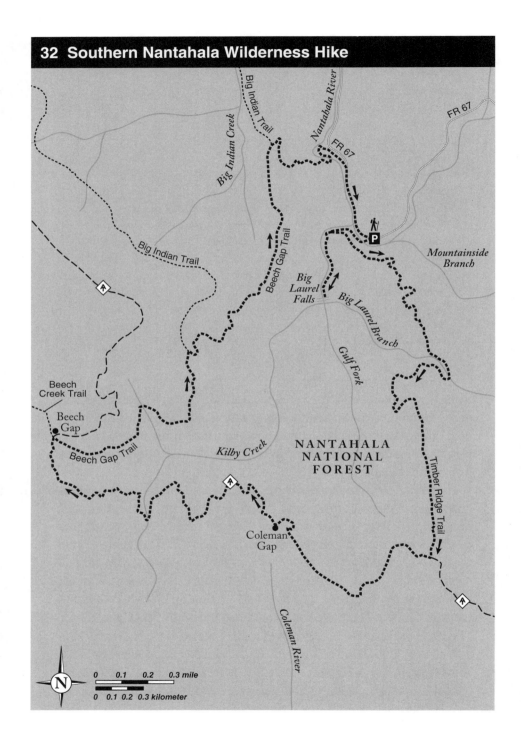

Autumn leaves adorn the scene at Big Laurel Falls.

Trail. The relatively faint track heads upstream on Mooney Creek a very short piece before switchbacking up a mossy, ferny forested ridge. Top out at 1.6 miles, descending back to Big Laurel Branch. Bridge the stream, well above the falls, at 1.8 miles. From here, begin working to gain the nose of Timber Ridge at 2.6 miles, among ferns and hardwoods.

Meet the AT at 3.0 miles. You are at 4,600 feet. Your trip along the AT will be fairly mild with no extensive ups or downs. Turn right here, southbound on the world's most famous footpath. Northern hardwoods of yellow birch, beech, and striped maple shade the trail. Descend to reach Coleman Gap in rhododendron at 4.0 miles. An abandoned trail leads south into Georgia from the gap. The AT, however, climbs slightly as it begins a pattern of winding in and out of the Nantahala River's uppermost headwaters, dribbling springs flowing from Little Bald above. Watch for a hillside covered in galax just before you pass the most robust tributary at 5.0 miles.

The walking is easy, and you saunter into Beech Gap at 5.7 miles. This pretty mix of grass, tree, and rhododendron makes for a nice, relaxing spot and also a potential campsite if you were backpacking this loop. Water can be had from the Beech Creek Trail leading left toward Beech Creek. Our loop leaves right from the gap on the Beech Gap Trail. The pleasant hiking continues on a gentle to level track, passing through a couple of small clearings. The path remains level until reaching an intersection at 6.7 miles. Here, the Big Indian Trail keeps straight on a roadbed, while the Beech Gap Trail leaves right. Another branch of the Big Indian Trail runs in conjunction here with Beech Gap Trail. Dive down to briefly level off at Kilby Gap at 7.2 miles. You are less than a half-mile from Big Laurel Falls—as the crow flies. Cruise north on Indian Ridge, on a dry crest of sourwood, blueberry, and mountain laurel. Drop steeply to reach a gap at 7.9 miles. Here, the Beech Gap Trail leaves right, while the continuation of the Big Indian Trail keeps straight. Turn right with the Beech Gap Trail, switchbacking a slope, deeper into the Nantahala River Valley. Come alongside the Nantahala River in scads of rhododendron at 8.3 miles. The path turns upstream to bridge the waterway on a sturdy wooden footbridge. Climb to reach FR 67 at 8.4 miles. Turn right here, walking the dirt road to reach the Big Timber trailhead and complete the hike at 8.8 miles.

Mileages

0.0   Timber Ridge Big Laurel Falls trailhead on FR 67
0.5   Big Laurel Falls, backtrack
1.0   Join Timber Ridge Trail
1.8   Cross Big Laurel Branch
3.0   Right, southbound on AT
4.0   Coleman Gap
5.7   Beech Gap
6.7   Stay right with Beech Gap Trail
7.9   Right again with Beech Gap Trail
8.4   Right on FR 67 after bridging upper Nantahala River
8.8   Timber Ridge Big Laurel Falls trailhead on FR 67

---

33 • JONES KNOB VIA THE BARTRAM TRAIL

Hike Summary: *Bag two view-laden peaks while walking the remote, lesser-trod Bartram Trail. Leave Jones Gap, passing through a meadow, then make*

33 JONES KNOB VIA THE BARTRAM TRAIL

Distance: 5.4-mile there-and-back

Hiking time: 3.0–4.0 hours

Difficulty: Moderate

Highlights: Stellar views, solitude, Bartram Trail

Cautions: Steep, open rock faces

Fees/Permits: No fees or permits required

Best seasons: Year-round; fall and winter for best views

Other trail users: None

Trail contacts: Nantahala National Forest, Nantahala Ranger District, 90 Sloan Road, Franklin, NC 28734, (828) 524-6441, www.fs.usda.gov/nfsnc

Finding the trailhead: From the intersection of US 23/441 and US 64 in Franklin, take US 64 east for 14.6 miles to Turtle Pond Road/NC 1620. Turn right on Turtle Pond Road, just before the left turn into Cliffside Recreation Area. At 1 mile, stay right, now on Dendy Orchard Road. In another mile, the pavement ends. Climb and then, 2.3 miles from US 64, turn left on FR 4522. There will be a Bartram Trail access sign here. Follow FR 4522 steeply uphill, dead-ending at Jones Gap and the trailhead at 2.0 miles. Alternate directions: From Highlands, take US 64 west 4.5 miles, just past the entrance to Cliffside Recreation Area, and reach Turtle Pond Road. Turn left and follow the above directions.

GPS trailhead coordinates: N35° 4.561', W83° 17.271'

the short ascent to Jones Knob, where a rock face opens stellar views. Backtrack to the Bartram Trail, then work your way to Whiterock Mountain. Here, an open cliff face presents views superseding those of Jones Mountain. The trek is not difficult either, with climbs and descents of just a few hundred feet each. And for the views you get, the solitude is very surprising.

The trail is named for 18th-century naturalist William Bartram. Inspired by his naturalist father, John Bartram, William set out in 1773 to explore the southeastern United States. For four years he cataloged and described the flora, fauna, and Indians of the region and is credited with identifying more than 200 native plants. His adventure was later published as *Travels of William Bartram*. Today, the Bartram Trail (BT) roughly follows his journey through the mountains of northern Georgia and western North Carolina.

This section of the BT traverses the Fishhawk Mountains, simply one

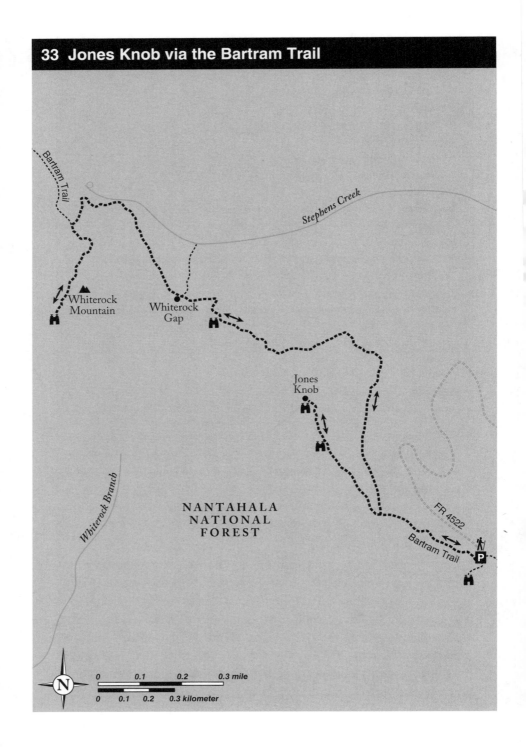

The Little Tennessee River Valley is shrouded in fog below.

of the most scenic ranges in North Carolina's national forests. These ancient highlands have sheer rock slopes overlooking Tessentee Creek Valley. Other parts are clothed in rich woods; still others have wildlife clearings that act as mountain meadows. The side trail to Whiterock Mountain will stun you and make you hold on for dear life, as its rock face curves from a high point down for hundreds of feet.

At Jones Gap, you'll see a trail signboard. As you face the signboard, a trail leads forward downhill to a rock face and warm-up vista. The yellow-blazed BT comes in from a pole gate behind and to your left. This hike leaves right around the pole gate, tracing a wide track. Follow the grassy lane flanked with fire cherry and locust trees, indicating recent reforestation. Oaks and maples are finding their place. Reach a narrow wildlife clearing at .2 mile. The clearing is mown by the forest service to enhance wildlife habitat. At the far end of the clearing, a side trail leads left .3 mile toward Jones Knob. Follow this rocky, narrow, single-track path up to a view before cresting on the open slab of Jones Knob. At your feet are sometimes-filled potholes. Beyond, you can overlook the

Tessentee Creek Valley and the striated face of Whiterock Mountain next door. And more mountains beyond.

Backtrack to the BT. It skirts the steep east slope of Jones Knob, winding among rocks, moss, and rhododendron with a hardwood overstory. Watch for thickly trunked rhododendron bushes. Regain the ridgecrest at 1.7 miles. Just ahead a side trail leads left to a rock face and views at 1.9 miles. Resume the BT. Look around the woods for abundant rock slabs. Descend just a bit more, switchbacking to reach Whiterock Gap at 2.0 miles. A wooden sign announces the elevation as 4,150 feet. A spur trail leads right 800 feet down to Stevens Creek. A level but potentially windblown campsite is located in the gap.

The BT leaves Whiterock Gap, ascending along the east side of Whiterock Mountain in a rich wildflower area. Swing around the northeast slope of Whiterock Mountain, passing a side trail right to a spring at 2.4 miles. After a brief uptick, reach the blue-blazed side trail leading left to the vista on Whiterock Mountain. Take it. Top out in a mix of rock slabs and low pines and oaks. Pass several rock faces, then descend to reach the granddaddy rock face of them all at 2.7 miles. It drops for hundreds of feet without interruption toward Tessentee Creek Valley. Be careful if the rock slab is wet. Gaze west across the Little Tennessee River Valley. Beyond that rise the Nantahala Mountains, running north-south. It is where the more heavily trod Appalachian Trail travels. Here, on the BT, solitude and great views are yours, in these Fishhawk Mountains. Beyond here, the BT travels past more outcrops and views. For more information about the BT, visit www.ncbartramtrail.org.

Mileages

- 0.0 Jones Gap
- 0.2 Wildlife clearing
- 0.3 Spur left to Jones Knob
- 0.6 Jones Knob
- 1.9 View
- 2.0 Whiterock Gap
- 2.5 Spur to Whiterock Mountain
- 2.7 Whiterock Mountain view
- 5.4 Jones Gap

Hike Summary: *Take a walk into Civilian Conservation Corps (CCC) and North Carolina national forest history on this hike. First, stroll alongside bucolic Cliffside Lake, where mountainous woodlands rise from its still waters and picnic areas beckon a stop. After completing that short family circuit, climb an adjacent ridge to a wooden shelter and a view of Cliffside Lake and mountains beyond. Cliffside Lake Recreation Area also offers fishing, swimming, and picnicking. Nearby Van Hook Glade has camping, too.*

Cliffside Lake is one of those old-fashioned national forest recreation areas exuding rest, relaxation, and a return to nature. The Nantahala National Forest facility was originally developed by the CCC back in the 1930s. Its trademark wood-and-stone shelters as well as rustic rockwork complement the natural setting. Here, Skitty Branch was dammed, creating a 9-acre lake forming the recreation area centerpiece. You will circle this scenic impoundment, open to fishing and swimming. The other loop travels trails developed by the CCC. Here, you hike to a highland shelter with a clear view of Cliffside Lake and mountains beyond. Even though Cliffside Lake is day-use only, Van Hook Glade Campground is within walking distance and can complement your experience. The whole area is great for family or group gatherings or simply for those seeking eye-pleasing scenery in the mountains. Be apprised that Cliffside Recreation Area is open April through October.

Pick up the Cliffside Loop, walk just a few feet, then reach Cliffside Lake, its clear waters reflecting the shoreline forest. The scenic impoundment stretches before you. Turn right here on a wide, gravel nature trail. Pass a fishing platform, then follow the trail behind the lake dam. Watch for a massive, old-growth white pine here. Just ahead, the Homesite Road Trail leaves right for US 64. Bask in a flat woodland walk under large-trunked mountain laurel, maples, and white pine. Stroll on, bridging South Skitty Branch. Ahead, a spur trail leads right to the picnic area turnaround. Cruise the north shore of Cliffside Lake, passing alluring picnic areas nestled along the shore in small clearings bordered by woodland. Short spurs lead up to the picnic area road.

At .8 mile, on the west side of the lake, reach a trail junction. Here a signed spur leads right up to a picnic shelter and restrooms. For now, go

Distance: Two loops, 0.8 mile and 1.9 miles each

Hiking time: 2.0 hours

Difficulty: Easy

Highlights: Quiet mountain lake, views

Cautions: Potentially confusing nest of short trails

Fees/Permits: Recreation area parking fee required

Best seasons: April through October

Other trail users: None

Trail contacts: Nantahala National Forest, Nantahala Ranger District, 90 Sloan Road, Franklin, NC 28734, (828) 524-6441, www.fs.usda.gov/nfsnc

Finding the trailhead: From the intersection of US 23/441 and US 64 in Franklin, take US 64 east for 14.7 miles to Cliffside Recreation Area. Follow the access road for .9 mile, then reach the fee kiosk. Split right here, then reach the swimming/fishing parking area. Park here. Alternate directions: From Highlands, take US 64 west for 4.5 miles, and the entrance will be on your right.

GPS trailhead coordinates: N35° 4.721', W83° 14.204'

left, immediately crossing Skitty Creek on a footbridge. Pass behind the swim beach, then return to the trailhead parking at .9 mile.

You have completed the first loop. Now, walk up the parking area access road, then split right. Ahead, you will see a trail sign indicating the Clifftop Vista Trail. Begin working uphill among rhododendron and oaks. Turn up the south slope of a dry ridge, meeting the main branch of the Clifftop Vista Trail after a quarter-mile. Turn right here and make a solid climb in hickory-oak woods. At 1.6 miles of your double loop, come to another trail junction. Here, the Clifftop Nature Trail leaves acutely right and downhill back toward the main recreation area. Just ahead, another spur leads right to the CCC-built shelter and vista point. The shelter makes a nice resting place after your climb. The tree-framed view looks down on Cliffside Lake and rising mountains beyond, including some cabins that weren't there when the CCC was developing this area.

After soaking in the view, keep straight on the Clifftop Vista Trail. Shortly, begin switchbacking downhill off the north side of the ridge in dense pockets of rhododendron. Curve back toward the lake, then meet the faint Potts Memorial Trail at 2.1 miles. Stay straight here, then meet the Skitty Creek Trail at 2.2 miles. Stay left, descending to bridge Skitty

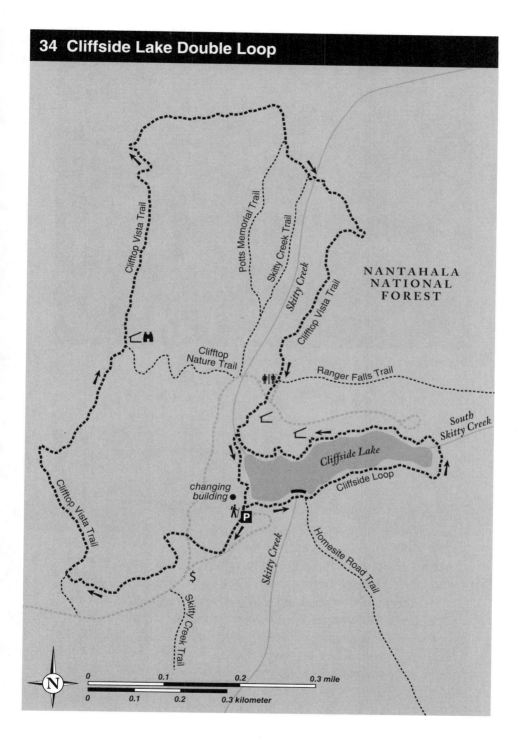

Clifftop Vista Trail

Potts Memorial Trail

Skitty Creek Trail

Skitty Creek

Clifftop Vista Trail

NANTAHALA
NATIONAL
FOREST

Clifftop
Nature Trail

Ranger Falls Trail

South
Skitty Creek

Cliffside Lake

Cliffside Loop

Clifftop Vista Trail

changing
building

Homesite Road Trail

Skitty Creek

$

Skitty Creek Trail

N

0   0.1   0.2   0.3 mile

0   0.1   0.2   0.3 kilometer

Cliffside Lake reflects the shoreline woods.

Creek. Climb briefly, then turn south in rich woods to reach picnic area parking at 2.5 miles. A spur trail leads left .5 mile to 25-foot-high Ranger Falls, a nice addition to this hike, especially in spring. Pass through the parking area, then come to a rustic picnic shelter with a chimney in the middle. Stay right here on a gravel path, descending to Skitty Creek. You have been here before. Cross the bridge over Skitty Creek, pass the swim beach, and complete the second loop at 2.7 miles.

Mileages

0.0   Cliffside swimming/fishing parking area
0.8   Left to bridge Skitty Creek
0.9   Complete Cliffside Loop, join Clifftop Vista Trail
1.2   Stay right with main branch of Cliffside Vista Trail
1.6   Shelter and vista
2.1   Potts Memorial Trail leaves right
2.2   Skitty Creek Trail leaves right, stay left
2.5   Main picnic area parking area
2.7   Cliffside swimming/fishing parking area

Hike Summary: *This hike near Highlands drops to four viewing perches of fiery—and long—Glen Falls, plus a mountain view for added measure. Follow a series of heart-stopping cataracts diving headlong through a steep valley divided by Horseshoe Mountain and Chinquapin Mountain. Your trip starts on the level to reach a mountain overlook, but the trail soon steepens as it makes loping switchbacks on a well-graded, stabilized path deep into the East Fork Overflow Creek Valley. Three of the four waterfall overlooks are developed decks.*

Claims of the height of Glen Falls vary. It's hard to see the falls in its entirety, for Glen Falls is a series of drops that collectively create the cataract. Interestingly, the four primary vantage points give the impression that you are at four different waterfalls. The disparate sections of Glen Falls are, well, disparate. From your first perch, you will see the top of the upper fall. It slides over a rock slab and drops off into the netherworld. Then, when viewing this same fall from its base, you see the falls head-on. It spills white as a curtain-type cataract, slowing when it meets angled bedrock. The next fall is a multitiered pourover that tumbles in varied forms and channels, according to stream flow. The final and least visited cascade is a chute-and-pool drop, with a single discharge over a stone face, stilling in a deep pool. Be apprised that many fools have been injured—and some killed—playing around on Glen Falls. Do not try to access the creek by climbing over guardrails and other barriers. The open rock slabs are slick and angled. One minute somebody is showing off, and the next minute they are lying mangled at the base of a cataract.

Leave the trailhead on the Glen Falls Trail. At this same spot, the Chinquapin Mountain Trail makes a 1.6-mile climb to great views, if you want to add mileage to this hike. The Glen Falls Trail heads straight on a wide, gravel all-access path. White pines, mountain laurel, and rhododendron form an evergreen backdrop. At .1 mile, the level trail comes to a cleared view. Here, the mountains stretch southeast beyond the Tar Heel State, while the Blue Valley lies below.

Begin your descent into the East Fork Overflow Creek Valley. Your walk is moderated by a wide, graded trail and wood steps, very unlike the wild crash course East Fork is taking. At .2 mile, reach your first observation deck. East Fork careens down an angled slope, then spills off beyond sight. This top-down view makes the fall hard to appreciate. Continue down the valley. Mountain laurel clings to the slopes. Just ahead the trail splits. Take the path leading acutely right, back toward East Fork. At .4 mile you will reach the second observation deck. This deck lies at the base of the upper falls. A sharp eye will spot the observation deck you were just at. The falls is much more impressive from here, spilling over a wide stone bluff, then making a more subtle, angled drop before flowing beyond vision again.

Return to the main trail. A long, loping switchback takes you to the next part of Glen Falls. Avoid shortcutting the switchbacks. It causes erosion on this popular trail in a very steep gorge. Come to an observation deck at .7 mile, standing directly beside the ripping waterway. This fall rolls in stages, stair-stepping and expanding over a wide rock face about 70 feet. Estimating the height of each fall is hard because you don't know where to start or end your calculations. Glen Falls is almost one continuous drop, but 210 feet is the length generally bandied about.

The developed part of the Glen Falls Trail ends here and is where most hikers turn around. Continuing on, the path morphs into a nar-

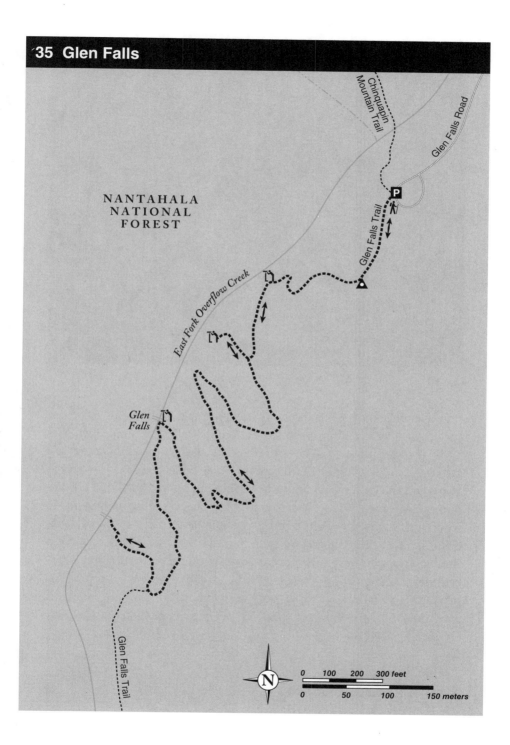

NANTAHALA
NATIONAL
FOREST

Chinquapin Mountain Trail

Glen Falls Road

Glen Falls Trail

East Fork Overflow Creek

Glen Falls

Glen Falls Trail

N

| 0 | 100 | 200 | 300 feet |

| 0 | 50 | 100 | 150 meters |

East Fork Overflow Creek is nearly one continuous falls.

row, irregular, rooty—but easily passable—track. Work well away from the stream. Reach an intersection at .8 mile. Here, the main Glen Falls Trail leads left to an alternate trailhead on FR 79C in Blue Valley. You stay right, angling back toward East Fork Overflow Creek. Burrow 'neath evergreen thickets, then emerge at the stream and a final fall. This one makes a simple, 15-foot drop into a plunge pool and is the only place where you can safely access the stream. Since this is the base of Glen Falls, sand and tree limbs and such aggregate from the collective wild tumble above. However, the pool is accessible, and you could take a dip, or at least allow children to play in the stream. Allow a little time for relaxation, since the return is more than 500 feet of climbing. On your way up, review the cataracts and see which part of Glen Falls is your favorite.

Mileages

0.0   Glen Falls parking area
0.2   First observation deck
0.4   Second observation deck

0.7   Third observation deck

0.9   Lowermost falls, backtrack

1.8   Glen Falls parking area

36 • WHITESIDE MOUNTAIN

Hike Summary: *This circuit hike climbs the crest of iconic, 4,930-foot White-side Mountain, where breathtaking panoramas stretch in three directions while you stand atop 750-foot granite cliffs. One of the Nantahala's signature hikes, this trek includes copious interpretive information explaining the peak's human and natural history. An old roadbed gradually takes you up the backside of the mountain. After reaching the crest, you walk along cliff after cliff after cliff, stopping at multiple overlooks. The trip down is shorter—and steeper.*

Whiteside is one of North Carolina's special mountains. And it has been that way a long time. Before North Carolina existed, the native Cherokee recognized Whiteside Mountain as a special place. Translated to English, its name became "White Bear," perhaps for its white cliffs and how it rose above the adjacent terrain. The Cherokee ceded the land by treaty in 1819. The peak itself wasn't settled, but simple farmers cultivated its foothills. By the early 1900s, Highlands and Cashiers had become summer destinations for those who could afford it. The Ravenel family bought Whiteside Mountain and much of the surrounding lands. They sold it to a company that ran tours on the mountain peak. The rocky roadbed, up which you hike, follows the old bus route to the top of Whiteside. Even while hiking along the crest, you can often see the roadbed on the backside of the cliffs. The land was logged over before it was purchased by the forest service and added to the Nantahala National Forest.

The forest has recovered nicely, and the hike makes for a pleasant and popular natural experience. Leave the parking area on a steep track with many steps. You are already nearly 4,400 feet high. Preserved hemlocks guard much of the early path. At .1 mile, begin the loop portion of the hike. Here, you join the old tourist bus route, now a wide and rocky trail, angling left. Blasted bluffs, covered in moss, escalate to your right, along with natural granite faces. The mountainside drops steeply to your left, though far less steeply than the mountain's south side, as you

36 WHITESIDE MOUNTAIN

Distance: 2.0-mile loop

Hiking time: 2.0 hours

Difficulty: Moderate, does climb 500 feet

Highlights: Multiple views from open cliffs

Cautions: Steep cliffs (with handrails)

Fees/Permits: Parking fee required

Best seasons: Whenever the skies are clear

Other trail users: None

Trail contacts: Nantahala National Forest, Nantahala Ranger District, 90 Sloan Road, Franklin, NC 28734, (828) 524-6441, www.fs.usda.gov/nfsnc

Finding the trailhead: From the intersection of US 64 and NC 107 in Cashiers, take US 64 west for 4.7 miles, then turn left on Whiteside Mountain Road. Follow Whiteside Mountain Road for .9 mile, and the trailhead entrance road is on your left.

GPS trailhead coordinates: N35° 4.824', W83° 8.650'

shall see. Yellow birch and maple rise overhead. Rhododendron lends a year-round evergreen tone. In spring, wildflowers color the forest floor.

Top out and level off at .9 mile. Here, a spur leads left to an easterly view into the upper Chattooga River Valley and beyond to the cliffs of Timber Ridge. The crags of the Devils Courthouse spur from the slope of Whiteside Mountain. Just ahead is your first vista looking south into Georgia and South Carolina, down the Chattooga River Valley. From here, join a foot trail heading southwesterly along the sheer south slope of Whiteside Mountain. The views start coming one after another as you straddle the edge of cliffs dropping hundreds of feet below. But fear not, for the forest service has installed cables running along the precipices. Though the cliffs drop straight down, the path itself remains fairly level.

Granite-topped mountains such as Whiteside were formed when streams of lava rose upward, forming a bubble of sorts, then cooled. The harder granite resisted erosion, while softer rock layers above it crumbled away over time, leaving these granite faces that grace much of North Carolina's Nantahala and Pisgah national forests. Here on Whiteside, the granite faces are most open facing south, but elsewhere, such as at John Rock and Looking Glass Rock, the most open sheer cliffs face north and west, respectively.

36 Whiteside Mountain

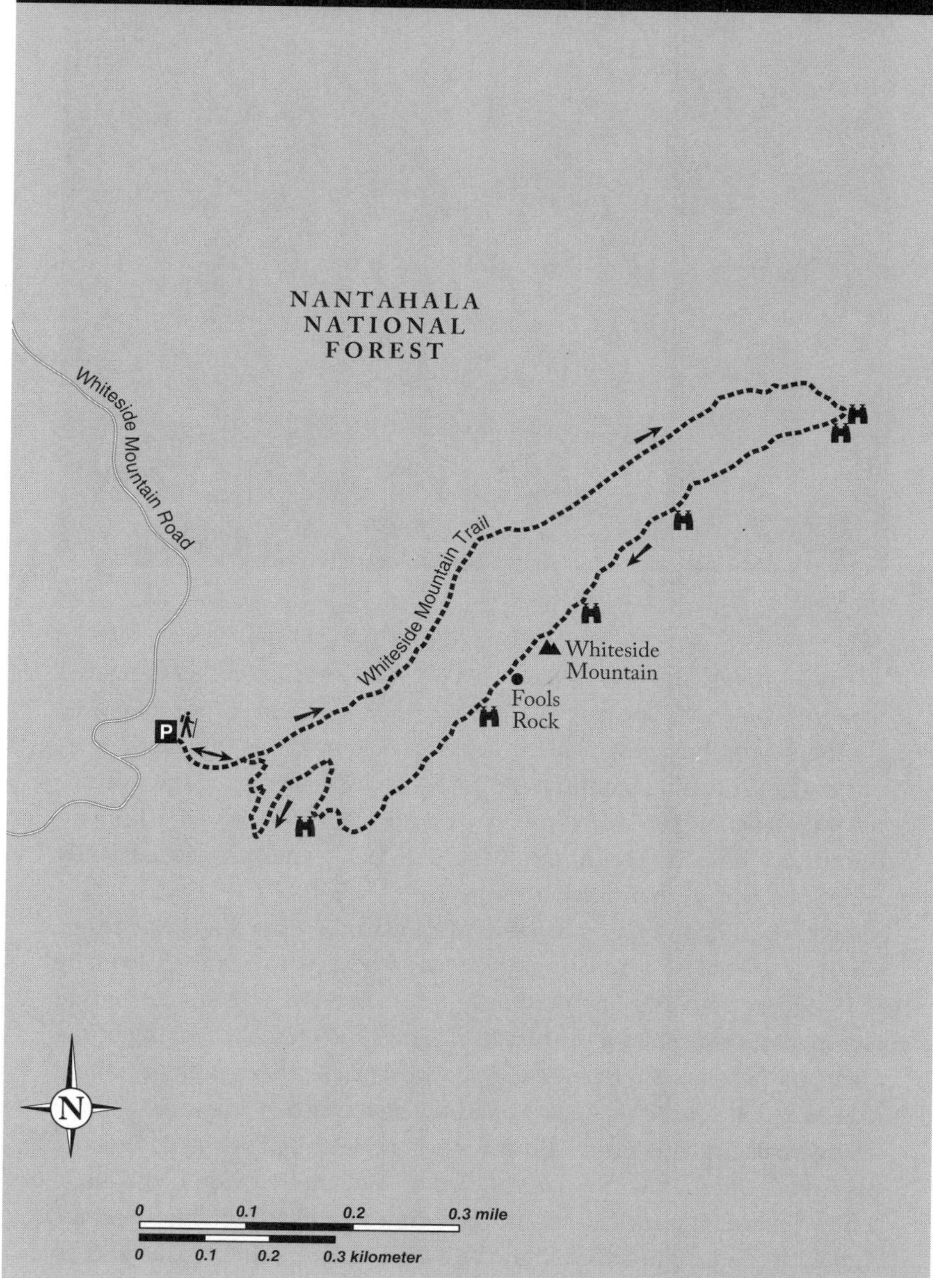
NANTAHALA NATIONAL FOREST
Whiteside Mountain Road
Whiteside Mountain Trail
Whiteside Mountain
Fools Rock
P
N
0
0.1
0.2
0.3 mile
0
0.1
0.2
0.3 kilometer

The foggy trail rises to Whiteside Mountain.

Interestingly, the mountainside is a nesting spot for endangered peregrine falcons. The south slope of the mountain is popular with climbers, who have established nearly a dozen routes up the dangerous crags. Whiteside Mountain is closed to climbing during the falcon's nesting season, generally January to June. The raptors were reintroduced to Whiteside Mountain in the mid-1980s and have successfully reclaimed part of their former range.

Oaks, locust, and pines thrive on this warmer, drier southerly slope. Chestnut trees still spring up astride the rock, only to be taken down by the ongoing chestnut blight. Shortly, you will come to Fools Rock. One day in May, more than a century back, some visitors were taking in the views up here on Whiteside. And the worst happened—a man named Gus Baty fell from Fools Rock! Somehow he clung to a small bush along a ledge, battered and bruised, but alive. Charlie Wright decided to rescue his friend. Charlie made his way down on a slope that would challenge today's gear-laden rock climbers, then endeavored to pull his friend up. And with the help of a third man, Will Dillard, they brought Gus Baty to safety. Peering down from Fools Rock sends a shiver through my spine as I think of doing what Charlie did—spontaneously descending the precipitous rock to save a friend.

The hike works down past Fools Rock, sometimes pulling back from the cliff. Spurs lead back to overlooks and shady relaxation rocks. At 1.5 miles, leave the south face of Whiteside Mountain and begin heading downhill in earnest. Pass a small rockhouse, then come to your final view at 1.6 miles. The outcrop extends westerly toward the town of Highlands. Continue descending in switchbacks. Steps ease the drop. Complete the loop at 1.9 miles. From here it is but a short backtrack to the trailhead.

Mileages

0.0 Whiteside Mountain parking and picnic area
0.9 Reach mountain crest and first vista
1.3 Fools Rock
1.9 Complete the loop
2.0 Whiteside Mountain parking and picnic area

37 • CHATTOOGA WILD AND SCENIC RIVER HIKE

Hike Summary: *Though this famed and federally designated wild and scenic river is more renowned in Georgia and South Carolina, the Tar Heel State claims its headwaters. Start the hike by climbing a low ridge to enter the upper gorge of the Chattooga. Come alongside the gorgeous waterway in ultra-rugged terrain on a slender path. Ramble deep in the watershed. Reach the confluence with Norton Mill Creek and a scenic iron bridge. Here, Norton Mill Creek drops in cascades to a large pool in the Chattooga, which is just emerging from a narrows. Enjoy swimming, fishing, and relaxing at this attractive locale.*

The Chattooga River is protected by a wild and scenic river corridor, which averages a quarter-mile wide across the river, in addition to its inclusion within federal lands. Auto traffic is blocked from the corridor, a few spots excepted. The Chattooga deserves this wild and scenic designation, and then some. Culled from the Nantahala National Forest of North Carolina, Georgia's Chattahoochee National Forest, and the Sumter National Forest of South Carolina, this select river corridor protects

37 CHATTOOGA WILD AND SCENIC RIVER HIKE

Distance: 5.4-mile there-and-back

Hiking time: 3.0 hours

Difficulty: Moderate

Highlights: Deep wooded gorge, swimming, fishing

Cautions: None

Fees/Permits: No fees or permits required

Best seasons: Late spring through early fall for swimming

Other trail users: None

Trail contacts: Nantahala National Forest, Nantahala Ranger District, 90 Sloan Road, Franklin, NC 28734, (828) 524-6441, www.fs.usda.gov/nfsnc

Finding the trailhead: From the intersection of US 64 and NC 107 in Cashiers, take NC 107 south for 1.7 miles, then turn right on Whiteside Cove Road. Follow it 4.1 miles to the signed trailhead on your left.

GPS trailhead coordinates: N35° 3.890', W83° 7.333'

one of the most significant free-flowing streams in the Southeast. The river itself is 50 miles long, starting on the Blue Ridge below Whiteside Mountain near Cashiers. It then heads south through North Carolina, then southwest, forming the Georgia–South Carolina border. Eventually, the Chattooga meets the Tallulah River, and together they form the Tugaloo River.

The Chattooga is still best known for being the backdrop of the Burt Reynolds movie *Deliverance*. It was around this time, in 1974, that the Chattooga was designated a wild and scenic river, a place where rafters, canoers, kayakers, and anglers enjoy this valley of massive boulders, clear trout-and-bass-filled waters, and deep forests. It is also a place where hikers and campers roam. Trails lace both sides of the river in Georgia and South Carolina, leaving the riverside trails in North Carolina lesser walked but no less scenic.

The elevation changes on this hike aren't much—less than 400 feet— but the trail in the gorge is irregular and rugged, despite improvements by the forest service. Plainly speaking, the canyon terrain is rough; therefore, just about any trail going through it is going to be primitive. Leave the parking area on a natural surface track, rising through mixed pine-oak-sourwood forest. Meet the edge of the Chattooga gorge at .4 mile. The echo of colliding rapids rises 200 feet from the river. Ascend

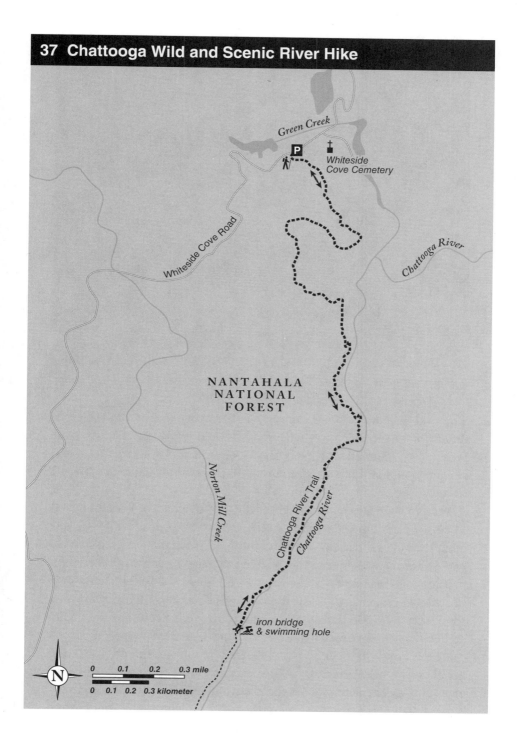

A picturesque iron bridge spans Norton Mill Creek.

along the wooded edge of the canyon, then turn away from the river. Enter a silent, scenic cove where substantial white pines tower over level land populated with holly, rhododendron, and a host of Southern Appalachian plant life. This mountain flat was surely logged or farmed in the past.

Pass an abandoned portion of the old Chattooga River Trail that used to start near Whiteside Cove Church, before the forest service developed the current parking area and rerouted the trail. Join an old roadbed glittering with mica. The walking is easy as you drift downhill, probing for a way down to the river. At 1.3 miles, the trail makes a pair of switchbacks; you're getting tantalizingly close. The Chattooga comes into view. Step over a tributary at 1.4 miles, then work around a cliff stabilized by a wooden wall. Look for bluffs across the gorge.

Come along the river at 1.7 miles. Its tannish waters roll clear over sandbars. In other places, trout lurk in deep, slow pools. Ample rain—80 or so inches per year—keeps the river moving and the adjacent vegetation lush and dense in summertime. Continue crossing small tributaries feeding the river. Shoals and still water alternate on the water-course, beckoning the hiker. At 2.0 miles, a short spur trail leads left to a rapid, pool, and river access. Here, the Chattooga River squeezes between large boulders, pounds its way through in a white froth, then silences in a huge hole ideal for swimming. Ample rocks avail adequate sitting spots.

Continue downriver, close to the bank, still in rugged terrain on a narrow, twisting track. Enjoy beauty at every turn. At 2.7 miles the path reaches Norton Mill Creek and its attractive arched iron bridge. The dense foliage gives way. From the bridge, you can look upstream at a two-tiered cascade where Norton Mill Creek is dropping to meet the Chattooga. A deep pool gathers just upstream of the bridge. Below the iron bridge, Norton Mill Creek widens and stair-steps down to meet the Chattooga River in a yawning, dusky pool. Walk down to the Chattooga, where white sands border the still water. Look upstream—the Chattooga has just squeezed between granite narrows.

The pothole-pocked boulders, tan sand, and graceful bridge all beckon a stop. The scene as a whole makes for a great destination. For those inclined, a small campsite lies on the far side of the bridge over Norton Mill Creek. From here, the Chattooga River Trail continues downstream for about 3.5 miles before ending at Bullpen Road.

Mileages

0.0   Parking area on Whiteside Cove Road
0.4   Reach gorge edge, then turn away
1.7   Come alongside the Chattooga River
2.0   Water access and swimming hole
2.7   Reach iron bridge over Norton Mill Creek, cascades, swimming hole; backtrack
5.4   Parking area on Whiteside Cove Road

---

38 • PANTHERTOWN BACKCOUNTRY LOOP

Hike Summary: This circuit explores the west side of the Panthertown Backcountry, visiting waterfalls and overlooks amid everywhere-you-look splendor. View steep Wilderness Falls, then hike below the Great Wall, deep in Panthertown Creek Valley. Climb Big Green Mountain for wide vistas. Backtrack, then stop by the wide Granny Burrell Falls. Climb away from Panthertown Creek and soak in a final view of Panthertown Valley from a mountainside rock slope.

This adventure delivers an excellent overview of Panthertown's beauty—high and low, with a net difference of just a bit over 500 feet between peaks and valleys. Your hike starts on the wide and gravelly Panthertown Valley Trail. The old road wanders easterly before meeting the Wilderness Falls Trail at .2 mile. Take a right on this single-track, hiker-only path, entering a lush vale carpeted in ferns. Come near a drainage, then tunnel beneath the sinewy arms of mountain laurel on a dry ridge. The trail opens onto a rock slab, then works its way down along Wilderness Falls, via a rerouted path that was once much steeper. Wilderness Falls is a long, narrow, granite slide cataract on Double Knob Gap Creek. It's hard to see the entire drop of 80 or so feet due to thick laurel that seems to knit itself together. Continue beyond the falls in rhododendron and black birch, leveling out along Frolictown Creek, one of the all-time great Carolina mountain names.

Intersect the Deep Gap Trail at 1.1 miles. It leaves right to cross Frolictown Creek and left toward Panthertown Creek. A spur trail goes forward and down to Frolictown Falls. This is an elegant, photogenic pourover. It spills about 15 feet over a smooth rock face shaded by lush greenery in a mossy, rocky cathedral. Sandbars border the plunge pool. Head left on the sandy Deep Gap Trail and meet the Great Wall Trail at 1.2 miles. Stay right here and wander easterly in a wide, flat, wooded valley. Rock-hop Frolictown Creek at 1.5 miles. Just ahead, reach yet another intersection. Here, the Granny Burrell Falls Trail leaves left. You will join this trail later. For now, keep straight on the Great Wall Trail as it heads south up the scenic Panthertown Creek Valley, cloaked in a verdant forest.

Granite slabs barricade both sides of the valley. The gray fortress of the Great Wall—the west side of Big Green Mountain—rises to your left, while Goldspring Ridge forms a rampart to your right. At 1.6 miles, pass a trail shelter that is actually the roof portion of an old barn. Continue up Panthertown Creek under tall white pines on an easy, level track. At 2.4 miles, leave the valley and begin your assault on Big Green Mountain. The slender track works uphill on steps of stone and wood. Some steps have been carved directly into the rock slabs. Reach a gap on Big

38 PANTHERTOWN BACKCOUNTRY LOOP

Distance: 7.4-mile loop with spur

Hiking time: 4.0 hours

Difficulty: Moderate to difficult

Highlights: Multiple views, multiple waterfalls

Cautions: Slick granite mountainsides

Fees/Permits: No fees or permits required

Best seasons: Fall through spring for best views

Other trail users: Bikers and equestrians on limited parts of the loop

Trail contacts: Nantahala National Forest, Nantahala Ranger District, 90 Sloan Road, Franklin, NC 28734, (828) 524-6441, www.fs.usda.gov/nfsnc, www.panthertown.org

Finding the trailhead: From the intersection of US 64 and NC 107 in Cashiers, take US 64 east for 1.9 miles to Cedar Creek Road. Turn left on Cedar Creek Road and follow it for 2.2 miles, then turn right on Breedlove Road (There is a sign for Panthertown Backcountry here). At 3.3 miles, Breedlove Road appears to dead-end, but veer left to join a downhill gravel track. Reach the trailhead in .2 mile more.

GPS trailhead coordinates: N35° 10.075′, W83° 2.407′

Green Mountain at 2.9 miles. Turn left here, uphill in oaks. Keep up the ridge nose. Reach a spur trail at 3.4 miles. Here the path leads left to a trademark Panthertown granite slab and a vista. The rock and forest of Goldspring Ridge stand clear. Other, potentially confusing spur trails split off the farther north you go on Big Green Mountain. Some lead to views on open slabs above the Great Wall after wandering under laurel. Others simply peter out. Be judicious in your route choices.

Backtrack from Big Green Mountain after exhausting the potential views, almost all of which are on the westerly or northwesterly side of the mountain. Head back down the Panthertown Creek Valley and reach the Granny Burrell Falls Trail at 5.9 miles. Head right, following Panthertown Creek downstream, on the Granny Burrell Falls Trail. Once again, mountain laurel and rhododendron gather in deep, dark thickets, recalling scary forests of children's books. At 6.1 miles, reach Granny Burrell Falls. The cascade gently slides about 10 feet over an open rock slab and gathers in a pool. Then the stream continues over open bedrock, not vertical by any means but simply flowing on as mountain streams do, finally stilling in a dark pool where sand gathers in surprisingly hefty quantities, enough for a beach.

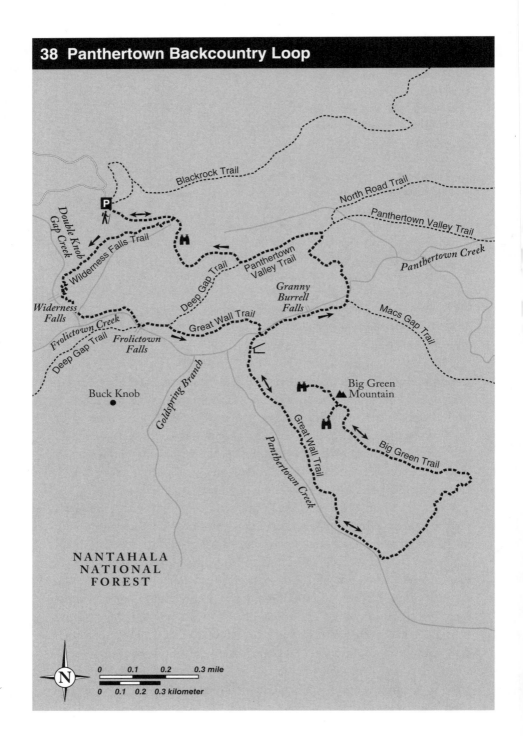

Frolictown Falls lives up to its intriguing name.

At 6.2 miles, meet the Macs Gap Trail. Follow it left to bridge Panthertown Creek, then enter a wide, planted white pine grove with campsites aplenty. Gently work uphill and north, leaving the pines to meet the Panthertown Valley Trail at 6.6 miles. Take this wide, rocky track left. The sky is open overhead as you walk near rock slabs. Pass the Deep Gap Trail at 6.8 miles. The trek offers one more surprise at 7.1 miles. Here, a rock slab opens to the southeast, revealing the Panthertown Creek Valley before you, as well as Big Green Mountain, where you were earlier, and Little Green Mountain; a host of mountains forming the Tennessee River Valley divides in the rising distance. This panorama lays bare the Panthertown landscape. At 7.2 miles, pass the Wilderness Falls Trail. From here it is a .2 mile backtrack to the trailhead.

Mileages

0.0   Western Panthertown trailhead
0.2   Acute right turn on Wilderness Falls Trail
0.8   Wilderness Falls
1.1   Deep Gap Trail and Frolictown Falls
1.5   Pass Granny Burrell Trail
3.7   Northernmost vista on Big Green Mountain Trail; backtrack
5.9   Right on Granny Burrell Trail
6.1   Granny Burrell Falls
7.1   Vista
7.4   Western Panthertown trailhead

39 • SCHOOLHOUSE FALLS LOOP AT PANTHERTOWN

Hike Summary: This hike visits three different waterfalls in the Panthertown Backcountry and adds a fine view for good measure. First, descend from Cold Mountain Gap and cruise past Macs Falls, a modest cascade. Hike along gorgeous Greenland Creek to reach Greenland Creek Falls, a tall, rock-faced cataract. You will then work your way up to Little Green Mountain, where extensive vistas await from an open granite mountainside. Finally, descend to popular Schoolhouse Falls, a classic curtain-drop cascade that spills into a large swimming hole.

Panthertown Backcountry has received much acclaim in recent years, and deservedly so. This loop shows off its primary features—an abun-

39 SCHOOLHOUSE FALLS LOOP AT PANTHERTOWN

Distance: 4.9-mile loop

Hiking time: 3.0 hours

Difficulty: Moderate

Highlights: Three waterfalls, views from open mountainside

Cautions: None

Fees/Permits: No fees or permits required

Best seasons: Spring for bold waterfalls and good wildflowers

Other trail users: Bikers and equestrians on limited parts of the loop

Trail contacts: Nantahala National Forest, Nantahala Ranger District, 90 Sloan Road, Franklin, NC 28734, (828) 524-6441, www.fs.usda.gov/nfsnc, www.panthertown.org

Finding the trailhead: From the town square in Brevard, take US 64 west for 15.7 miles to NC 281. Turn right onto NC 281 north and follow it for .8 mile, then turn left on Cold Mountain Road, just after passing the Lake Toxaway Fire and Rescue Station, on your right. Follow Cold Mountain Road for 5.6 miles, then turn left on a marked gravel road just before reaching Canaan Land residential development. Follow this marked gravel road .1 mile, then turn right on a signed gravel road. Follow it .1 mile to dead end at the trailhead.

GPS trailhead coordinates: N35° 9.474', W82° 59.946'

dance of waterfalls, open granite slabs that present stellar views, and plush forests that carpet the land. A trail system has been developed and is well marked and maintained by the Friends of Panthertown, a volunteer organization keeping this slice of the Nantahala National Forest in great shape.

Leave the trailhead on the hiker-only Greenland Creek Trail, passing around a pole gate and bisecting the infamous powerline cut that splits in half the entire Panthertown Backcountry. Reenter woods and descend a rib ridge for Greenland Creek under upland hardwoods. At .3 mile, a user-created spur trail leads right down to Macs Falls. This smaller cascade delivers tea-colored water over a rock slab into a plunge pool. The area is difficult to access.

The sandy track sidles alongside Greenland Creek, heading upstream amid laurel thickets, doghobble, galax, black birch, and white pines. Meet Macs Gap Trail at .7 mile. It leaves left back for the trailhead. Stay right here, heading upstream along Greenland Creek to another intersection at .8 mile. Here, Macs Gap Trail splits right. For now, keep straight on the Greenland Creek Trail, twisting among streamlets and

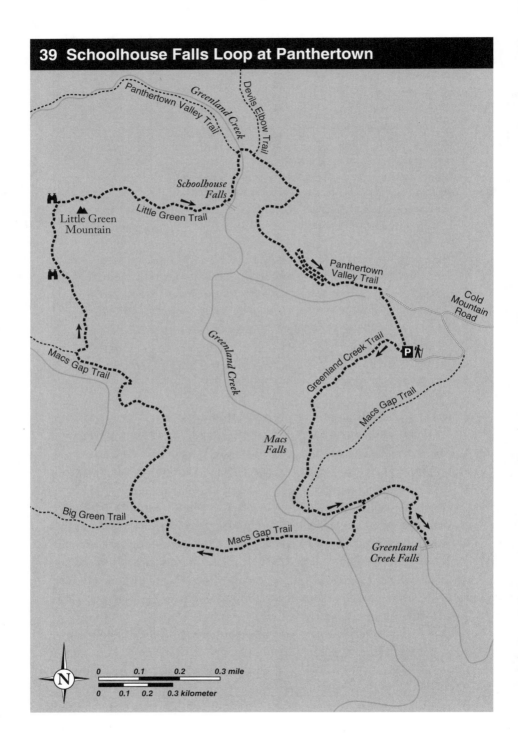

Schoolhouse Falls spills into a massive pool.

arbors of laurel on a rooty, muddy track. Emerge at Greenland Creek Falls at 1.1 miles. The two-tiered cataract pours 30 feet over a widening rock face into a plunge pool deep enough for a dip! Large boulders make for ideal photographer perches. The open sky overhead contrasts with the dark forests through which you've been hiking.

Backtrack from the falls and rejoin the Macs Gap Trail. Ford Greenland Creek. The path ascends to cross a tributary of Greenland Creek and works up another feeder branch, this time atop rocks slabs bordered by yellow birch. Level off at a woodsy intersection at 2.1 miles. Stay right with the Macs Gap Trail. Top out on a forested knob at 2.3 miles. Your descent from the knob is exceeded by a stream diving to meet Panther-town Creek. Switchback to another intersection at 2.7 miles. Stay right with the Little Green Trail. Climb steeply in oaks on wood-and-earth steps. You are soon rewarded as the Little Green Trail opens onto a granite face adorning the west slope of Little Green Mountain, interspersed with low-growing sedges and brush occupying thin-soiled cracks. Walk out there. Pine-framed panoramas open of Blackrock Mountain, rising with a rocky face across Panthertown Creek Valley.

Now comes the tricky part—staying on the correct path. Keep north along the upper edge of the granite slab, in and out of pine copses. User-created paths dead end. Watch for painted arrows on the rock slab. Better views appear on the next open slope, a bigger, more north-facing granite slab. The gray-and-black stone face begs exploration. Outcrops demand to be stood upon. This is a place to tarry. At 3.2 miles, leave right from 4,100-foot Little Green Mountain, descending on a narrow path in crowded vegetation, east, for Greenland Creek.

The rapid descent from laurel into rhododendron soon brings echoes from Greenland Creek to your ears. Reach the valley floor at 3.6 miles and a trail junction. A spur trail dips right a short distance to Schoolhouse Falls. Here, it isn't the falls itself that makes the scene, but rather, the scene makes the falls. A gravel and rock viewing area opens to a huge pool, far outstripping the modest size of Greenland Creek. A frame of greenery borders the tan but translucent, still water. At the rear, Schoolhouse Falls systematically pours a drape of white 20 feet over a smooth rock face, where the froth disappears into the aforementioned ochre pool. No wonder it is the most popular destination in Panthertown Backcountry.

The hike then turns downstream along Greenland Creek, spanning a boardwalk to meet the Panthertown Valley Trail at 3.9 miles. Turn right here, bridging Greenland Creek on a wide bridge. Just ahead, the Devils Elbow Trail leaves left. Stay straight on the multiuse path. Work up a pair of lung-friendly switchbacks. Emerge onto the powerline clearing, then reenter woods, bordering national forest property. Make an abrupt right here at 4.7 miles. Skirt the national forest property boundary in woods on a slender path, completing the hike at 4.9 miles.

Mileages

0.0   Cold Mountain Gap trailhead
1.1   Greenland Creek Falls
2.7   Right with the Little Green Trail
3.2   Leave Little Green Mountain
3.6   Schoolhouse Falls
3.9   Right on Panthertown Valley Trail
4.9   Return to trailhead

Hike Summary: This short trail leads to one of the most visited falls in North Carolina's national forests. Leave the large parking and picnic area near the South Carolina state line and walk an asphalt path to an all-access view of this massive, 400-plus-foot, multitiered cataract. From there, take wooden steps to a closer view of this amazing white froth. If you want to add miles to your hike, a connector path leads to the Foothills Trail, a long-distance path traversing South Carolina's Sumter National Forest in addition to part of the Nantahala National Forest.

Whitewater Falls is perhaps the most-oft photographed waterfall in North Carolina. The massive cataract has been adorning tourism brochures as long as the Highlands-Cashiers area of North Carolina has been attracting vacationers and those seeking to escape the heat of the southern lowlands. Deserving of its star status, Whitewater Falls drops a total of 411 feet in an irregular series of chutes, pitches, and slides, ever widening until ending in a fog of mist and spray. The aptly named Whitewater River continues its crash course, entering South Carolina and finally slowing in the still waters of Lake Jocassee. Most of the upper Whitewater River watershed is protected within the Nantahala National Forest.

The forest service has built a large parking and picnic area to accommodate waterfall visitors. But if you visit during off times—such as mornings or weekdays—it can be quiet. From the parking area you can enjoy a cleared view down the Whitewater River Valley into the Cherokee Foothills of South Carolina. There are also picnic and restroom facilities here. Start your hike on the asphalt path at the lower end of the parking area, passing open, shaded, and sheltered picnic tables astride a grassy lawn. A steep wooded mountainside rises to your left.

By .2 mile you have reached the all-access overlook of Whitewater Falls. A cleared view stretches through a frame of trees to the cataract down below. First, Whitewater Falls drops in a relatively slender chute, then it tumbles down a less steep angle, widening over bedrock, saving the best for last, where it fans out and becomes steeper, loudly following gravity's orders, slowing in a jumble of boulders perpetually soaked in waterfall spray.

If you want a closer look, take the 152 steps (landings are included

40 WHITEWATER FALLS

Distance: .6-mile there-and-back

Hiking time: 1.0 hour

Difficulty: Easy

Highlights: Two views of gigantic falls

Cautions: Steps to lower viewpoint

Fees/Permits: Parking fee required

Best seasons: Year-round

Other trail users: None

Trail contacts: Nantahala National Forest, Nantahala Ranger District, 90 Sloan Road, Franklin, NC 28734, (828) 524-6441, www.fs.usda.gov/nfsnc

Finding the trailhead: From the intersection of US 64 and NC 107 in Cashiers, take NC 107 south, entering South Carolina and intersecting SC 413. Turn left on SC 413 and follow it back into North Carolina and the parking area on your right. Shortly after reentering North Carolina, SC 413 turns into NC 281.

GPS trailhead coordinates: N35° 1.818', W83° 0.972'

as steps) to the lower overlook. It presents a closer view, still not as close as most falls, but as close as the forbidding terrain allows. Here, preserved hemlocks frame the setting. The white froth is closer, and the din of the falls rises brasher. To your right, the set of stairs leaving the lower overlook links this perch to the Foothills Trail.

It is 111 more steps to reach the Foothills Trail. The trail begins to switchback via more steps into the depths of the Whitewater Gorge. Downstream you see giant boulders clogging the river as the water loudly forces its way downstream. After a half-mile, an iron suspension bridge allows you to cross the Whitewater River and adds a great watery view. The Foothills Trail goes on.

The Foothills Trail may be the most unsung, underused, and underrated long trail in the Southeast. It traverses the lowermost Southern Appalachians in North and South Carolina, through state parks, national forests, and state-owned preserves. In these lands are high ridgelines, wild and scenic rivers, deep rock gorges, wilderness areas, mountain lakes, clear trout streams, towering forests, and a number of other incredible waterfalls, stretching from one end of the path to the other.

The Foothills Trail is well marked and well maintained, and it makes for an excellent extended trek with its ample camping opportunities.

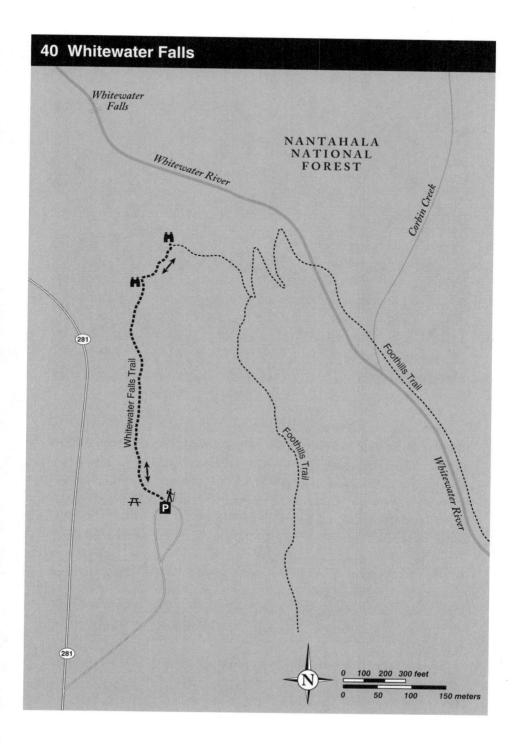

Whitewater Falls

Whitewater River

NANTAHALA
NATIONAL
FOREST

Corbin Creek

Foothills Trail

Whitewater River

Whitewater Falls Trail

Foothills Trail

281

281

P

0   100   200   300 feet

0   50   100   150 meters

N

Whitewater Falls is arguably the most spectacular cataract around.

Several decades back, local folks recognized the natural beauty and hiking potential along the border of the Carolinas, and they realized a path connecting these resources would be a great way to both enjoy and protect them. No one knows the exact originator of the idea, but several persons and agencies converged to begin the "Foothills Trail." The first miles were laid out in Sumter National Forest back in 1968. As time wore on, more agencies got involved, culminating with Duke Power Company laying out much of the heart of the trail. Duke Power has since sold their lands to the two states. Today, the Foothills Trail extends 77 miles from South Carolina's Oconee State Park to Tablerock State Park, passing through the Nantahala National Forest here in the vicinity of Whitewater Falls. For more information, visit www.foothills trail.org.

The Foothills Trail links the two primary waterfalls of the Whitewater River. Technically, this is the upper falls of the Whitewater River, but it is simply referred to as Whitewater Falls. The other primary cataract, downstream, is known as Lower Whitewater Falls, generally acclaimed at 200 feet, but it seems higher to me. Lower Whitewater Falls can be viewed via the Bad Creek Access, operated by Duke Power. Simply take NC 281 south from the Whitewater Falls parking area. After you enter South Carolina, the gated access will be on your left. The Foothills Trail connects you to the Lower Falls spur.

Mileages

0.0 Whitewater Falls parking and picnic area
0.2 All-access waterfall vista
0.3 Lower viewing platform; backtrack
0.6 Return to trailhead

Uwharrie National Forest Hikes

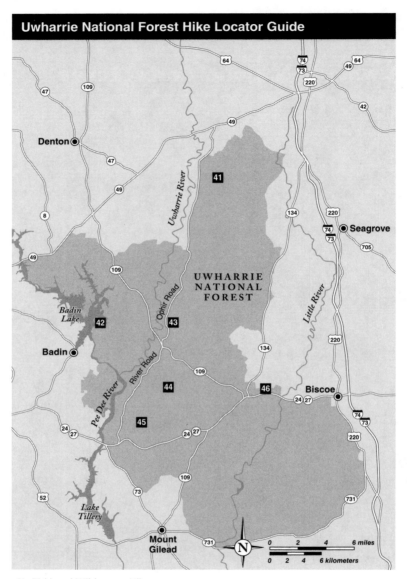

Uwharrie National Forest Hike Locator Guide

41 Birkhead Wilderness Hike
42 Vistas of Badin Lake
43 Uwharrie Trail
44 Upper Dutchmans Loop
45 Lower Dutchmans Loop
46 Densons Creek Loop

Hike Summary: *This circuit explores a federally designated wilderness—the only one in the Uwharrie National Forest—in purportedly the oldest mountain range around, the Birkhead Mountains. On this loop you will trace old roads built by early Carolina settlers and explore slender footpaths. First, follow a ridgeline before dropping to Robbins Branch, a wildflower-filled vale you will rock-hop numerous times. Climb to the Birkhead Trail, walking an ancient spine to reach the historic Bingham plantation site. The Hannahs Creek Trail takes you back to the trailhead as you visit more settler evidence along the way.*

The Birkhead Mountains Wilderness covers nearly 5,000 acres. This loop explores most of it. Established in 1984 at the northern end of the Uwharrie National Forest, the trails explore linear wooded ridges divided by small, pure streams. Though the Birkhead range doesn't exceed 1,000 feet in elevation, the steepness of the hills will surprise and challenge unaware hikers. As the United States swept eastward from the coast, the Birkhead range was farmed, homesteaded, and cut over for timber. Today, the tract exudes a sense of wilderness, but vigilant hikers will see the human imprint, including old roadbeds, homesites, rock walls, and even an erect chimney beside the trail. You will also pass the Christopher Bingham plantation site. In 1780, Mr. Bingham came to what was then the West and cultivated the Birkheads. Look for piles of stones and leveled land.

The trails are well marked with blazes and signage at intersections. From the parking area, take the trail heading north, the Robbins Branch Trail. The hiking is easy on an old roadbed shaded by ridgetop woodlands. Roll over eroded soil vehicle berms, built prior to the wilderness designation yet still showing. At .3 mile, reach a trail junction. Here, your return route, the Hannahs Creek Trail, leaves right. Stay left, still on the Robbins Branch Trail, rising in a thick forest of pines. At .9 mile, look for a conspicuous tree to the right of the trail. Here, a hardwood grows vertically, then horizontally, then vertically again, forming a resting seat. The tree was likely bent by another tree that fell on top of it but has since disintegrated back into the soil. Winter views of adjacent hills open to your east and west. At 1.4 miles, the trail tops out. Here, exposed quartz forms what is referred to as the "White Walkway," a

41 BIRKHEAD WILDERNESS HIKE

Distance: 6.9-mile loop

Hiking time: 4.0 hours

Difficulty: Moderate to difficult

Highlights: Bluff views, wildflowers in season, wilderness

Cautions: None

Fees/Permits: No fees or permits required

Best seasons: Year-round

Other trail users: None

Trail contacts: Uwharrie National Forest, 789 NC 24/27 East, Troy, NC 27371, (910) 576-6391, www.fs.usda.gov/nfsnc

Finding the trailhead: From the intersection of US 220 and US 64 in Asheboro, take US 64 west for .2 mile, then keep forward, joining NC 49 south. Follow NC 49 south for 6 miles to turn right on Science Hill Road (the left turn at this intersection is Tot Hill Farm Road). Follow Science Hill Road for .2 mile to reach Lassiter Mill Road. Turn left on Lassiter Mill Road. Do not turn left into the signed Thornburg trailhead of Birkhead Mountain Wilderness at 2.7 miles; rather, drive a total of 5.6 miles on Lassiter Mill Road to the second signed left turn into the Birkhead Mountains Wilderness. Join a gravel road and follow it for .6 mile to dead end at the trailhead.

GPS trailhead coordinates: N35° 35.40', W79° 56.90'

pale pebble path unique to this trail. Look for a large quartz rock beside the trail here.

At 1.6 miles, meet the Thornburg Trail. It leads left over Silver Run Creek to the Thornburg trailhead. Turn right, descending toward Robbins Branch, to shortly pass an old rock wall on trail left. This wall was built to clear what once were fields and slow down erosion on the slope. The current forest cover makes it hard to imagine a farm here. At 1.9 miles, reach and rock-hop Robbins Branch. You are heading upstream in a rich, heavily wooded valley with verdant spring wildflowers. Mountain laurel and holly are found in abundance. At 2.0 miles, step over Robbins Branch twice in succession. Cross it a fourth time. Finally, at 2.7 miles, leave Robbins Branch, curve easterly, and ascend, steeply at points, to meet the Birkhead Trail. Turn right here, southbound. Oak trees dominate the ridgeline. At 3.5 miles, the hike crests at 900 feet. Meet Camp 5 and a large fireplace on trail right. A yellow-blazed trail leads east to North Prong Hannahs Creek. Undulate among rock outcrops. At 4.4

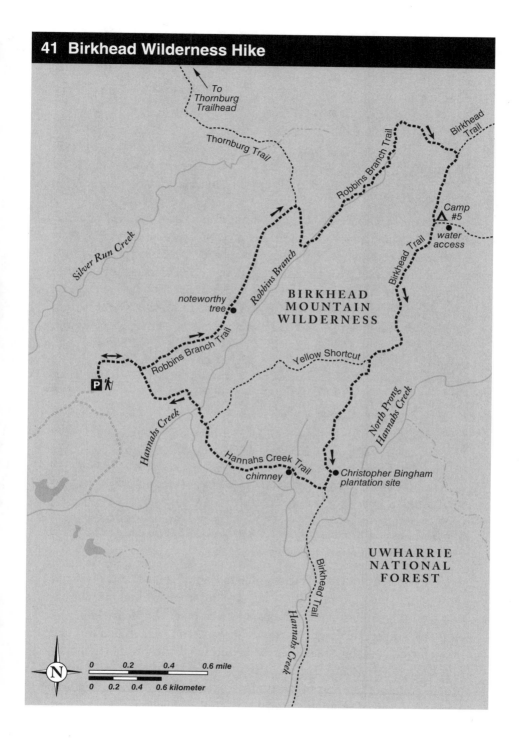

To
Thornburg
Trailhead

Thornburg Trail

Robbins Branch Trail

Birkhead
Trail

Camp
#5

water
access

Silver Run Creek

Robbins Branch

noteworthy
tree

BIRKHEAD
MOUNTAIN
WILDERNESS

Birkhead Trail

Robbins Branch Trail

Yellow Shortcut

P

Hannahs Creek

North Prong
Hannahs Creek

Hannahs Creek Trail

chimney

Christopher Bingham
plantation site

UWHARRIE
NATIONAL
FOREST

Birkhead Trail

Hannahs Creek

N

| 0 | 0.2 | 0.4 | 0.6 mile |

| 0 | 0.2 | 0.4 | 0.6 kilometer |

Quartz abounds in the Birkhead Wilderness.

miles, a shortcut trail leads right a mile to Hannahs Creek. Stay forward on the Birkhead Trail to find the signed Christopher Bingham plantation site at 5.1 miles. Descend a bit more to meet the Hannahs Creek Trail at 5.2 miles. Turn right on the Hannahs Creek Trail, rolling through hills above Hannahs Creek. Begin looking for settler evidence. At 5.4 miles, step over a tributary of Hannahs Creek. Find an erect double-hearth chimney, remains of a settler's homesite. At 5.8 miles, step over another branch of Hannahs Creek. At 6.0 miles, a yellow-blazed shortcut leads right back up to the Birkhead Trail. Ahead, rock-hop Robbins Branch after passing a settler's stone fence. Climb to meet the Robbins Branch Trail at 6.6 miles. From here, retrace your steps .3 mile to the trailhead.

Mileages

0.0	Robbins Branch trailhead
0.3	Stay left with Robbins Branch Trail
1.6	Thornburg Trail leaves left
1.9	Reach Robbins Branch
2.7	Leave Robbins Branch
4.4	Shortcut leaves right
5.1	Bingham plantation site
5.2	Right on Hannahs Creek Trail
6.0	Pass other end of shortcut
6.6	Complete loop, left on Robbins Branch Trail
6.9	Robbins Branch trailhead

42 • VISTAS OF BADIN LAKE

Hike Summary: Luckily for us, a portion of the Uwharrie National Forest borders Badin Lake, a hill-rimmed impoundment of the Pee Dee River. This hike travels its shores, wandering waterside woods with aquatic vistas most of the way. You will also pass developed national forest facilities before turning inland and trekking through hills. But you'll find more shoreline to enjoy on the final part of this attractive circuit hike.

This hike can be your excuse for tying several recreation opportunities together into one nice national forest package. Here at Badin Lake you can camp, fish, swim, boat, and of course, hike. The trailhead—Kings Mountain Point—offers restrooms, picnic facilities, a small nature trail, and fishing platforms. A campground host is located here for everyone's safety—if only other trailheads were this full of amenities. Also, the trail passes two alluring national forest campgrounds, Badin Lake and Arrowhead. They may tempt you to add an overnight campout to your lakeside hike.

As you look out toward the tip of Kings Mountain Point, the Badin

42 VISTAS OF BADIN LAKE

Distance: 5.1-mile loop

Hiking time: 3.0 hours

Difficulty: Moderate

Highlights: Lake views, fishing opportunities

Cautions: None

Fees/Permits: No fees or permits required

Best seasons: Year-round

Other trail users: None

Trail contacts: Uwharrie National Forest, 789 NC 24/27 East, Troy, NC 27371, (910) 576-6391, www.fs.usda.gov/nfsnc

Finding the trailhead: From Troy, take NC 109 north for 10 miles to NC 1153/Reservation Road and a big sign for Badin Lake Campground. Turn left on NC 1153 and follow it for .4 mile to turn right on Moccasin Creek Road/FR 576. Follow it for .6 mile, then turn right on McCleans Creek Road/FR 544. Follow McCleans Creek Road for 2.7 miles to reach a T intersection. Turn right on Badin Lake Road, aiming for Kings Mountain Point. At .2 mile, veer left onto FR 597A. Follow FR 597A for .5 mile to reach an intersection. Keep forward on Group Camp Road/FR 6551 to dead end at .8 mile, reaching the Kings Mountain Point Picnic area.

GPS trailhead coordinates: N36° 5.73', W80° 11.56

Lake hiking trail leaves from the upper part of the parking area. Walk southbound, toward Badin Lake Campground, on a single-track path passing amid shaded picnic tables. White blazes mark the trail. Leaves, rocks, and roots form the natural surface path. An abundance of exposed milky white quartz peeks from the forest floor. Pine-oak woods with sweetgum rise above holly and dogwood. At .2 mile, after curving around an embayment, look back, north, to Kings Mountain Point. Note the lakeside clearings used by bank anglers.

At .5 mile, step over an intermittent stream just before reaching Badin Lake Campground. Here, a spur trail curves around the campground between the campsites and the shoreline. However, the Badin Lake Trail continues straight at this intersection to bisect the campground access road and then rejoin the alternate campground loop. Resume cruising the shoreline.

At .8 mile, reach a point and a good lake vista. Look south to a cove and west toward open water. At 1.4 miles, slalom through a particu-

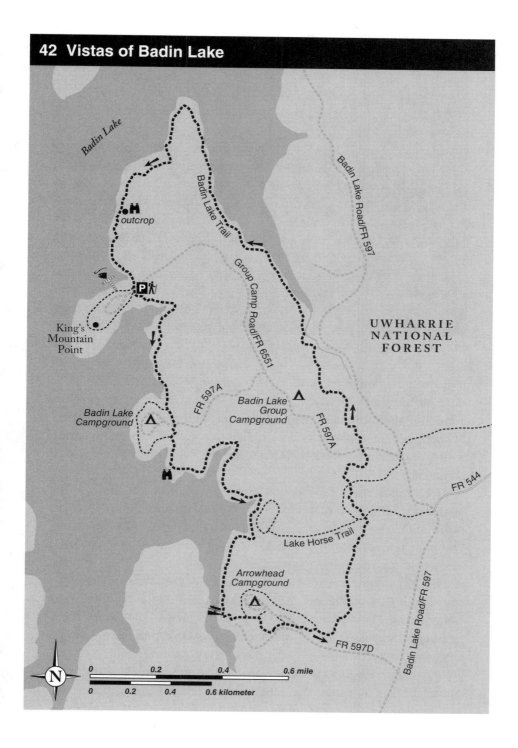

Badin Lake

Badin Lake Trail

Badin Lake Road/FR 597

outcrop

Group Camp Road/FR 6551

King's
Mountain
Point

P

UWHARRIE
NATIONAL
FOREST

FR 597A

Badin Lake
Campground

Badin Lake
Group
Campground

FR 597A

FR 544

Lake Horse Trail

Arrowhead
Campground

Badin Lake Road/FR 597

FR 597D

N

| 0 | | 0.2 | | 0.4 | | 0.6 mile |

| 0 | | 0.2 | 0.4 | | 0.6 kilometer |

The shores of Badin Lake open to hilly panoramas.

larly rocky section of trail while circling around a cove. The trail crosses multiple intermittent streambeds, and others flow full time while straddling the shoreline of Badin Lake. Most of them can be easily rock-hopped, yet some places will be marshy or mucky, especially during winter and spring. You are walking along the Beaverdam Creek arm of Badin Lake.

At 1.8 miles, reach Cove Boat Ramp. Walk on pavement toward the restroom, then veer left and look for steps leading uphill to the trail's resumption. The path has been mostly level this far, but now you climb. The path temporarily leaves Badin Lake at Cove Boat Ramp, passing Arrowhead Campground to enter its mini-trail network. At 1.9 miles, reach a junction near Arrowhead Campground. Keep forward, joining a paved path. The paved path going left loops around the far side of the campground. Shortly pass a spur path leading left to the campground restrooms. Stay right. At 2.1 miles, cross the Arrowhead Campground entrance road. At 2.2 miles, reach the far end of the Arrowhead Campground loop trail. Keep forward, now on a natural surface trail that curves north. From here the path winds through wooded piney hills and hardwood hollows before returning to the lake. At 2.4 miles, reach a hilltop in a young forest; shortly drop to cross an old forest road. At 2.6 miles, cross the green-blazed Lake Horse Trail, then cross it a second time at 2.7 miles. Circle around an old clearing. At 2.9 miles, cross FR 597A. Work through some steep hills, going mostly downhill from this point. At 3.5 miles, you sidle alongside the largest creek of the hike. Private property is located on the other side. Shortly reach Badin Lake again. Houses are located on the far side of the widening embayment.

Enjoy more shoreline hiking while passing through some boat-accessible campsites. These camps can be confusing, as user-created trails spur off, but you stay with the blazes and stay along the shore. At 4.4 miles, reach the peninsula's northern tip. Views are abundant from this point. From here you turn south. The trail passes through arguably the steepest and most rugged terrain of the hike before reaching Kings Mountain Point. Bisect several rocky gullies shaded by pines and moss. At 4.8 miles, the path crosses an open rock outcrop with a superlative lake vista to the west. From here it is but .3 mile to the trailhead and the loop's end.

Mileages

0.0   Kings Mountain Point
0.5   Badin Lake Campground
0.8   Lake vista
1.8   Cove Boat Ramp
2.1   Cross Arrowhead Campground entrance road
2.9   Cross FR 597A
4.4   Reach peninsula's northern tip
4.8   Vista from rock outcrop
5.1   Kings Mountain Point

43 • UWHARRIE TRAIL

Hike Summary: The Uwharrie Trail is the Piedmont's long-distance hiking opportunity. This path extends almost 20 miles and provides an opportunity to backpack among the streams and hills of the Pee Dee River watershed. Even if you don't backpack, consider hiking this gem by sections, as several trailheads offer access throughout the length of the trail. It starts near the community of Ophir, then climbs extremely rocky Dark Mountain. From there it continues south, crosses Tower Road, then ambles south into the greater Spencer Creek Valley before emerging at NC 109. The trail explores many other waterways, including superlative Watery Branch, before reaching Yates Place Camp. The lower part of the path continues alternating between wooded hills and rich streams until emerging at its southern terminus on NC 24/27.

To hike the Uwharrie Trail in its entirety was a long-standing dream of mine. The reality was more rewarding than I anticipated. I hope it will be that way for you. Over the course of 20 miles, you will find the trail moves in patterns. First it will climb a rocky hill, then drop into a watershed, all of which flow westerly to meet the Pee Dee River, at this point impounded as Badin Lake. The streams often have flats used for camping. The trail then rises to another hill and drops into the next stream south. In places, the route was laid out to keep it within the confines of the national forest property, since private parcels are scattered within the Uwharrie. Also, you will cross closed forest roads. On the southern half of the hike, a growing network of mountain bike trails crosses the Uwharrie Trail. Stay with the white blazes of the Uwharrie Trail and you will be fine.

Start the hike with one of your steepest, rockiest climbs. It leaves directly from the northern trail terminus. Here, the Uwharrie Trail—a single-track path for almost its entire length—works up the slope of Dark Mountain. Top out at .8 mile. Soak in westerly views of the mountains across Badin Lake; there are hills to the east, too. Continue southbound, ridge-running in oaks and pines, tracing the white blazes. Work off the steep slope, descend into a boggy flat, and cross Tower Road at 2.0 miles. Climb away from Tower Road, working around the side of Horse Mountain. Drop to bisect holly-and-laurel-choked Panther Branch at 3.2 miles. Climb into dry hills of pine and oak. Scattered quartz adds white to the forest floor.

The Uwharrie Trail joins north-south-running Morris Mountain. Undulate along its crest. Pass through a gap at 4.4 miles. After a descent, meet a connector trail leading right to Morris Mountain Campground at 5.8 miles. Resume dropping, reaching a flat and footbridge over Spencer Creek at 6.0 miles. This is the largest creek along the path. Climb away from the bridge, only to descend into rocky and azalea-rich Cattail Creek at 7.3 miles. Turn upstream, rising to a knoll, then roll into the NC 109 trailhead at 8.0 miles. Cross the paved road and work down to bouldery Cedar Creek at 8.6 miles. The path ascends, squeezing be-

43 UWHARRIE TRAIL

Distance: 19.8 miles end to end

Hiking time: 13.0 hours

Difficulty: Difficult

Highlights: Backpacking, wildflowers, winter views from multiple hilltops

Cautions: Wet areas beside creek, rock-hops

Fees/Permits: No fees or permits required

Best seasons: October through May

Other trail users: None

Trail contacts: Uwharrie National Forest, 789 NC 24/27 East, Troy, NC 27371,
(910) 576-6391, www.fs.usda.gov/nfsnc

Finding the trailheads: To reach the south terminus, the NC 24/27 trailhead, from Troy,
take NC 24/27 west for 9.5 miles to the signed trailhead on your right. To reach the
north terminus from the NC 24/27 trailhead, continue west on NC 24/27 for 1 mile to
River Road. Turn right on River Road and follow it for 8.5 miles to turn left on NC 109
north. Follow NC 109 north .2 mile, then veer right onto Ophir Road. Follow Ophir
Road for 5.0 miles to Flint Hill Road. Turn right on Flint Hill Road and follow it 1.7 miles
to reach the Jumping Off Rock trailhead on your right.

GPS trailhead coordinates: NC 24/27 trailhead N35° 18.65', W80° 2.61'; Jumping Off Rock
trailhead N35° 28.80', W79° 57.08'

tween private property parcels, then dives among outcrops into Watery Branch, one of the most attractive streams in the forest. Work up the vale clad in pine and mountain laurel. Step over Watery Branch at 9.8 miles, keeping south to join a tributary at 10.5 miles. Climb still, crossing Dusty Level Road, and meet the spur trail to Yates Place Camp at 10.9 miles.

The Uwharrie Trail keeps south to meet the Dutchmans Creek Trail at 11.4 miles. It offers an alternate route to the NC 24/27 trailhead. The Uwharrie Trail will cross it twice along the way. The path goes up and down amid small drainages, reaching upper Dutchmans Creek and a level camp 12.9 miles. Leave the creek and ascend to your second meeting with the Dutchmans Creek Trail at 14.1 miles.

Stay straight on the Uwharrie Trail at this four-way trail junction. Cross an open grassy forest road. Begin a rocky descent to rock-hop Big Island Creek at 14.9 miles. Step over the heavily vegetated creek twice more to make a 350-foot climb of rocky Dennis Mountain, topping out at 16.1 miles. Just as quickly descend to Upper Wood Run. Turn up this

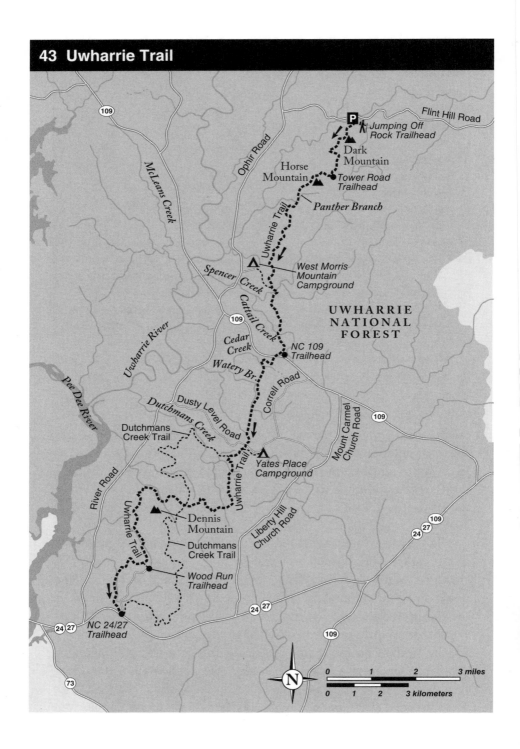

A backpacker relaxes after a long day on the Uwharrie Trail.

dusky, alluring vale, bridging it at 17.4 miles. Rise to make a trail junction at 17.7 miles. A connector trail leads left to the Wood Run trailhead. Southbound on the Uwharrie Trail, your next stream is rocky Wood Run Creek, which you meet and hop at 18.4 miles. Keep up the valley to pass under a powerline at 19.4 miles. Rise to a hill and finish the entire trail at the NC 24/27 parking area at 19.8 miles.

Mileages

0.0	Jumping Off Rock trailhead on Flint Hill Road
0.8	Dark Mountain, views
2.0	Tower Road trailhead
3.2	Panther Branch
5.8	Spur to Morris Mountain Campground
6.0	Bridge over Spencer Creek
7.3	Cattail Creek
8.0	NC 109 trailhead
8.6	Cedar Creek
9.8	Leave Watery Branch
10.9	Spur to Yates Place Camp

---

44 • UPPER DUTCHMANS LOOP

Hike Summary: *This circuit penetrates some of the most rugged terrain in the Uwharrie National Forest. After leaving Yates Place Camp, the hike drops to meet the Uwharrie Trail, where it turns south, rolling through hills to cross upper Dutchmans Creek. From there, the trail surmounts a knob and cruises to a hilltop flat. Drop into the Little Island Creek drainage, enjoying the flowery valley. The challenges then begin as you scale rocky hills aplenty to make lower Dutchmans Creek. A rewarding walk up this mountain-esque rill closes the loop. Ample campsites and streams add backpacking possibilities.*

The southern end of the Uwharrie National Forest has two long trails that form a figure 8—the Uwharrie Trail and the Dutchman's Creek Trail. This is the northern loop of that figure 8. It is a popular and rewarding hike used by Piedmont hikers and backpackers, and it makes for a great training hike for those wishing to tackle the bigger mountains situated in North Carolina's national forests to the west.

From the Yates Place Camp, walk westerly down a closed and gated forest road just a short distance. A sign points right for the connector foot trail leading to the Uwharrie Trail. The connector passes under a transmission line, then meets the Uwharrie Trail at .3 mile. Turn left at this intersection, southbound on the Uwharrie Trail, in mixed pines, oaks, dogwoods, and tulip trees set on sloping hills. At .8 mile, intersect the Dutchmans Creek Trail and begin the loop portion of your hike. Stay left on the Uwharrie Trail, descending into the first of many holly-and-mountain-laurel-filled drainages. Prescribed fire is a regular tool here, and you will see blackened tree trunks astride the trail. Step

44 UPPER DUTCHMANS LOOP

Distance: 9.4-mile loop

Hiking time: 5.5 hours

Difficulty: Difficult

Highlights: Wildflowers, streams, big woods aura

Cautions: Wet areas along trail

Fees/Permits: No fees or permits required

Best seasons: October through May

Other trail users: None

Trail contacts: Uwharrie National Forest, 789 NC 24/27 East, Troy, NC 27371, (910) 576-6391, www.fs.usda.gov/nfsnc

Finding the trailhead: To reach the Yates Place Camp trailhead from downtown Troy, take NC 24/27 west a short distance to reach NC 109 Bypass. Turn right on Business 109 Bypass and follow it .8 mile to turn left on NC 109 north. Follow NC 109 north for 4 miles to turn left on Correll Road/NC 1147 and follow it for 1.8 miles to a T intersection. Turn right here, on Dusty Level Road. Follow it for .7 mile to reach the Yates Place Camp trailhead at .7 mile.

GPS trailhead coordinates: N35° 21.89', W79° 59.38'

over a clear, rocky stream at 1.2 miles, then reach another branch, separated by chestnut-oak-clad hills, at 1.7 miles. Continue roller-coastering south, rock-hopping yet another streamlet at 2.0 miles. One more hill separates you from upper Dutchmans Creek and a large flat and campsite at 2.3 miles.

From here the Uwharrie Trail climbs nearly 200 feet before drifting downhill and reaching an intersection at 3.6 miles. This four-way trail junction is the center of the figure 8. There is a level campsite at this point, but there is no nearby water. This loop turns right, joining the Dutchmans Creek Trail as it crosses a closed forest road and begins descending toward Little Island Creek. Dip through shallow drainages and hills to make Little Island Creek at 4.6 miles. This is one of the bigger Uwharrie streams, and it requires a dexterous rock-hop in spring if you want to stay dry-footed. Continue down the rhododendron-laden valley. Cross the stream twice more in succession.

At 4.9 miles, make a steep charge up a rocky-to-the-extreme hill. Top out at 5.3 miles, huffing and puffing. Look left for winter glimpses of Badin Lake. The path begins a downgrade. And as often is the case, the trail goes where you think it won't or shouldn't go. These unusual twists and

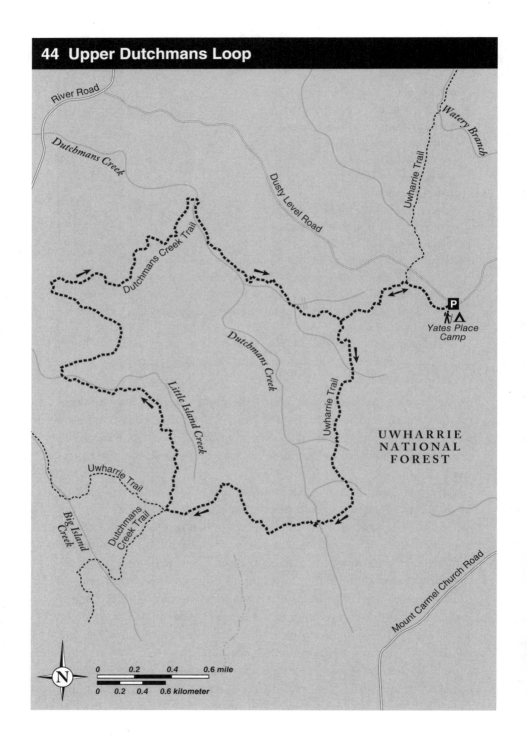

Chickweed brightens the trailside in spring.

turns keep the path on national forest property. Drop to a small stream among old dug pits and reach a low point at 6.0 miles. Now begin a 350-foot climb, broken by a couple of short descents, reaching the high point of the entire loop, Lick Mountain, elevation 815 feet, at 6.8 miles. Glimpses open of the hills on the far side of Badin Lake and the Pee Dee Valley. Check your brakes because here comes a prolonged descent. Be glad you aren't doing the loop in the opposite direction. The sounds of Dutchmans Creek begin drifting to your ears, as it gurgles over rocks and forms small shoals.

Reach the bridgeless crossing of Dutchmans Creek at 7.3 miles. At normal water levels you can rock-hop across, but in spring it may be a wet-footed crossing. Pass through a camping flat, then turn upstream, astride the left bank. Mountain laurel, rhododendron, pines, and oaks shade the rocky rill, which alternates in pools and shoals toward its mother stream, the Pee Dee River. At 7.6 miles, the trail crosses over to the right bank of Dutchmans Creek near a big pool. After tunneling into mountain laurel, it quickly skirts back over to the left bank. The Dutch-mans Creek Trail then leaves Dutchmans Creek and continues easterly, up a smaller tributary. The scenery remains alluring. Step over a pair of

streamlets, the second of which has a waterfall upstream of the crossing. Leave the water at 8.3 miles, passing an old homesite to the left of
the trail. At 8.6 miles, the Dutchmans Creek Trail ends. You have completed the loop. From here it is .8 mile back to Yates Place Camp and the
trailhead.

Mileages

- 0.0 Yates Place Camp
- 0.3 Left on the Uwharrie Trail
- 2.3 Cross upper Dutchmans Creek
- 3.6 Right on Dutchmans Creek Trail
- 4.6 Little Island Creek
- 5.3 Top of knob
- 6.8 High point of hike
- 7.6 Lower Dutchmans Creek crossing
- 8.3 Cross last stream
- 8.6 Left on Uwharrie Trail
- 9.1 Right on connector
- 9.4 Yates Place Camp

45 • LOWER DUTCHMANS LOOP

*Hike Summary: This circuit combines the lowermost Uwharrie Trail and
Dutchmans Creek Trail to form a long day hike or an ideal one-night backpack
trip from the popular NC 24/27 trailhead. Take the Dutchmans Creek Trail
northbound, rolling over a series of mostly easy hills before dipping into Big
Island Creek. From here, rise to a flat and then join the Uwharrie Trail, where
you alternately walk along attractive creeks—with wildflowers in season—
divided by taller pine-oak hills. Campers will find sites plentiful along the
entire loop.*

An abundance of campsites, located in flats along streams large and
small, makes this loop backpacker-friendly, though it can easily be
done as a day hike. I've even seen trail runners on it. You may encounter
mountain biking trails in this vicinity. Bicycle paths are being built into
this area of the Uwharrie National Forest and will continue to expand
and crisscross the Uwharrie Trail hiking network. Also, this loop crosses

45 LOWER DUTCHMANS LOOP

Distance: 11.6-mile loop

Hiking time: 6.5 hours

Difficulty: Difficult

Highlights: Good backpacking loop, creekside hiking, wildflowers

Cautions: Wet areas beside creeks, rock-hops

Fees/Permits: No fees or permits required

Best seasons: October through May

Other trail users: None

Trail contacts: Uwharrie National Forest, 789 NC 24/27 East, Troy, NC 27371, (910) 576-6391, www.fs.usda.gov/nfsnc

Finding the trailhead: From Troy, take NC 24/27 west for 9.5 miles to the signed trailhead on your right.

GPS trailhead coordinates: N35° 18.65', W80° 2.61'

closed and gated forest roads along the way. All intersections are well marked and the trails are signed, so navigation should be but a small concern for hikers.

Leave the trailhead on the yellow-blazed Dutchmans Creek Trail and start your counterclockwise circuit. Holly, oak, hickory, and tulip trees shade the path, along with white oak, pine, and azalea. Dogwoods are plentiful as well. The path bridges a little streamlet at .3 mile, then turns east, rising among hills broken with small watercourses that may run dry during late summer and fall. At 1.3 miles, the path crosses a sunken and eroded roadbed, only to turn and cross it again. The Dutchmans Creek Trail has now turned north, still rolling through the low hills and small streams. At 2.1 miles, leave a streambed, making a climb. Level off at 2.4 miles, near a clearing in the forest. At 3.0 miles, pass under a large powerline clearing. The elevation changes among these low hills are unremarkable and the walking is easy.

At 4.0 miles, you will see a wetland pond to your left. This was perhaps an old homesteader's stock pond that has since filled in and partially grown up with trees. Frogs will be peeping in the woods here during the warm season. This hilltop wetland is a rare component of the Uwharrie National Forest ecosystem. Ahead, the path slaloms through a boulder-strewn hilltop. At 4.5 miles, your ridge-running ends, and you drift north off a knob into the deep Big Island Creek watershed. This

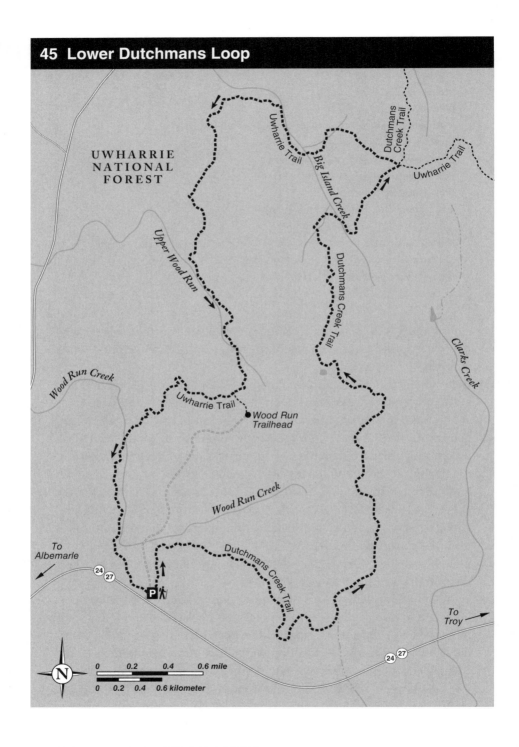

UWHARRIE
NATIONAL
FOREST

Uwharrie Trail

Dutchmans Creek Trail

Uwharrie Trail

Big Island Creek

Upper Wood Run

Dutchmans Creek Trail

Wood Run Creek

Clarks Creek

Uwharrie Trail

Wood Run
Trailhead

Wood Run Creek

To
Albemarle

24 27

Dutchmans Creek Trail

P

To
Troy

24 27

0   0.2   0.4   0.6 mile

0   0.2   0.4   0.6 kilometer

N

A well-outfitted city dweller tackles a rocky section of trail.

steeply cut valley allows views of the hills rising north and west. The path remains rocky. Step over a tributary of Big Island Creek, cloaked in cane, at 5.0 miles. Turn down this tributary, reaching Big Island Creek at 5.2 miles. This upper part of the stream, in a flat, is easily rock-hopped. Turn up the valley only to leave it with a steep climb at 5.4 miles. Boulders and rocks are strewn along the slender hogback you ascend.

At 5.9 miles, reach the four-way junction where the yellow-blazed Dutchmans Creek Trail and the Uwharrie Trail cross. Leave left from this flat area with a campsite, now joining the white-blazed Uwharrie Trail, southbound. Cross an open grassy forest road and begin descending in rocky oak woods. Enter a bloom-filled valley—dogwoods, azaleas, and smaller wildflowers. Cross this tributary twice, then reach Big Island Creek at 6.6 miles. This is a rock-hop. Turn downstream amid holly, mountain laurel, and beard cane. Continue down this basin, crossing the stream twice more, before turning south and leaving Big Island Creek at 7.3 miles. A half-mile climb of rocky, chestnut-oak-filled Dennis Mountain, gaining 350 feet, grabs your attention. But before you can say "level off," the Uwharrie Trail dives southward, aiming for Upper Wood Run. A tributary of Upper Wood Run opens a hollow for you to reach Upper Wood Run at 8.5 miles. This time you go up the creek in scads of tightly growing laurel and pine on an irregular ascent. Bridge Upper Wood Run at 9.2 miles, then turn away from the stream to reach an intersection at 9.5 miles. Here, a connector trail leads left a quarter-mile to the auto-accessible Wood Run trailhead. The descent into the next stream, Wood Run Creek, is much milder. Cross this sizable, rocky stream in a laurel thicket at 10.2 miles. Surprisingly, the trail climbs a hillside, resuming up the valley above the creek. Dip back along Wood Run Creek, then pass under a powerline at 11.2 miles. The Uwharrie Trail makes a final push up and away from the creek. The buzz of NC 24/27 drifts into your ears. Emerge onto the large NC 24/27 parking area at 11.6 miles.

Mileages

0.0	NC 24/27 trailhead
1.3	Cross sunken roadbed twice
3.0	Pass under a powerline
4.0	Wetland pond
5.9	Left on Uwharrie Trail at four-way intersection
6.6	Cross Big Island Creek
8.5	Upper Wood Run
9.5	Connector trail leaves left for Wood Run trailhead
10.2	Cross Wood Run Creek
11.2	Pass under powerline
11.6	NC 24/27 trailhead

Hike Summary: *This is an excellent Uwharrie National Forest sampler hike, exploring the forest's hills and hollows. Start behind the ranger station near Troy, descending to trickling Spencer Branch. Then up you go, cruising hardwood knolls before dipping into the wide, wooded wildflower flat of Densons Creek. A short spur leads to the waterway, where you can peer down the shoalbroken stream as it passes a sheer bluff. Next, gain a view from atop the bluff after climbing its heights. A final woods ramble leads you back to the ranger station.*

This is one place in North Carolina's national forests where you should be able to easily obtain a trail map, since you will be starting this hike behind the Uwharrie National Forest ranger station. Actually, the ranger station has a specific handout for the Densons Creek Trail that includes interpretive information to enhance your hike. This path was originally constructed by the Youth Conservation Corps in the 1970s. Since then it has gone through some ups and downs, including storm damage, but is now in fine shape. In many ways the trail is a microcosm of North Carolina's Piedmont national forest. It has small, rocky, and mostly clear streams dividing wooded hills previously used for subsistence agriculture, grazing, and mining. Evidence of these past uses can be seen in old wagon roads, homestead sites, or grown-over pits. Here, as elsewhere in the Uwharrie, white quartz brightens the trailside in quantities unseen elsewhere. The pale white rocks seem to jump out at you frequently along the way.

Note the giant broken millstone at the trailhead. Leave the ranger station and picnic tables before dropping into a tall forest of white oak, holly, dogwood, and sweetgum. After just a few feet, the trail splits; stay left, beginning a clockwise loop. Continue making your way down toward Spencer Branch. The single-track path leads deeper into a hollow where beech trees and mountain laurel thrive. At .2 mile, a short bridge leads over Spencer Branch. Turn down the hollow, passing the site of an old sawmill.

At .3 mile, reach a trail junction. Here, the Short Loop leaves right back toward the ranger station. Your loop stays left and turns up a clear tributary of Spencer Branch. The noisy streamlet keeps you company while rising through thickets until you cross this watercourse by bridge

46 DENSONS CREEK LOOP

Distance: 2.1-mile loop

Hiking time: 1.5 hours

Difficulty: Easy to moderate

Highlights: Bluff views, wildflowers in season

Cautions: None

Fees/Permits: No fees or permits required

Best seasons: Year-round

Other trail users: None

Trail contacts: Uwharrie National Forest, 789 NC 24/27 East, Troy, NC 27371,
(910) 576-6391, www.fs.usda.gov/nfsnc

Finding the trailhead: From Biscoe/Troy/Carthage exit on I-73/I-74 south of Greensboro,
take NC 24/27 west for 5.5 miles to the Uwharrie National Forest Ranger Station on
your right. The Densons Creek Trail starts behind the ranger station near some picnic
tables.

GPS trailhead coordinates: N35° 21.72', W79° 51.76'

at .4 mile. The Densons Creek Trail leaves the moist vale for drier hilltop woods cloaked in pines and oaks. Note the abundance of exposed quartz here. The blackened trunks of trees indicate that this area is regularly subject to prescribed burn. These forests are managed with prescribed burns to keep fuels down, to keep exotic plants at bay, and to help wildlife.

The loop tops a hill, then descends toward Glenn Road, which you cross at .8 mile. Angle left across the quiet, two-lane drive, then ascend a circular knob. Come near some fields that act as wildlife clearings. These clearings create edges between forest and field. On these edges, foods such as wild berries grow, attracting wildlife from turkeys to bobcats.

At 1.0 mile, a spur trail leads left down to the Town of Troy Nature Trail system. Keep straight, descending to a flat along Densons Creek. Loblolly pines rise high here. This bottom is a favorable wildflower habitat, featuring trout lilies, violets, and mayapple. Bridge Spencer Branch at 1.2 miles. Here, the trail splits. Stay left and walk just a few feet to reach an overlook of Densons Creek. Here, you can peer downstream at shoals, an island, and a high bluff, a place of repose.

Return to the main loop, then climb sharply to the bluff top to gain a

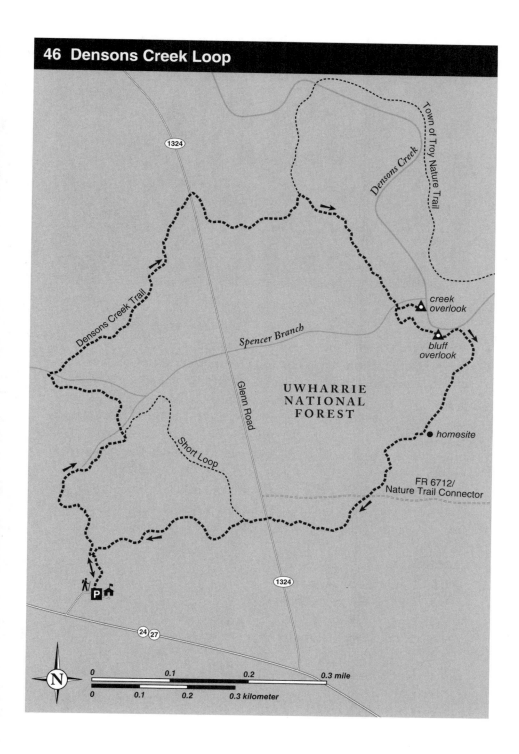

46 Densons Creek Loop

1324

Densons Creek

Town of Troy Nature Trail

Densons Creek Trail

Spencer Branch

creek overlook

bluff overlook

UWHARRIE
NATIONAL
FOREST

Glenn Road

homesite

Short Loop

FR 6712/
Nature Trail Connector

1324

P

24 27

N

0   0.1   0.2   0.3 mile

0   0.1   0.2   0.3 kilometer

Wild azalea is fixing to bloom.

second view, a decidedly different vantage, of Densons Creek. Continue cruising atop the bluff before turning away, continuing to ascend. At 1.5 miles, in a flat, reach an old homesite. You can see a broken-down rock chimney, perennial flowers blooming in spring, and other evidence of a quiet way of life now forgotten. Continue climbing, and at 1.6 miles you will reach FR 6712. It acts as a connector to the Town of Troy Nature Trail. Resume the single-track path to shortly cross Glenn Road. Continue rolling in pine, hardwoods, and holly to meet the Short Loop at 1.8 miles.

Keep up the forest walk; you are almost back. In winter, the ranger station will come into view before you complete the loop portion of the hike. Backtrack to the ranger station, finishing the circuit.

Mileages

- 0.0   Uwharrie ranger station
- 0.3   Short Loop leaves right
- 0.8   Cross Glenn Road
- 1.0   Town of Troy Nature Trail system leaves left
- 1.2   Spur leads to creekside vista of Densons Creek
- 1.3   Bluff top vista of Densons Creek
- 1.5   Homesite
- 1.8   Meet Short Loop
- 2.1   Uwharrie ranger station

Croatan National Forest Hikes

Croatan National Forest Hike Locator Guide

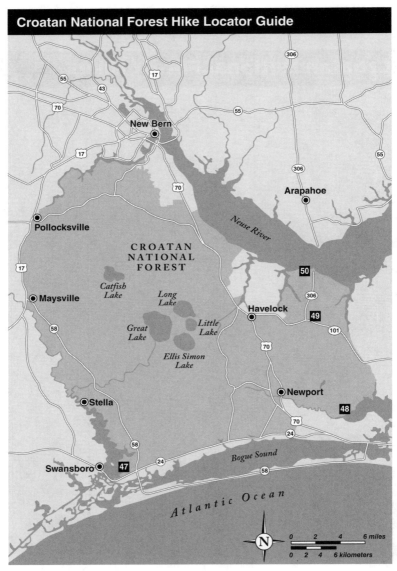

47 Cedar Point Tideland Trail
48 Neusiok Trail: Oyster Point to Blackjack Shelter
49 Boardwalks of the Neusiok Trail
50 Neusiok Trail Beach and Bluff Hike

47 • CEDAR POINT TIDELAND TRAIL

Hike Summary: *One of the finest interpretive walks in the entire North Carolina national forest system, this trek explores the Croatan's coastal shore. First, you will walk through maritime Carolina forests. Come along serpentine tidal streams bordered in spartina grass. Impressive arched bridges crossing these estuarine waters deliver extensive views. The last part visits hardwoods on terra firma.*

A glance at a map of the United States shows few national forests touching coastal areas. But here in North Carolina, we have the Croatan, which presents outdoor recreation opportunities, including hiking, along the continental edge. Here at the White Oak River, you can explore this rare meeting of salt water and national forest.

The greater Cedar Point Recreation Area has a fine campground, open year-round, which can enhance your experience. At the trailhead, picnic tables are situated under pines, and a boat ramp opens to the White Oak River. Paddlers often ply the nearby waters, even wandering under the elevated boardwalks on which you are about to walk. Restrooms and potable water are available as well. This national recreation trail is broken into two loops. The shorter loop is packed gravel its entire way and is wheelchair accessible. Benches and interpretive information are scattered throughout the hike.

Leave the parking area on a packed gravel track to enter maritime woods of cedar, pines, wax myrtle, and stunted live oaks. The proximity of salt water and frequent storms keep the forest in check here. At .1 mile, stay left to begin the loop portion of the hike. Soon join a bridge-like boardwalk that rises to span a tidal stream bordered with spartina grass. Depending on the tidal cycle, the water may be going in or out. Enjoy the salt marsh environment from the elevated wooden structure. To your left, the waters of the White Oak River widen in the distance. You are but a few miles from the open Atlantic Ocean. In the foreground are salt pannes, areas where the ocean dries after storm surges leave standing seawater, creating a barren but unique habitat of salt-tolerant plants.

Stay left at .2 mile. The short loop leaves right. As you traipse through the maritime hardwoods, intermittent views open of Swansboro, standing across the river. It is home to a fleet of commercial fishing boats. At

.3 mile, a spur trail leads left to the open shores of the White Oak River. Enjoy a panorama of the shoreline, looking near to a network of tidal creeks and far across the main river. As you continue the loop, stroll atop another elevated boardwalk. The view from the top reveals changing ecotones, rising from salty waters to spartina grass flats up to hilly wooded shoreline. Birders may be able to spot raptors such as osprey and hawks, songbirds like mockingbird or Carolina wren, and shorebirds such as herons. Fiddler crabs will be scurrying about open mud flats.

At .6 mile, come to a second shoreline panorama. Overlook Dubling Creek, one of many tidal streams. A final boardwalk takes you over more salt flats and streams. From these elevated boardwalks you can look down and understand the veinlike network that creates these waterways coursing through the spartina grass.

At .7 mile, the hike leaves the tidal marsh region and joins a sloped freshwater forest solidly entrenched on the mainland. The woods thicken; pines increase in number. Holly, laurel oak, and cane join the fray, as do water oak and maple. These trees will display colorful leaves in November. You aren't through walking boardwalks yet, as the trail

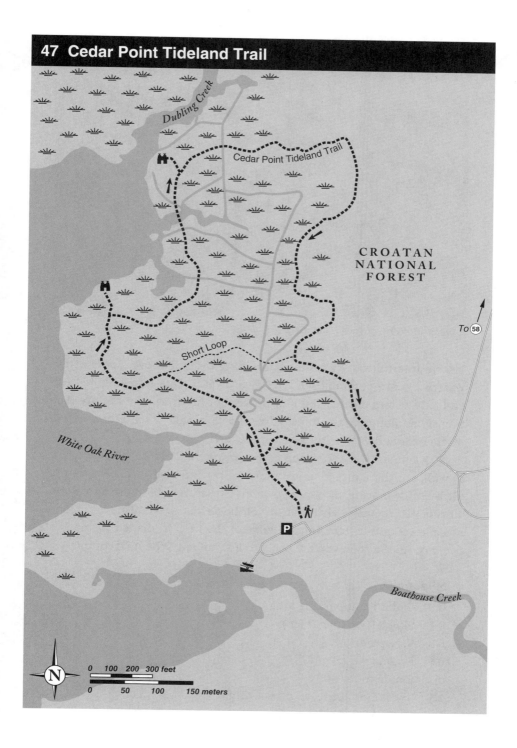

Dubling Creek

Cedar Point Tideland Trail

CROATAN
NATIONAL
FOREST

To 58

Short Loop

White Oak River

P

Boathouse Creek

0   100   200   300 feet

0   50   100   150 meters

N

A bridge offers a vista over tidal waters.

bisects intermittent streambeds draining the hill above. Some of the waterways are perennial and are fresh water. This mingling of fresh and salt waters creates the rich nursery of life that marshes are. The trail sidles alongside the forest edge, allowing looks toward the wetland in the near and White Oak River in the far.

At 1.1 miles, the short loop comes in on your right. You may want to walk out there just to enjoy another elevated boardwalk. Notice the ultra-sturdy nature of these wooden structures, built to withstand storms that regularly visit this part of the Carolina coast. The main loop stays left. Continue circling the edge of the marsh, shaded by many a live oak. All too soon you are back at the trailhead, the hike complete.

Mileages

- 0.0   Cedar Point parking area
- 0.2   Stay left on longer loop
- 0.3   Viewpoint
- 0.6   Second viewpoint
- 0.7   Rejoin mainland
- 1.1   Short loop comes in on your right
- 1.4   Cedar Point parking area

Hike Summary: Starting at the southern terminus of the Croatan's showcase path, take the Neusiok Trail to a vista of tidal Newport River, then turn up the estuarine Mill Creek Valley. Overlook the interconnection of maritime woodland and wetland before entering pine forests. Your destination is Blackjack trail shelter, an overnighting camp along the freshwater portion of Mill Creek.

As American citizens have become wealthier, we have chosen to move into scenic locales--the seacoasts and the mountains--of which North Carolina has both in ample supply. Fortunately, North Carolina also has national forests near the sea and in the highlands. These national forests are now very valuable in terms of their land worth as well as the habitats they preserve. This hike on the Neusiok Trail explores some treasured coastal terrain as it transitions from tidal shores to piney flatwoods.

The Neusiok Trail is the pride and joy of the Croatan National Forest. It extends over 20 miles end-to-end, linking the Newport River to the Neuse River, gigantic tidal waterways on the North Carolina coast. Interestingly, this is also part of the Mountains-to-Sea Trail, the Tar Heel State's master path, linking this oceanic environment to the craggy heights of the Southern Appalachians in the state's western realm.

Leave the parking area on the Neusiok Trail, heading south. In just a short distance, reach a live oak grove and a small, sandy canoe landing. Here, you can overlook the Newport River stretching out toward the barrier islands of the coast. From this camera-friendly spot, Oyster Point, you will turn north and head up the Mill Creek Valley. The single-track path winds beneath pines, bay trees, holly, and laurel oaks, an oft-burned, fire-dependent woodland. Dogwoods brighten the forest in spring. The path edges along the Mill Creek marsh, where picturesque live oaks overlook spartina grass flats centered by the ceaseless tidal action of lowermost Mill Creek. A maritime forest rises on the far side of the horizontal wetland. This nexus of fresh and salt water doubles the habitats comprising your hiking backdrop.

Cruise directly alongside the marsh before turning away, circling around a titi thicket bisected by a small stream feeding Mill Creek at .8 mile. The forest is surprisingly hilly as uplands rise from the Mill Creek flats. Turn westerly, bordering another tributary of Mill Creek. At 1.0

48 NEUSIOK TRAIL: OYSTER POINT TO BLACKJACK SHELTER

Distance: 4.8-mile there-and-back

Hiking time: 2.5 hours

Difficulty: Moderate

Highlights: Tidal environment and swamp-bordered pinelands

Cautions: None

Fees/Permits: No fees or permits required

Best seasons: September through May

Other trail users: None

Trail contacts: Croatan National Forest, 141 E. Fisher Avenue, New Bern, NC 28560, (252) 638-5628, www.fs.usda.gov/nfsnc

Finding the trailhead: From the intersection of NC 101 and US 70 in Havelock, take NC 101 east for 11.6 miles to Old Newberry Road. Turn right and follow Old Newberry Road for 3.7 miles to reach a T intersection with Mill Creek Road. (You will hit Mill Creek Road at 1.7 miles a first time. Don't veer left at this first intersection.) Turn right on Mill Creek Road and follow it .2 mile to turn left onto FR 181 at the sign for Oyster Point Campground. Follow FR 181 for 1.0 mile to dead end at the trailhead and Oyster Point Campground.

GPS trailhead coordinates: N34° 45.64', W76° 45.70'

mile, the Neusiok Trail emerges onto FR 181. The path turns right here, bridging the tributary via road. The track then turns right, back into the forest, resuming its incarnation as a single-track footpath. Wander over hills, looking south to enjoy elevated partial views of the open Mill Creek marsh in the yon, broken with small isles of cedar.

Turn back north, entering evergreen thickets of wax myrtle and titi, part of the pocosin ecosystem so prevalent on the Carolina coastal plain. A couple of boardwalks lead you through a freshwater wetland. The Neusiok Trail emerges onto Mill Creek Road at 1.7 miles. Continue northbound on the Neusiok Trail, rising into high pines and a few scattered oaks. The walking is easier here, in the flats, though adjacent wetter depressions exhibit pocosin characteristics--a more acidic, nutrient-deficient environment supporting pond pines and a sparse, shrubby undergrowth. These depressions generally have no water outlet, so they remain wetter than adjacent terrain.

At 2.0 miles, step over a streamlet on a boardwalk. Keep north, with the rustling of pines in the breeze singing in your ears. In the high-

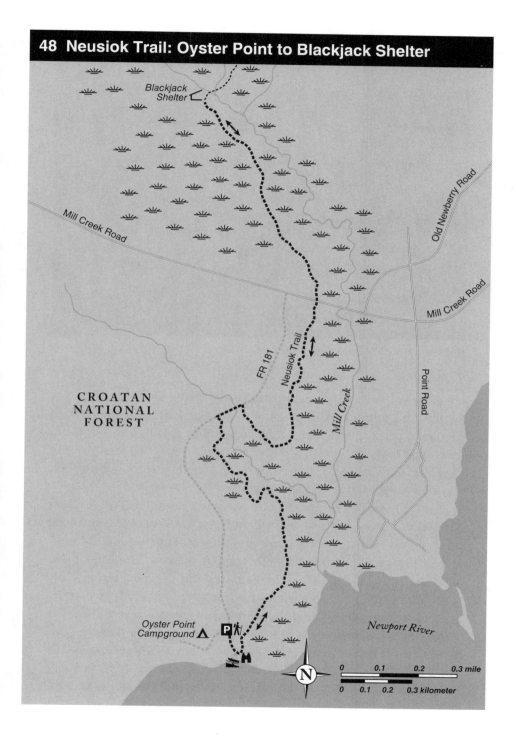

This relaxing view is from Oyster Point.

est areas you will see longleaf pines rising royally toward the sky. The freshwater portion of Mill Creek is lurking to your right underneath evergreen copses. Here, the tannic waters flow slowly over woodland debris and roots, slowing in silent, dusky pools. Ferns find their place in the moist margins and amid the pines. At 2.2 miles, another boardwalk takes you over an intermittent stream.

At 2.4 miles, the Neusiok Trail turns right toward Mill Creek. The Blackjack Shelter stands under evergreens at this turn. It is a smallish, three-sided wooden structure, open in the front, suitable for four campers. A fire pit and hand-pump well complete the campsite. This is one of three shelters located along the Neusiok Trail. It was built by the Carteret Wildlife Club. These shelters are ideal during the cooler months and during rains, but during the warmer, buggy time you will need a screen netting of some sort to keep the skeeters at bay. Campers can obtain their water from the pump well or nearby Mill Creek cloaked in dense growth. At least bring a lunch or snack to enjoy here, even if you aren't camping. From here, the Neusiok Trail continues north to cross FR 124 and NC 101.

Mileages

0.0   Oyster Point trailhead
0.8   Boardwalk over freshwater streamlet
1.0   Briefly join FR 181
1.7   Cross Mill Creek Road
2.0   Boardwalk
2.2   Boardwalk
2.4   Blackjack Shelter
4.8   Oyster Point trailhead

49 • BOARDWALKS OF THE NEUSIOK TRAIL

Hike Summary: This hike traverses wild wetlands of the Croatan, much of it over long, elevated boardwalks that add interest to this coastal hiking experience. Walk southbound on the Neusiok Trail, reconnoitering piney woods. Begin a long section of wetland forest, spanning much of it by boardwalk, one of which is a half-mile long! Rise to longleaf flatwoods, a decidedly different environment, and reach the Dogwood trail shelter, your turnaround point.

This is a fun hike. Since the Croatan is a coastal national forest, it is no surprise that it has wetlands interspersed within its 161,000 acres bordered by the Neuse River, Bogue Sound, and the White Oak River. You will be walking the heart of the Neusiok Trail as it traverses a forest that is periodically inundated. These periods of wetness make the boardwalks necessary, and many of them are built and maintained by volunteers who keep the Neusiok Trail in hiking shape. By following the boardwalks, you will reach NC 101. Then the landscape changes with just a few feet of elevation. Here, longleaf pines dominate the scene, towering above the trail. Here you will find the Dogwood Shelter, an overnighting locale perched above a wooded swamp. It is one of three shelters along the 20-mile Neusiok Trail.

Head south from NC 101 on the Neusiok Trail, following the trail markings, which may be circular white dots or rectangular metal tags nailed to trees. Loblolly pine woods, along with oaks, bay trees, and beard cane, border the trail, which soon comes along a small housing development bordering the national forest. Because of the nearby military bases and people's desires to live in a coastal environment, de-

49 BOARDWALKS OF THE NEUSIOK TRAIL

Distance: 7.0-mile there-and-back

Hiking time: 4.0 hours

Difficulty: Moderate

Highlights: Wetland boardwalks, pine flatwoods, trail shelter

Cautions: None

Fees/Permits: No fees or permits required

Best seasons: September through May

Other trail users: None

Trail contacts: Croatan National Forest, 141 E. Fisher Avenue, New Bern, NC 28560, (252) 638-5628, www.fs.usda.gov/nfsnc

Finding the trailhead: From the intersection of NC 101 and US 70 in Havelock, take NC 101 east for 5.3 miles to NC 306. Turn left on NC 306 and follow it 1.9 miles to the Neusiok trailhead on your right.

GPS trailhead coordinates: N34° 54.08', W76° 49.12'

mand for housing and land in this area continues to grow. The Neusiok Trail circles the edge of this development in woods. The trail itself has irregular undulations--watch your footing. You will likely hear jets from the adjacent Cherry Point Marine Corps Air Station. Come to your first boardwalk at .3 mile. Note how the trees in this wet strand have buttressed bases to help keep them upright when the soil is saturated and the trees are susceptible to windthrow.

The path leaves the housing development but continues bordering private property, now wooded. The red paint blazes you see on trees mark the Croatan National Forest boundary. Dip to another boardwalk at .7 mile. Evergreens such as titi are more prevalent in the wetter margins. At 1.0 mile, the Neusiok Trail is circling around a swamp to its right. Pass over another boardwalk at 1.1 miles. Some of the longer boardwalks are named, and you reach one of these at 1.7 miles. This one is called Cottonmouth Spa. It makes a serpentine course, perhaps inspiring the name, and extends over one-tenth of a mile. Beyond the Cottonmouth Spa boardwalk the Neusiok rises to pine flatwoods dominated by longleaf evergreens. The thickness of the understory depends on how recently fire has come through. Notice the blackened trunks of the regal pines.

Emerge onto a wide, grassy forest road at 1.9 miles. It acts as a lin-

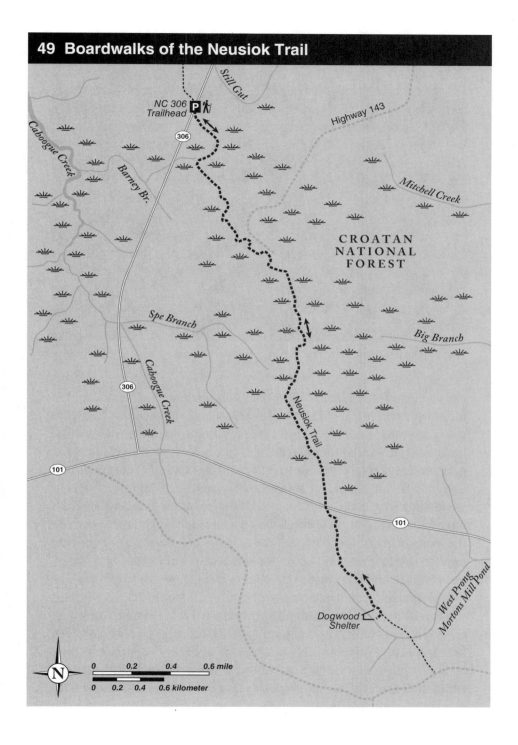

Long boardwalks characterize this section of the Neusiok Trail.

ear wildlife clearing. Angle right here and resume single-track trail in forest. At 2.0 miles, begin another boardwalk, then reach the Toad Wallow boardwalk. Undergo a brief span of ground hiking. Just ahead the longest boardwalk of them all begins. As you walk this elevated plank path, notice how it was built in different stages at different times and even in different forms, yet altogether it spans a half-mile over wetland woodlands that make the Croatan distinctive among North Carolina's national forests. This boardwalk took a lot of time and effort. Recognize the value of every step. The purpose of these boardwalks is not only to provide dry footing but also to prevent hikers from creating a rutted, muddy track and altering the ecosystem through which we walk.

The amazing boardwalk ends at NC 101 at 2.7 miles. Cross the road south and resume traversing the ground surface on a footpath under sweetgum and oaks. The footpath feels a little strange after so much boardwalk. Rise imperceptibly to longleaf flatwoods. Note the tall longleafs overhead as well as the younger pines regenerating the forest. At 3.5 miles, reach the short spur to Dogwood Shelter. The side path quickly reaches the three-sided wood enclave situated on a hill overlooking swampy West Prong. Dogwoods grow in the vicinity, giving the shelter its name. A fire ring and pump well complete the picture. Enjoy the boardwalks of the Neusiok a second time on your return trip.

Mileages

0.0	NC 306 trailhead
1.0	Circle around swamp on trail right
1.7	Cottonmouth Spa boardwalk
2.1	Toad Wallow boardwalk
2.7	Cross NC 101
3.5	Dogwood Shelter
7.0	NC 306 trailhead

50 • NEUSIOK TRAIL BEACH AND BLUFF HIKE

Hike Summary: Considered by locals to be the most spectacular section of the Neusiok Trail, this hike begins at Pine Cliff Recreation Area. Hike along bluffs overlooking the enormous and tidal Neuse River, the waterway for which the trail is named. Enjoy expansive aquatic vistas, then drop off to hike sand beaches dotted with moss-draped cypress trees. Next, turn to bask in woodland hills divided by steep freshwater drainages. Come along Cahoogue Creek to reach Copperhead Landing Shelter, perched on a hill above the tidal stream.

Pine Cliff Recreation Area is one of the most scenic spots in the Croatan National Forest. Situated on a bluff at Cherry Point, it displays commanding views of the Neuse River, a huge tidal waterway extending for miles in both directions. Several picnic tables are scattered under trees overlooking the river. Take note of the sturdy wooden picnic shelter, originally constructed in the 1930s by the Civilian Conservation Corps. But your attractive starting point is only the beginning of the beauty here. Join the Neusiok Trail as it travels westerly along the bluff line above the Neuse River under pines and sycamores. A sandy shoreline borders the water below. Take care to avoid nearby horse paths, which occasionally intersect the Neusiok Trail. After a quarter-mile, bridge cypress-bordered Gum Branch. Work your way along the Neuse River bluff. Shortly cut to the beach, crossing a tannic, tea-colored stream that cuts through shoreline sand the last few feet to meet the Neuse.

Distance: 7.6-mile there-and-back

Hiking time: 4.5 hours

Difficulty: Moderate

Highlights: Tidal river views, beach hiking, trail shelter

Cautions: None

Fees/Permits: No fees or permits required

Best seasons: September through May

Other trail users: None

Trail contacts: Croatan National Forest, 141 E. Fisher Avenue, New Bern, NC 28560, (252) 638-5628, www.fs.usda.gov/nfsnc

Finding the trailhead: From the intersection of NC 101 and US 70 in Havelock, take NC 101 east for 5.3 miles to NC 306. Turn left on NC 306 and follow it 3.3 miles to turn left onto FR 132, and a sign for Pine Cliff Recreation Area. Follow the forest road to dead end at Pine Cliff after 1.4 miles.

GPS trailhead coordinates: N34° 56.33', W76° 49.31'

Walk along the beach border, where an accomplished photographer can do wonders among the cypress trees and their strange knees rising from the sand. Cruise along the beach. If rain hasn't fallen lately, the loose sand can slow your progress, but who is in a hurry here? Note where trees that once stood on the bluffs have fallen on the tan beach in picturesque fashion. At times, the Neuse River is so wide you can hardly see across it. Continue working along the shore. Remember to look back and view the ferry that crosses the river from Cherry Point to Minnesott Beach.

Storm damage may push the trail up to the bluff, or it might continue on the beach. Stay with the white circular blazes or the rectangular metal blazes. Both indicate the Neusiok Trail. Relish this national forest beach walk amid Spanish-moss-draped trees. Cross another small stream at .9 mile. At 1.0 mile, the Neusiok Trail ascends from the beach back to the bluff. Inattentive hikers may accidentally join the equestrian trail network. Sometimes the path will have to work around swamps that are at river level. At 1.6 miles, the Neusiok Trail leaves the bluffs and beaches for good. The attractive scenery doesn't end after you leave the river. Rolling hills cut with freshwater streamlets provide another ecotone to enjoy. Ramble among beech trees, sweetgums, holly,

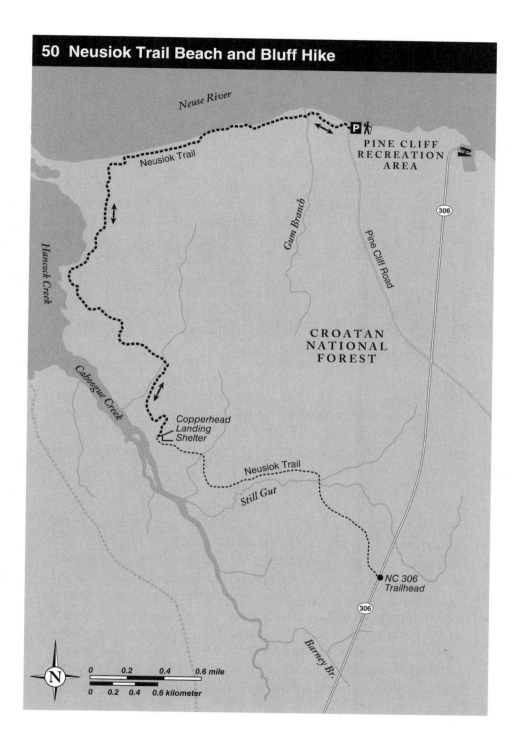

Cypress trees and sand border the wide Neuse River here.

oaks, and pines. The hiking trail swings within view of Hancock Creek, a large estuarine waterway that seems small only in comparison with the Neuse River. Cherry Point Marine Corps Air Station stands on the far side of Hancock Creek. Your southbound track rolls over wooded swales separated by moister margins.

At 2.4 miles, the Neusiok Trail curves around an inlet cloaked in spartina grass, indicating a tidal nature. At 2.5 miles, dip into a freshwater wetland shaded by cypress, saw palmetto, bay trees, and cedar. A short boardwalk crosses the wettest margin. Then you rise to hilly hardwoods and pines, only to reach another low wetland at 2.8 miles. Maples, holly, bay trees, and cypress border this creeklet. Continue the roller coaster, rising again to piney woods before reaching the biggest freshwater stream at 3.2 miles. A long boardwalk spans this wooded wetland that seems a world apart from the beaches of the river and the pine-clad hills that rise around it in three directions. The Neusiok Trail begins aiming for Cahoogue Creek, a tributary of Hancock Creek. But first it swings around one last wetland. Then, at 3.8 miles, meet the Copperhead Landing Shelter. This, like the other two shelters along the Neusiok Trail, is a three-sided wooden affair with a shed roof. It is open on the front and overlooks Cahoogue Creek. A pump well and fire ring complement the shelter. This is certainly the most scenic setting of the three shelters. A trail leads to the spartina grass and Cahoogue Creek; but it's pretty mushy down there, and the tidal waterway is shallow near the shore. Those camping here overnight will be treated to a scenic setting sun over Cahoogue Creek. But even if you don't camp, this is a good destination and turnaround point. Also, you will likely agree that this is one trek hikers certainly won't mind backtracking, enjoying the spectacular and vastly unique Croatan National Forest scenery a second time around.

Mileages

- 0.0   Pine Cliff Recreation Area
- 0.3   Bridge Gum Branch
- 1.6   Leave the Neuse River
- 2.4   Circle spartina-grass cloaked inlet
- 3.2   Boardwalk over freshwater stream
- 3.8   Copperhead Landing Shelter
- 7.6   Pine Cliff Recreation Area

Index

Note: **Bold** page numbers refer to maps and photographs.

KERI ANNE MOLLOY

Johnny Molloy is a writer and adventurer based in Johnson City, Tennessee. His outdoor passion was ignited on a backpacking trip in Great Smoky Mountains National Park while he was attending the University of Tennessee. That first foray unleashed a love of the outdoors that led Johnny to spend over 3,500 nights backpacking, canoe camping, and tent camping over the past three decades.

Friends enjoyed his outdoor adventure stories; one even suggested he write a book. He pursued his friend's idea and soon parlayed his love of the outdoors into an occupation. The results of his efforts are over 50 books and guides. His writings include hiking guidebooks, camping guidebooks, paddling guidebooks, comprehensive guidebooks about a specific area, and books about true outdoor adventures throughout the eastern United States.

Though primarily involved with book publications, Molloy writes for varied magazines and websites and is a columnist and feature writer for his local paper, the *Johnson City Press*. He continues writing and traveling extensively throughout the United States, pursuing a variety of outdoor endeavors.

A Christian, Johnny is an active member of First Presbyterian Church in Johnson City, Tennessee. His non-outdoor interests include reading, American history, and University of Tennessee sports. For the latest on Johnny, please visit www.johnnymolloy.com.

Other **Southern Gateways Guides** you might enjoy

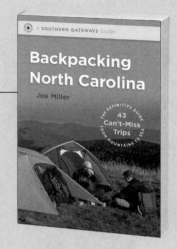

Backpacking North Carolina The Definitive Guide to 43 Can't-Miss Trips from Mountains to Sea

JOE MILLER

From classic mountain trails to little-known gems of the Piedmont and coastal regions

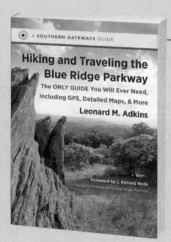

Hiking and Traveling the Blue Ridge Parkway
The Only Guide You Will Ever Need, Including GPS, Detailed Maps, and More

LEONARD M. ADKINS

The most up-to-date resource for Blue Ridge Parkway travelers

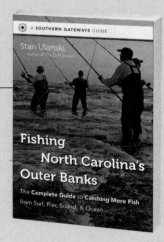

Fishing North Carolina's Outer Banks
The Complete Guide to Catching More Fish from Surf, Pier, Sound, and Ocean

STAN ULANSKI

Improve your fishing techniques (and success) by learning the science of the sea

Available at bookstores, by phone at **1-800-848-6224**, or on the web at **www.uncpress.unc.edu**